Advance Praise for GODS OF NOONDAY

"Very few childhoods are this exotic, and even fewer are retold in such beautiful language as Elaine Orr does in this book. If her heart is still partly marooned in her exotic childhood world, her mind made it possible for me to live there, too, and understand. A fascinating memoir with language rich enough for a poem, plot rich enough for a novel."

Doris Betts, author of *Souls Raised from the Dead*

"In a voice by turns intimate, engaging, melancholy, familiar, lyrical, and fraught with the tender distance of learning, Orr portrays a white girl's life in the Nigeria of the 1960s and 1970s, postcolonial, yet far from free. Hers is a rich memoir of childhood mystery, adult illness, and triumphant recovery."

James Morrison, author of *Broken Fever*

"Truly learned, incredibly fascinating, Elaine Orr's *Gods of Noonday* melts the Atlantic divide as we read the story of this unique personality located in two different worlds. Here is a rare example of a memoir that turns experience into knowledge and teaches without being prescriptive, in the process giving us an unmistakable portrait of the remarkable power of human dignity."

Toyin Falola, author of *Yoruba Gurus*

GODS OF NOONDAY

*For, whether the love of one's country be real or imaginary,
or a lesson of reason, or an instinct of nature, I still look back
with pleasure on the first scenes of my life, though that pleasure
has been for the most part mingled with sorrow.*

OLAUDAH EQUIANO

GODS *of* NOONDAY

A White Girl's African Life

ELAINE NEIL ORR

UNIVERSITY OF VIRGINIA PRESS   CHARLOTTESVILLE

University of Virginia Press
© 2003 by the Rector and Visitors of the University of Virginia
All rights reserved
Printed in the United States of America on acid-free paper
First published 2003

9 8 7 6 5 4 3 2 1

LIBRARY OF CONGRESS CATALOGING-IN-PUBLICATION DATA

Orr, Elaine Neil.
  Gods of noonday : a White girl's African life / Elaine Neil Orr.
    p.   cm.
Includes bibliographical references.
  ISBN 0-8139-2209-7 (cloth : alk. paper)
  1. Orr, Elaine Neil. 2. Nigeria—Biography. 3. Children of missionaries—
Nigeria—Biography. 4. Americans—Nigeria—Biography. 5. Nigeria—Social life
and customs. 6. Chronic renal failure—Patients—United States—Biography. I. Title.
  CT2528.O77 A3 2003
  966.905′092—dc21

                                                        200300213

TO MY FAMILY NEAR AND FAR

Contents

Acknowledgments

No one cheered the writing of this book more than my parents, Lloyd and Anne Neil. Beyond my own memory, my mother has been my greatest resource, providing stories, names, connections, and her library of Nigerian books. She reports to mutual friends that she "doesn't look that good in Elaine's book," and yet she believes this memoir has restored my soul. In recent years, she has stayed with me in the dangerous territory of living relationships, and I am forever grateful. My father drew maps and diagrams and provided names, stories, and history, and delighted in my happiness as I recovered my heart's country. Years ago, he took the photograph on the cover. My sister, Becky, helped me remember details and moods.

I wish to thank my husband, Andy, who has traveled a long road with me, and my son, Joel, who came back with me.

Mara Faulkner told me to write this book. Nick Halpern read it in draft three times and was so enthusiastic, I believed in myself. Paige McCormick, sister MK, confirmed my experience and made me bold with her love of this project. I am grateful to my Nigerian brothers Chimalum Nwankwo, Obed Anizoba, and David Gaultney for reading segments or all of the narrative and urging me on. Mary Evelyn Fredenburg, Don and Gwen Reece, Eunice Smith Bland, Yinka Jolaoso, Okey Ndibe, and Rebecca Nagy read the manuscript or parts of it, or advised me on history, names, and spellings, and all offered important insight.

I am grateful to friends in the English department at North Carolina State University for support throughout the writing of this book. For help at pivotal points, I am grateful to Angela Davis-Gardner,

Maria Pramaggiore, Lucinda MacKethan, Jim Morrison, John Kessel, Sharon Setzer, Dawn Keetley, Eyal Amiran, Andrea Mensch, Carmine Prioli, Jim Clark, and Jon Thompson.

I wish to thank Margaret Zahn and Tom Lisk for assistance with course reductions when I was ill, an adjustment that allowed me to keep working and writing, and Mary Helen Thuente for assistance in the last stages.

Thanks go to Peggy Payne, who helped me shape the story, to Joelle Delbourgo, my agent, who always believed in the book, to Lee Smith, who advised me in times of trouble, and to Cathie Brettschneider, acquisitions editor at the University of Virginia Press, who has loved the book from the first. Mark Saunders, Trish Phipps, Martha Farlow, and Ellen Satrom lent grace and energy to the project.

I am grateful to John Morillo and Patricia Lynn for technical assistance.

A leave from North Carolina State University in the spring of 1997 gave me time to begin this book, and a fellowship from the North Carolina Arts Council (2001–2002) gave me time to finish. Thanks, finally, to Matt Zingraff, Dean for Research in the College of Humanities and Social Sciences at N.C. State, for funds to prepare photographs for the book, to David Hughes for his excellent reproductions, and to the International Mission Board of the Southern Baptist Convention for permission to use some photographs from its archives.

I am grateful to my transplant team at Duke Medical Center and to the family of a donor I do not know.

A dupe o.

NOTE

I have written Yoruba proper nouns, for example, Ogbomosho and Oshogbo, as I knew them as a girl, though I now know they are anglicized. In spelling Nigerian-language words, I have sought to follow what seems to me standard practice among contemporary Nigerian writers addressing international audiences. The names of some people in the book have been changed.

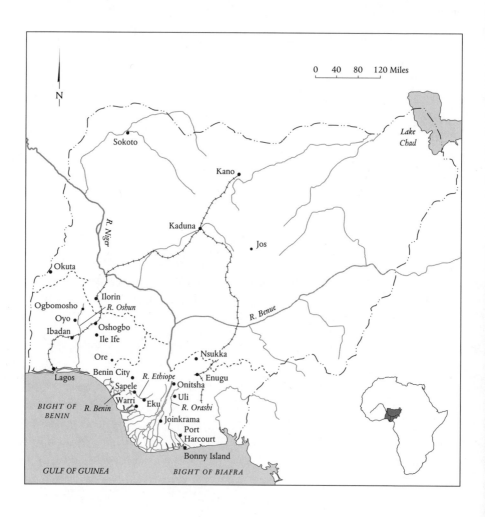

Nigeria in the 1960s

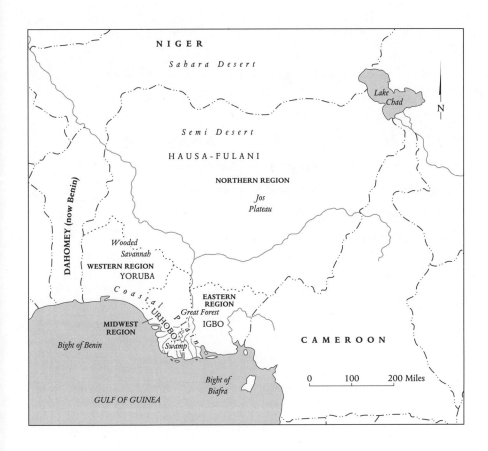

I tell you the truth like a watercolorist who has her own vision. This is what I remember, except for the facts about the mission and Nigerian history and the Biafran War, which I have sought to convey as accurately as possible. My sister would tell the story differently, as would anyone else who appears here.

Prologue

To get to the clinic from the parking lot at Duke Medical Center, you can walk through an enclosed elevated passageway or you can stay outside, cross the street, and walk on the concrete path until you get to the clinic and enter. I choose the outdoor path even though, at 9:30 A.M., the temperature is nearing eighty-five degrees and I can feel the heat strobing around my feet. I always prefer to walk outdoors. Here I can see the dignified stone buildings and the yellow daylilies and feel a sudden breeze that lifts my hair. I can almost believe I'm in Africa. Two men sit on a bench and I know they will watch me as I pass. I don't look sick, and I always walk with purpose as my father taught me. So I imagine they think I am visiting some other less lucky person. But I am the patient, reporting for a visit with the transplant doctor.

I like Dr. Collins. He is African American, and his face is handsome and kind. Everything about him is balanced. He is not in a hurry. So I wait for the requisite fifteen minutes, have my blood drawn, wait some more, see Dr. Collins, who answers a few questions I've jotted down, and then I'm on my way, cleared to remain on "the list," that awful, wonderful list that means you are relatively healthy and have good insurance so you can have an organ transplant.

As I leave the clinic, walking back out into the summer light, I am blinded for a moment. And in that brief disorientation, I hear a voice, sharp and full, like a series of musical notes; it seems to come from the air above me. But it is actually behind and I turn quickly, stumbling as I look back. The woman almost runs into me. She is dressed entirely in yellow: a yellow print blouse with puff sleeves that are cut out just at the shoulders so that her brown skin shows through, a solid yellow wrap, even yellow sandals, though her feet at the back spill over, and she is large, not just in her body but in her manner. I smile, and she smiles back quickly before calling out again. As she passes, I see she is hailing her son, who has gone out before us and is running down the path. She half-runs after him, though she seems almost to be in slow motion, her arms lifting into the air and coming back down, like wings of a huge monarch butterfly. I pick up my pace because I want to hear her voice again. As she approaches the child, one arm goes out before her and she swoops him up, laughing, and as she hoists him to her shoulder, his face is now toward me and he is absolutely delighted. Now she stands and waits because there are others in her party coming up behind us. When I reach her, I stop, ostensibly to admire the boy. But what I want, really, is to make her speak, to hear that voice again.

"Where are you from?" I ask, directly, for this is what I have learned to do in North Carolina whenever I hear someone from West Africa. She answers, "We live in Cary," once a town outside Raleigh but now a tidy upscale suburb.

But this isn't what I mean. "No," I correct her. "Where are you from originally?" And she sturdies herself. "I am from Africa," only it's more like *Ah-free-ka,* with the emphasis on the *Ah* and the *ree* vibrating on her tongue. Still she doesn't take me seriously. "No," I venture, more sternly this time, "what country?" And now she says, relaxing, "I am from Nigeria." She draws it out: *Nigh-jyyy-rria.*

Tears come to my eyes and then my body warms, as if I have had a transfusion. "I know," I tell her, "I was born in Ogbomosho." Every Nigerian knows Ogbomosho, in Yoruba land.

"Ah," she replies quietly, as if this is a mystery, and we stand for a moment in recognition of a kinship impossible to speak. She is from Ibadan, just down the road from my original home. Her name is Joanna. Finally her husband approaches, for he is in no hurry at all; he wears one of those West African print shirts with the embroidered necks and sleeves to the elbows, and you can see his stomach protruding slightly. "Johnny," she calls out, "this woman is a Nigerian." I am as happy as the child was moments earlier.

So few people know me. I am white. I have blonde hair and blue eyes. I teach American literature in the English department of North Carolina State University. No one in my neighborhood would imagine that I grew up in Africa. For years, even I forgot where I am from. So I am thankful for Joanna's discernment. In Nigerian thinking, anyone born in Nigeria *is* Nigerian. She may be a bad Nigerian or a lost Nigerian, but she is still a Nigerian.

In the car, driving home, I am no longer in North Carolina. The clean lines of the interstate fall away, making room for the footpaths of Africa. Even the trees do not exist for me, this despite the fact that it is midsummer and they are reaching their green apex and surely expect my applause. They are not palms. In my illness, I have looked for my foundation, and it is not in America. It is in Africa. Now there is no other place than Nigeria, no other place than the river and the compounds and the brown villages, nothing but the mango trees and the reaching snakes and the grass taller than children and the sudden huge wind introducing the rains. I know no other place. This is where I live in my mind. This is the dream I enter every night. I am traveling with a porter. He is carrying my bags as we approach a city. It is an old city, huge and flat, reaching from a central valley up the hills around it like a lake trying to rise. I see it spread out around us, the low brown houses, their foundations several feet below the laterite road, the brown walls, the brown piazzas and courtyards, the brown roofs. When I look skyward, I see that even the low-hanging clouds are brown, the reflection of the village. I am at home here, in the dream where the sky and the ground come together under my skin and run through me like blood. Nothing is closer to me than the smell of the Yoruba market and the taste of guavas just plucked from the tree and the drums of Ogbomosho at night, appealing to Shango, god of lightning, for the early rains.

Nigeria calls like a buried box, a treasure, a promise.

It calls to natives and visitors alike.

It calls to all who are born there, especially to those who are born there. You can watch the children listening. You can turn your own head in the wind and catch the vibration, see the way the boy leans against a tree with one leg cocked and crossed in front of the other, his mouth at work with a chewing stick. He knows that wherever he goes, he will return here. Such children have a knowledge that goes back far enough to carry them forward. The buried box, the treasure, is the knowledge of their own sacred grove or holy land, *igbodu* in Yoruba.

Nigeria is the place of my hidden self that is truer than my public self. It is the country of my heart. But having left Nigeria and Yoruba land long ago and having remained absent from my holy land, I have become broken.

So it is not by chance that I read a book in which I learn about Itefa, also called the Establishment of the Self. Diviners work with a young boy, reading his personal set of palm nuts to discern the child's "inner head" and prepare him for life. As with many Yoruba rituals, this one is a journey, a journey back in order to go forward.

I can imagine the ritual, the young boy, the diviner's hands. It is night and the company is outdoors, just beyond the house, its plastered outer walls cool as bones. The boy's mother is close. Still his fingers itch. Stars appear like lanterns at a distance, and then the group begins to move, snakelike, back and forth across the front yard, halting at moments to clear the trouble spots—I can see the diviner's arms splitting the air. Finally to the back yard, headed for a grove enclosed by palm fronds, the sacred place of rebirth where the diviner speaks ancient words. And everyone dancing, eyes on the ground, for in traditional Yoruba dance, you watch where you step, everyone together working the ground. And then the splash of cool water in calabashes for the ritual washing of the palm nuts. Finally, the boy and his mother on their knees carrying an iron staff on their heads, a sign of the hardships of life, stopping at the entrance to the grove, for only the boy and the diviners can enter to see the miracles.

In my life, only two directions are possible: death or rebirth. I prefer the second, which is why I am on the list for a transplant, two transplants actually, a pancreas to cure the diabetes I have suffered for twenty years and a kidney for end-stage renal disease resulting from diabetes. But I also require another sort of healing, a more primary cure, which is why my spirit roams at night, looking for its homeland.

As I read on, I learn that sometimes older Yorubas are reborn, those like me whose lives have been splintered and strewn about like a broken calabash. Walking on their knees, all of them carry the iron staff. But when they emerge from the grove, their heads are painted white. This African whiteness means the person is now together, not broken and scattered.

Apparently, problems are typically serious before an adult Yoruba seeks the healing of Itefa. I wonder if end-stage renal disease qualifies. I think so. Or rather, my rebirth has already begun in chance meetings and dreams. After running into Joanna, I encounter a Yoruba man in my local grocery store. Two young Igbo women show up in a course I am teaching in American literature. I think a band of angels has come to carry me home.

O Thou Fount of Every Blessing

I RUFFLE THROUGH old black-and-white photos of my family, of our houses. Finally I call my mother. "Aren't there more pictures? There must be." She isn't sure so I travel in my car up US 1 to Wake Forest, the American village in which she and my father retired. And in an old metal drum—the sort we used to transport our loads from Africa to America and back, for my parents were Southern Baptist missionaries—I find a small, poorly focused snapshot. In it, I stand tall, lean, and nine years old beside the River Ethiope. "This is it," I say out loud. "This is it."

Because my most sacred place, my most native ground, is that very river, the Nigerian spring I swam in as a girl, a river near the village of Eku, my second Nigerian homeplace after Ogbomosho, the bustling city of my birth.

In the afternoons, after his day at the hospital, my father would come looking for me on his black Raleigh bicycle. The sun would be coasting midway between high noon and sunset. He might find me with my best friend, David—both of us muffled in sweat—beside the eroding tennis court that was black and green with algae, for we lived in the rain forest. But now it is the dry season, and Dad coyly inquires of us if we would like to go swimming. He might as well ask a drowning man if he would like saving. Not taking the time to answer, the two of us throw up our swords and rifles, really the long pods that fell from the flamboyant tree, and race down the compound road to our houses to change into our swimming clothes. If David's younger brothers, Stevie and Bruce, were with us, they were eating our dust by now.

The pride of the Eku mission compound wasn't actually on the compound. It was the River Ethiope that wound through the neighboring countryside, a darling stream beginning at the base of an iroko tree, rolling up in the coastal plains, and running like a native path to Sapele and the estuary called the River Benin and eventually to the Atlantic Ocean. Named after one of the first successful trading ships to find its way into this part of the Nigerian interior, the river passed not far from my front yard, but it was separated from our compound by a rubber plantation and swamp so that we had to drive up the road about nine miles to Abraka, where there was a Western-style landing under the protection of a local boys' school.

Often it is the case in one's youth that getting to a destination is half the fun, and this was true of our trips to the river. With my father driving our 1957 sierra gold Chevrolet station wagon and our legs sticking to the protective plastic that covered the car seats, David and I would call off the names of the villages as we passed through them:

Okorori
Sanubi
Oria
Erho
Urhovia

Along the way, our car was tailed by a band of children waving furiously and calling, *"Oyinbo, oyinbo, oyinbo,"* white person. I could understand why they did this once—there weren't that many white children around to yell at—but why they did it every time we went through their town was mystifying. Perhaps they wondered about us, since they kept announcing our strangeness but we just kept coming, like wasps after a rain. Sometimes a young boy would have a stick and a large thin metal cylinder, and he would keep the thing rolling alongside the car all the way through the village, his eyes always on the cylinder and his feet with eyes of their own. But the older youth would hold back, like elders who have seen through the magician's trick or who never let themselves be lured to the show. The smallest children might have only beads around their hips, and sometimes their bellies were too big. At the time I did not know why.

It took a while on those roads to cover nine miles, sharing the one lane of pavement with cyclers and walkers and goats, and we saw all kinds of visions along the way. We might spot a line of people just appearing through the bush, carrying loads of firewood and water and cassava, and of course we simply hadn't seen the path though it was there, and so they had been walking perhaps miles but had only just come out of the dense forest and into our sight. A mysterious world of interaction was occurring beyond our line of vision. We were like moviegoers who only got the previews.

Or we might see the devotees of the Mamy Wata (or Mammy Water), women doused from head to foot with white powder and carrying white basins on their heads filled with cowrie shells and kola nuts and other treasures. They were on their way to make sacrificial gifts to the water deity. I see those women now, right this minute—they are in my eyes forever—standing up on a little brown hill, casting their look at us momentarily as we pass. These apparitions startled my eyes and left me wondering. I had nothing in my own world with which to compare them, certainly not the women at the local Baptist churches who were members of the Women's Missionary Union and who dressed *aso ebi,* or all alike, in elegant gold blouses and wraps and always a gold necklace and who smelled like spanking new fabric.

At other times we might see Egungun, or Masquerades, the encounter so brief I wondered if I had fallen asleep and dreamed. These were masks riding men, large wooden sculptures painted red and white and decorated with an animal face, bearing manes of "hair" six feet long, always trailing yards of billowing cloth. Egungun paraded and danced, telling villagers their best stories or scaring children into better behavior or making fun of rival nations, like the Hausa, for instance. The masks might bolt at our car with cutlasses, their legs kicking up as if they had never heard of gravity. Or they might imitate the palm wine drinkard and fall over and over only to right themselves perfectly and, using their cloth, turn themselves inside out. Sometimes you could almost smell them, like cinnamon and pepper and dark wet earth. These were sprung spirits, more powerful to me than the local preacher at our church, whose words fell out of his mouth and onto the floor until they were scooped up by the translator and returned to him. Egungun spoke loudly, but through movement, like a silent hurricane. Moments later we might spot the Cherubim and Seraphim choir singing in white solemn procession down the side of the road. Many a pothole urged us forward in anticipation of the river.

Finally, we reached Abraka, turning left at what looked to me like a post office, though there were never any people there—perhaps it was a deserted colonial office—and then down a white sandy road that was gutted in the middle. On the left was a farm. The land on the right had been converted into a sandlot and was sometimes dotted with parked trucks. But just next to the road tall grasses grew so close that if I stuck my hand out the window, I could feel the slim stalks hit against my skin. I submitted to this pain because there was something sweet about such a slender hurt. At last, near the river, the natural vegetation of palms and hardwoods and thick forest undergrowth returned, and we would round a curve, pass through the gate, and drive the car nearly into the river before stopping. The old man who guarded the landing was like a chameleon. At first you wouldn't see him, but then he would stand up under the towering tree that sheltered his seat and begin a measured approach into the sunlight as if to say, "Remember, I am watching." Never had he the hint of a smile.

One landing up or down in either direction and you were in the midst of whole villages of local folk doing their wash and taking their baths alfresco. As you approached the water, you could hear their voices upstream coming down on that swift current. Remembering that music now, I realize we were hearing Nigerian speech as it might have sounded had white people never come here. The voices went up and down and up again, almost like the playing of scales, full of mothers' commands and young men's jokes and children's games.

I should have fallen down on my knees every time I saw that stream. Emerging from the car, I was ever stunned to see that any earthly thing could be so clear, so fresh, so gorgeous. Nothing you could *tell* me about God was equal to the proof of God provided by the mere existence of so lovely a river. The Nigerian musician King Sunny Ade sings a song in which he claims we do not know where the breeze comes from, *we only know the source of the river.*

The Ethiope was a river beyond poetry, iridescent, the water clear as glass, its white sandy bed interrupted at certain depths by rich green river grasses that swayed like the village women dancing. Depending on the angle and time of day, the river's colors were green and more green, a fluffy white like cotton from the kapok tree, the blue of the woodland kingfisher, or granite beneath a threatening sky. At certain times of year, white lilies with yellow centers ornamented the water's edge. This was a river lovelier than the diamonds of Sierra Leone, lovelier than the gold of this country Nigeria, lovelier than the kings' stools of Ghana, lovelier than any of us who bathed in it.

The Ethiope is the water that baptized me and sanctified me and made me whole. It was cold enough to knock you silly when you jumped in, but then you swam for the opposite shore, crazily, your eyes open so you could mark your progress against the swift current, and you could see logs like huge fallen monuments and greenery on the river bottom twenty-five feet below and a school of fish parting at your approach and veering off at forty-five-degree angles and all the while you pulled for your life against the river that would not let you alone, and when you kicked finally that last time you lifted your arms and grabbed hold of the mossy tree trunk that leaned out over the water and you came up spouting and spraying. Afternoons at the river were the happiest times I have had—in the company of the people I loved the most—and I believed when I was young that I would live by this river forever, that I would learn to breathe underwater, that I would build a hut by its side, that I would never let it go.

Sometimes David and I would swim down to the next landing, or better yet we would catch a ride on the huge hardwood logs that came gliding downriver, two or three grand mahoganies or irokos or African walnuts, banded together and directed by a lone pilot. We would dive out toward the logs, pull for several strokes before reaching the great raft, and then hoist ourselves up. The logs, pungent with sap, were headed for Sapele, where there was a sawmill and a factory for turning out veneers and plywoods. Sometimes, floating like that, you could catch a glimpse of a shrine up in the bush overlooking the bank, a small hut with an open door and maybe a bowl in front of it on a table and wood sculptures. I remember that there was always something bright white at these shrines, maybe a white enamel bowl, or maybe the Mamy Wata devotees had sprinkled the whole thing with white powder. The current would carry you down before you could really see what it was you were seeing. Still those shrines made it clear how small people are in relation to the great rain forest. You could see acres and acres of dense woods and then, like a hiccup, this small human-made dwelling. But then it wasn't really like a hiccup because the shrine seemed to fit. It was more like a child's brown hand with a white handkerchief waving.

Approaching the next landing, David and I would stand up, salute the driver, and dive in. And then we would walk the sandy road back to our accustomed spot. The sand was boiling hot here in the open, so we jumped from one clump of grass to another, speeding across the sand when we had to, then ran like crazy when we got close to the river and careened out over the current like madmen.

In my present life I search for evidence that I am not merely dreaming, some outside source that will confirm for me the existence of my sacred grove. I discover a photograph of the Ethiope in a book from my library, and so ebullient am I over the find that I end up losing my handbag with my wallet and keys and all forms of American identification. But I don't care, because what I have found is truer to me than my own handwriting. The caption reads: "Transport of logs by water: the river Ethiope, Sapele, Nigeria." Gray and indistinct, the image is so poor I doubt any reader has ever paused for a moment to examine it. But it might as well be a photograph of a child born to me and lost in infancy.

I search the picture hungrily for visual reminders of what I once knew. In the middle distance I make out a man in a canoe. Such men in such boats were a common sight to my eyes, gliding by as we swam, sometimes stopping to sell a yellow pineapple or the day's catch of fish, which we would purchase to sup on later that evening at home. Such men would say only, "two shillings," taking the coins, handing us our provisions, and then nodding almost imperceptibly before dipping their paddles back in the water. The tree line in the picture is as necessary to me as the spelling of my name: palms outdistanced by hardwoods, the hardwoods' upper branches opening out to the sky.

I will know one day that I am coming home when I fly back to Nigeria and break through the clouds and see below nothing but those palms and hardwoods, palms for as far as I can see.

Family

I AM HAUNTED by an early memory so sweet and so sad. It tells me that I long for Nigeria because it is the place from which all hopes and dreams and griefs emerge.

We are on a round drive surrounded by trees. They seem to be leaning slightly inward as if in sympathy or as if they hoped to overhear our faint speech. They were large trees brimming with leaves, and yet they threw no shadow except directly underneath. So I think it must have been late morning or even noon, and I suspect it was a weekday because no one else was around. Looking down at my dress I saw the color already fading out of it. My own skin seemed to be evaporating so that the pale blue of the dress and the light salmon of my skin were swirling away down the laterite road. I did not know what it was that had left us there, my father and sister and me, standing as if for a photograph in front of our station wagon. We might have been there waiting like that for minutes or hours—I don't know which it was.

Becky was straight and prim in her cotton dress, her short brown hair parted on one side and held with a barrette, her mouth closed tightly, and her hands holding on to the pleats in her dress. My own wispy blonde hair was parted in the middle in what my mother called a pixie cut. I had begun by this time to grow out of my childhood plumpness. Still, my eyes only reached my daddy's waist, and looking up at him through that hard African sunshine was like looking up into the face of God. You had to cup your hands and squint and still you didn't see much. I would have had to back up to see him properly, but I was staying close. Besides, I knew how he looked in his short-sleeved cotton shirt and khaki shorts and high-top socks and laced shoes, everything proper and fine and selected with care, his tall, thin body and whimsical face with the dent in the middle of his chin like someone had pressed a pencil into it. Up close I saw his hands, his clean square nails, his gold wedding band and his silver wristwatch. He is a man for all African seasons. I already know he will never be ill.

I stand in my shorts and shirt with my stomach pushed slightly forward and touch my hair, which is hot on my head. We could be in church the way we're standing here. I might be listening to my mother playing the piano in the seminary chapel, "Crown Him with Many Crowns," and Yoruba voices swelling in sonorous praise.

But we are not in church. We are standing in front of Frances Jones Memorial Convalescent Center, a lying-in hospital for white American missionaries, the very building in which I was born in 1954, in the middle of the rainy season, a month overdue, just as the guavas were ripening. Frances Jones is a fancy place where important meals are served on white tablecloths by Nigerian men in stiff uniforms with gold buttons. But we are not here for dinner.

My mother has been gone from home, and we have come to get her. I am not afraid. I have no cause to be. I have my family. We live in a pretty bungalow up on the other side of the mission compound. My father is a "big man on seat" at the hospital: the business manager. My mother teaches in the nursing school, but more than that she rules our home, and all the other missionaries think she is very wise. The two of them stand above Becky and me like umbrellas in the afternoon sun. So even though my father seems wistful and quieter than usual, I am not afraid. I am simply perplexed because, after all, nothing is ever wrong with our family. And I am a little anxious, not so much about what had happened, because I don't really know what it means that my mother has had a miscarriage. Anxious instead to please, to strike just the right balance between melancholy and cheer.

It was that year and maybe that very day that Chinua Achebe's slender novel *Things Fall Apart* came off the presses in Great Britain. None of us knew about that novel. What we were hoping for was to put things back together.

Looking back, I think it was on that day I first became aware of an incompleteness, an emptiness somewhere, a gap between parents' love and the future they could not secure. It wasn't just the loss of the baby my mother had been carrying, a fatality from a bout with malaria. It was the knowledge that things could go wrong. I had the vague and unsettling sense that we had somehow lost ourselves, the perfection of the four of us.

Finally my mother appeared in the doorway of Frances Jones, leaning on someone's arm. Everything showed in a burst of white light as if we were caught in the elongated moment of a camera's flash. Perhaps after this event I felt even more intensely the sweetness I tasted in our home because now it seemed a more elusive thing.

Traditionally, West Africans believe in the coexistence of spirits not born, human beings, and ancestors who live beyond this life. In other words, all times are one and spirits never cease to exist. Born to die to this world, the *abiku* child is said to belong to a society of spirit children who call it back to their embrace. So that lost baby was an *abiku*. I consider now that babe who almost came but did not and whose sudden absence marked my consciousness like the cut of a knife on a young tree, and I think that near-infant must still be in Nigeria, perhaps in the vicinity of those trees at Frances Jones. When I think of that lying-in hospital now, I imagine it empty of human action with only the spirits remaining. I imagine screened doors flapping in the wind, leaves piled up in the corners of rooms, and lizards, unmolested, sleeping in sunlit halls. I know none of this conjecture is true. It's just that I have always been aware, as far back as I can remember, that the life I was born to could not last. Or at least I think I have, because my sense of life has always been that I could make few claims on what I loved the most.

Of course our *abiku* is not alone. Other missionary women lost babies in Ogbomosho. And the Nigerian women in that town lost many hundreds and thousands of babies. Long before Frances Jones, the first Baptist missionaries to Nigeria lost their own first babe— Mary Yoruba Bowen. *This morning about 9 o'clock the spirit of our only earthly treasure took its flight.*

Now I like to think of those infant spirits comforting one another, cradling each others' heads and combing each others' hair with the juice of pineapple. I hear their laughter early in the morning when the heat has not yet commanded everyone's attention and the breeze runs over the grass like a young duiker and the humans are not yet awake and the babes fly around in their naked dance. And later in the day when the sun is high and they are hot and tired, I hear them telling stories, speaking of the mothers they had whom they loved, speaking of their beauty. I like to think that we did not lose them entirely. In fact, years later, I returned to West Africa briefly with my husband, Andy, and conceived my only child, a son named Joel, knowing that the spirits were still there.

I am myself an *abiku* because part of me has always been claimed by Africa and will never come to America. This is why my body has already begun to leave me.

Memories Like Palm Nuts

I REACH FOR more memories:

"You better run. You better run, Elainski. I'm going to get you. Here comes the wolf!"

It's Daddy. He's on his hands and knees. Becky and I are in our cotton nightgowns, soft from many washings and smelling like water droplets singed by the iron. It's so dark outside the windows seem to be pushing into the yellow light of our living room. Becky jumps from black tim-tim to couch, leaving me behind. When I try to follow, I have to step down to the floor—my legs are too short for the jump. Lucky for me, the wolf has followed her and I make it to safety. I keep pulling my legs up under my gown, one at a time, I'm so afraid—or is it delighted—that they may be grabbed by this wild animal in the house. When the monster turns around, I scramble from the couch, running behind Becky into the spare room. Here we leap onto the extra bed, scuttle across, and stretch ourselves flat against the wall: "Oh, no. He's going to get us!" We fall in a heap as the great wolf pounces, pulling our legs out from under us, gobbling us up. And so we're hauled off to bed. It is the sweetest ending. We're captured, and we're safe, rapturous under the sheet that falls on us like a cloud. When we say our prayers, it's to the sound of Yoruba drums echoing through our screens from the other side of the compound fence. The color of the sound is burnt sienna. I'm too young to be frightened by God or eternity or even by Egungun. From outside our bedroom, the light in the dining room shines like Mary.

Sometimes, in the middle of the night, I wake up, my legs aching. When I call, my father comes first, bringing a glass of water. But when I cry with pain, my mother holds me in the living room in one of the mahogany mission chairs next to the square table with the inlaid wood top that holds the radio and turntable. She and Daddy are still up, and I hear insects jousting with the porch light, pinging against the screened door. I'm given one aspirin, and then we sit there, half rocking, she rubbing my knees and calves, reassuring: "It's those growing pains again. You're growing so fast. You're getting too big." And my exposed legs dangle down, confirming her diagnosis. Why is it, I wonder, that my growing pains always came at night? I had gone to bed feeling so safe, and now I was feeling overextended, literally.

I wish I could say I was a precocious child. I wish I had a story of learning to read. But I have no early memory of any alphabet. Perhaps I was between languages:

Cowrie shell
moon bead
kola nut
cutlass

Marimba
dodo
calabash
juju

Mixed in with my emerging English were some Yoruba words—*e kaaro:* good morning; *e kaabo:* welcome; *e kushe o:* good work; *a dupe:* thank you for saluting me; *o dabo:* good-bye. And there were a handful of words that held such currency, no one remembered if they were English or Yoruba—words like *petrol, dash, sack, machete.* These I picked up like pennies from the ground. I never called my parents Baba and Mama, but I understood the designations. For example, some nursing students from the rain forest passed our house once, laughing at my mother who was watering a small palm tree in the front yard during the dry season: "Ah, Mama! Come to Eku; we will show you palm trees!" The emphasis would be on *trees,* not *palm.* I learned Nigerian accents in my ears if not on my tongue. The languages sound like music, which is why they can be talked on drums.

The first book I remember was a heart-shaped leaf that grew on a small tree beside our house. We would pluck these and fold them in half and pretend they were hymnals and sing from them.

Listen: a story! Let it come, let it go. God made a small girl and he lowered her from the heavens onto a little land. She had with her a pencil and a mirror. With the mirror she studied her face and with the pencil she drew the world around her: palm trees and guava trees, savannahs and rivers, compounds and houses. She studied her face so much and drew so swiftly that she did not know where her face ended and the world began. She was the world. The world was in her.

My true alphabet was found outdoors, in fruits and flowers, in dry grass and sandy roads, in the shapes of trees and the wiriness of the grasshopper. I remember with love the sight of dry season grass meeting the road. Because the grass, like the sand, was a light, almost transparent brown, this meeting was observable not in terms of hue but of texture: the stubble of grass, the silkiness of packed sand. I learned from frangipani trees that beauty is fragile and not to be trusted. The limbs look sturdy enough, but they break easily, exuding a sticky white substance, and the flowers are so sweet to smell they give you headaches. Palm trees, on the other hand, bend almost to the ground in a storm but do not break. But they are also unattainable, their limbs high up as the hawks. Nigerian men climb them with a contrivance of ropes to collect the fruit and trim the fronds, a feat I never saw a white man attempt.

For children who like to climb, guava trees are the best, the limbs thin but sturdy and smooth to the touch. They branch often, making progress easy and affording many niches for feet and bottoms. Not only that, but you can pluck the fruit easily. Though finding a ripe guava in a nearby tree was difficult because we tended to eat them as soon as they hinted at maturity. Sometimes a guava would be shrouded by leaves and then maybe the wind would blow and you would spy it there in all its yellowness and claim it for your own mouth and that was a gift from God.

Along with the guava tree beside our bungalow, there was a small stand of guavas in an untamed grove across the road. This was the secret garden I shared with Gary Lynn Williams, another MK (or missionary kid), and Abike, my Yoruba nursemaid. When you walked into it, a wall of green closed behind you, and within, the light flickered through the leaves like minnows swimming, falling across your arms and clothing so that it seemed you were in a kaleidoscope. Looking up into those trees was like looking up into the vault of a great church, the way the limbs arched and interlocked. Everything was soft and green and brilliant and safe. Here we were hidden from the view of the rambling crowd.

From before I can remember, plants were company to me and I made my own *oriki,* or praise songs:

Caladiums are more trustworthy than God
Croton are braggarts
Mangos are noble
Pineapple is standoffish
Orange trees are sentinels
Bamboo is a trickster
Flame trees are beautiful without being proud
Elephant ears are gentle
Pepper plants are turncoats
Golden trumpet is a good friend
Pawpaws are silky
Barbados flower is frivolous with good cause
Hibiscus is the mother of the Gods
Guava trees are brothers
Gloriosa is grace

Of actual books, I remember the sounds of *Peter and the Wolf* spooking out of an LP record in our living room after dark in Ogbo-mosho. I also owned a large picture book, *Earth's Wonderful Gardens: Marvels of Plant Life in Colour,* that I must have gotten for Christmas when I was about three. Early on, my mother recognized my love of plants. Indeed, I often scolded Becky when we were helping to garden because she didn't know the difference between a weed and a cultivated seedling.

Here is a girl with her head bent over an open book. A perplexed look. On the pages before her: pictures of little people from Europe—the blond-

haired boy in wooden shoes from Holland, the blue-eyed peasant girl in a pink scarf—and pictures of plants from places like Africa with a caption that reads: "many of the plants in our gardens have been brought from far-away countries." Listed as examples of exotic plants: papaya, sweet potatoes, coconut, breadfruits, yams, bananas, the fruits in her back yard. A shift in consciousness, a sea change. She is far away. And who, then, is close? And where is the center? She doesn't believe the words and closes the book, digging into her surroundings like a tick.

I remember growing up a watched solitary girl. This is because in my early Ogbomosho years I had only a few playmates but many parents, not just Mother and Daddy but all the other missionary aunts and uncles and Sam and Ishola, our cooks, and then Abike, who always accompanied me when my sister was off with friends. I have no memory before Abike. It seems to me she was with me from the beginning, watching out for me but also allowing me to wander. And so I had space without being abandoned, freedom without being left to chance.

A teenager, Abike seemed to me to occupy a perfect never-never age between the slipperiness of childhood and the governance of adulthood. She was perfectly calm without threat and vigilant without worry. I was enamored by her hair combed neatly into fascinating plaits, topped sometimes—when she came to visit on holiday—with a magnificent headdress. On work days she wore dresses like mine; but hers were uniforms of green-checkered fabric that buttoned up in the front with a white collar and white cuffs on the sleeves. Abike spoke English, and she could switch midstream into Yoruba like a hand turning over. I can see her running easily across the yard, her feet cast back and at an outward angle, the light bottoms of her feet showing. My mother tells me that in my earliest years Abike would wheel me all around the compound every morning in a large black carriage until I fell asleep. I must have spent a great deal of time staring up at African skies. Later, I graduated to a navy blue canvas stroller. It was Abike who was with me the time I fell on the hard concrete floor of our porch and was knocked unconscious. She was the one who called me back to life. Once, I sharpened all of my crayons into a huge pile of shavings: turquoise blue, thistle, sepia, mulberry, orange yellow. "Ee-lane, what ah you doin'?" she demanded. But then she casually cleared the evidence into a trash can with one broad swipe of her arm.

Abike and our cook Sam laughed together when she supplied me with a huge glass of water (which I called *l'adel l'adel*) because I swallowed with such eagerness my throat sounded toadish with each gulp. I seemed to have had a need to say things in duplicate as a girl to assure enough of whatever it was I craved. At the dinner table, my family sat in the breezeway-like back room, whose outer wall was mostly screen. It was like an African room, halfway outdoors, so in the evening you communed with the moon. While Becky was inching cautiously through her first helping of chicken pot pie, I was requesting more. "How much do you want?" my father would ask, already humored, and I would answer bravely, "Three, four," which simply meant, "more than you're planning to give me."

On our walks, Abike and Becky and I often passed Frances Jones on the way to Edna Rachel and Susan's house, Edna Rachel being my first girl friend. The convalescent center was long and rectangular, with two wings sticking straight out from the central building, the whole thing raised several feet off the ground to protect the residents, I guess, from mosquitos, or perhaps to get them closer to God. Frances Jones was painted pale green, and across the front there was a deep screened veranda where ferns and caladium overflowed their huge clay pots. Bougainvillea almost hid the side entrance, it hung so heavily. The veranda itself was decorated with columns and archways, high-ceilinged, with the screen lacing it all together. Among the leaves of the asparagus fern, an inquisitive girl like me could find small red balls that smashed nicely between her fingers. And Dr. White lived here—she had delivered me at birth—so I visited with my mother every once in a while. Dr. White liked me. Sometimes we got to sit in a back room that opened onto a private garden and she would actually talk to me like a person.

"What have you got in your pocket?" she might ask, but she was wrong because I didn't even have a pocket. Instead, I had my hand under my dress, fingering my navel as I often did whether I was with my birthing doctor or just wandering around in the yard. It sort of tingled when I touched it. Dr. White was not offended but extended her hand, so I drew mine out and held hers and she walked me out to the garden to see the salmon-colored hibiscus that was blooming. There were adults who made you feel ashamed, and there were those who did not, and she did not.

Everything about Frances Jones spoke of abundance, and sometimes I think that my later hungers were a natural response to having been born there. After all that loveliness and fullness, most any other place was a lean remembering.

Often I did not see the big events coming or I did not understand them. In retrospect, I think I studied forgetting because the present seemed fine to me and I had no need for news of other worlds.

One day, for example, I found myself hiding with Gary Lynn under a double bed in his house, next door to ours. He was hiding because he had been bad and when his parents got home from the hospital he might get a spanking. Gary Lynn was always getting into trouble for things like shooting other MKs with his BB gun. Before long, I began to think that I was in trouble too and laughed out of nervousness. Suddenly Gary Lynn was pushing into my ribs: "Go, go," he commanded, and I did, charging out of the room and out of the house, bounding across the yard and up my front steps and through the screened door that slammed loudly behind me. For a moment I thought I was in trouble because Daddy was home and he looked at me without his usual delight. "Quiet," he instructed, lifting his forefinger. "We're listening to the radio." Leaning into the room from the kitchen were Sam and Ishola. So I stood still in my tracks, wiping back my wet bangs, my heart aloud in my ears.

A Nigerian man was talking through the static, but I only caught a few words, something about "giant steps," which I recognized from the game "Mother, May I." And then he used other words I vaguely knew like "freedom" and "nation." I didn't think I would be able to stand there much longer; I needed to go to the bathroom.

My parents seemed happy when the speech was over, Mother saying something like "Awolowo is very eloquent." She always talked like that. I was pleased that she was occupied with things other than Gary Lynn's mischief and my slamming the door. "Ah, madam, tis a big day for Nigeria," Sam agreed. And he laughed the way the Yoruba sometimes do when they are very serious. I did not know it at the time, but in my preschool years, Nigeria was wresting its independence from Britain, and Awolowo, our regional premier, was one of the country's big men. Speaking on the radio, his voice was reaching high and low because the radio was ubiquitous in Nigeria. Perhaps Awo spoke with forked tongue; all of the premiers puffed nationhood but also panted for themselves and their region. My parents would have been wise to take the radio static as a sign—how are things going to work if you've got several bosses in one country and many people who don't want a boss?—but I think they missed the clue. Sam did not and that was why he laughed.

When I came out of the bathroom, my mother asked only if I had washed my hands, and I offered them for her to smell the Ivory soap. Things were going well. We were all reassured.

꙳ꙮ

End-stage renal disease doesn't just slip up on you, at least not if you're reporting to a doctor. You see it coming like a rotten place expanding in the siding of your house. There's too much protein in your urine. Even with diuretics you begin to retain fluid, especially as the day goes on. If you press your ankles, your fingertips leave indentations. Your blood pressure gets out of hand. You begin to be sick to your stomach.

Sitting in the hospital waiting room the night I was admitted, I saw people as if on a television screen with the sound turned off. The exit sign blinked like a bad eye. Andy was not with me. We were in a civil war, separated at the time, my choice, if you can call it that. How many times had I driven away? Perhaps I thought that if I left him and our life together I could escape the disease that was stalking me. Or perhaps in leaving, I was only signing the breakdown of my body.

The next morning I was wheeled into surgery, the turns of the bed in the hall like a journey into a maze. A surgeon planted two shunts in my body, a temporary one in my neck for hemodialysis and a more permanent one in my abdomen for peritoneal dialysis. I would go to the clinic for hemo while the abdominal shunt healed sufficiently for me to begin the dialysis that I would do at home, four times a day, every day, until and if I could get a transplant.

My mother bravely drove me to the clinic. I was struck by how many of the patients were African Americans. First we were weighed so the technician knew how much fluid to "pull off." Then we were hooked up, in rows, to dialysis machines. My mother says we looked like people in a detention camp. All the decisions were made by someone else. In your station, one of many, you sprawled in an aquamarine plastic recliner. The room was bright but cold. Masked, robed technicians were our ministers. Perhaps the room felt cold because our blood was being sucked out and sent at great speed circulating through the artificial kidney—you could see it through the tubing. Here I was again, the minority white person among black people. But our prospects did not seem as good this time as they were in Nigeria when I was young and the federation was looking forward to independence and the country was taking off like a young cobra. Most of us in the dialysis clinic slept through the treatment because dialysis wears you out, exhausts you, leaves you limp, less like a cobra and more like a discarded skin. We were skins there. We were not intellects.

Coming back from Edna Rachel's in the afternoon, Abike and I would pass under the lovely teak trees on the seminary drive with the leaves big as plates and the tree trunks painted white from the base about five feet up. The dirt would be settling into the creases of my neck as the breeze met our faces. Later that evening I would show these rings to my daddy as I prepared to bathe. They were the badge of a day well lived.

I guess Abike must have thought me an ugly child: I was white and heavy and slow to perambulate. Apparently, my mode of operation around more agile peers was simply to pull them back down to my level. It must have seemed odd to her that such a child could be

so favored. If this was the case, her self-control was remarkable because she was always kind to me though not especially overindul-
gent. She sometimes laughed when I cried. But this was not a mark
of cynicism; it was a lesson in survival. Looking back, I wonder what
she heard when she returned to the city of Ogbomosho in the late
afternoon. The three great nations that had been pressed into British
Nigeria—the Yoruba, the Hausa-Fulani, and the Igbo—were vying
for control of the emerging national government. In villages, bribes
spiraled like whirlwinds.

Just recently, I learned that after working for us some months,
Abike herself was preparing to go to midwifery school but then she
discovered she was pregnant. I have no memory of this fact. I don't
remember ever seeing her baby though she continued to be my nursemaid. No doubt her mother cared for the new grandchild. I wonder
why it was that Abike did not, at least on occasion, bring her child
to play with me. I am sorry I missed the opportunity. Because as I
look back, I want the Nigerian sisters and brothers I was not allowed
to have. I want the thick taste of akara and groundnut stew in my
mouth.

I covet so many I missed and those I missed in part, like Abike.
And all of my parents, so many of them lost to me for so long, American and Nigerian, I will them back to me, or rather, I carry myself
back to them.

The Rough Guide

As I WRITE, I see a storm cloud gathering on the Guinea coast, weather fronts converging from west, north, and east. And out of this confluence a story emerges, slowly at first and then memories gather rapidly like machine-gun fire. And sometimes the memories burn because now I understand so much more.

For me at least the beginning is Ogbomosho, a large dusty town in Yoruba land proper, perhaps the largest city in the region after Ibadan, though my mother always called it a big village, the idea being that it was not much westernized when I was born there. The population as I write is over a million, at the time of my birth, perhaps two hundred thousand. What I most recall about the city itself is the sun slamming down, ricocheting off the tin roofs of mud-and-plaster houses and shops that reduplicated one another endlessly down a thousand bicycle paths, splashes of puddles during the rains, and a hundred women on their way to market. Ogbomosho is located in the partially wooded savannah district of southwestern Nigeria, about 225 miles north of the coastal port and then national capital of Lagos. There were patrol officers in red fezzes directing traffic at Idumota Square in Lagos and high-rise buildings, but we would leave those behind as we traveled back home after a visit. About midway to Ogbomosho, we would enter the city of Ibadan, where a great university had been founded in 1948. The one-lane paved road between cities was often overtaken by a moving river of Brahmin cattle on the way to market or by the menacing antics of overloaded lorries. These were decorated with showy sayings like "Go Slow" and "Fear Not" and "Sunshine Transport" and "Being a

Man Is Not a Day Job" and were always filled beyond capacity with women traders and young boys going to school and fatigued men returning to their villages and, of course, goats and chickens. First-class passengers sat in the front. These trucks appeared on the horizon like stunned beasts pummeling down the road with a rage for revenge, as often as not the driver leaning out the window to pilot his vehicle.

Not until 1997, while researching this book, did I begin to understand the sources of some of these sayings. "Go Slow," for example, is not just a word of caution to oncoming cars and neither is it simply a colloquialism for "traffic jam." Instead it recalls the "Go Slow" strike of 1944 in which Nigerians, including telegraph workers, civil technicians, and railway workers, fought for better wages from the British. "Go Slow" was a slogan of resistance that still held currency when I was growing up in Nigeria in the fifties and sixties. I just didn't know that at the time. As with the news about Abike's pregnancy, which I knew about only much later, this detail signifies how, in many ways, I was shielded from so much of what went on around me in the pumping dust that was Nigeria in those days. As I write this memoir, these hidden moments of a history I thought was mine come to light, and I begin to see that much of what I took for granted was being fought for by someone else, and what my family stood for in a world that was for me brand-new was already an old and fading story.

The first thing to understand about the land mass known as Nigeria is that many nations inhabited it before it was "invented" by the British. The second is that once the British arrived, they favored the North and the Hausa-Fulani people, maybe because of the cooler weather of the plateau region and certainly because the aristocratic Northerners were happier with imperialism than were the more democratic Yoruba and Igbo of the South (southwest and southeast; later called West and East). More than 250 languages are spoken in Nigeria—and I don't mean dialects—so the modern nation was born divided. As for me, the Ogbomosho of my birth lay within the folds of Yoruba land, the emerging Western state, and the regional sway of Obafemi Awolowo and his party, the Action Group. Because in early life I did not learn Nigerian geography but rather imagined my place on the national map, I first believed that Yoruba land encompassed most of the country. The huge Northern state was diminished in my mind by its absence from my experience. I knew of it primarily through the Fulani herders on the road, headed south, their bodies slight and agile. And I knew the Hausa traders, tall, elegant men who brought beautiful works of art to sell to the missionaries, laying out their wares on a mat on the veranda—moon-bead necklaces and mahogany letter openers and beautifully carved elephants—praying to Allah as regularly as the hibiscus that opened in the morning and closed in the late afternoon. When I was older, I tried without success to convert these men to Christianity, sharing little pamphlets in English about steps to salvation. I even scolded my parents for not doing likewise. We were undoubtedly Southern and Yoruba in our orientation.

At 8 degrees latitude, 4 degrees longitude, Ogbomosho, like all of the Nigerian South, experiences a nearly direct sun at noontime every day of the year. But the climate is not unbearably hot, perhaps because no one has been told to think so. And yet according to *West Africa: The Rough Guide* purchased in my local bookstore, Ogbomosho is "horrible in every way: ferociously busy, massively congested and in a state of permanent commercial mayhem along its manic main road, bottlenecked with traffic, fumes and dust." Whose eyes are these, I wonder. The dust is the only descriptor I recognize; though on second thought, I remember bottlenecked traffic and fumes as well, and that was forty years ago. It's just that I don't remember any of this as horrible. What I conjure instead is the beat of life around me. Here is a woman wearing one print wrap over a different print dress but the colors are coordinated, maybe green, yellow, and orange, and she wears orange tasseled beads around her neck and a matching headdress that is bigger than a crown. Here is another woman in a blue and pink and yellow patterned wrap, a yellow blouse with a smaller print in blue and pink, a blue scarf and blue flip-flops. Here is a woman in a black and blue striped wrap, a white lace blouse and a blue and orange headdress, red peppers in mounds laid out in front of her on a blue tarp, a small mountain of cassava in the background. Here is a man in slacks with a large loose tunic of the same print, all pale yellow, and he sports a white fedora and on his feet two-tone leather shoes. Here are Peugeots and Volkswagens and Fiats and an occasional Mercedes. Here is an advertisement on the side of a bar: *Guinness is good for you; hot or cold.* Here is a smell of goats and chickens and dried fish and smoking meat and urine and ancient dust. Here is highlife music and honking horns and the whishing sound of a bicycle passing by the car window, the jingle of the bicycle bell. Here is the Mobil Oil petrol station with Pegasus the horse emblazoned on the front of the building. None of this was horrible. Or if it was, I beg to be required to endure such horror again.

The Rough Guide proves useful to my sojourn, even if its reporting is less than enthusiastic. Though these books are meant to assist the traveler embarking on a future trip, for me this one works inversely, leading me backward and upstream into my past. The commentary continues: "But if you can bear to stop, [Ogbomosho] has a large market with a reputation for Yoruba cloth; it also boasts a very good Baptist Hospital." The first time I read this phrase—a very good Baptist Hospital—I am transfixed, as if I am witness to the burning bush. What flash through my mind are the bell tower, the carpenters' shed, the walkways linking the wards, at the hospital entrance a stand of red canna lilies unswerving as the queen's guard, in the air the high thin smell of formaldehyde.

That is *my* hospital, I want to say. I know that place.

Like an archeologist, I dig further, reading everything I can find on Nigeria. For the first time, I study the white "discovery" of my homeland. Sometimes you have to go far back in order to make sense of the present or even your personal past, certainly to divine your future. I dust off the story of the Scottish explorer Mungo Park, who first saw the Niger in 1796. I unearth Richard Lander, who realized that this river, beginning in a ravine on the border of Sierra Leone and Guinea, ends up in Nigeria, emptying into that section of the Atlantic called the Gulf of Guinea. And I ponder W. B. Baikie, who established the first real settlement by the British at the Niger-Benue confluence, becoming the first of thousands of English civil servants in this territory. By 1898, the rough borders of what is now Nigeria were drawn. In 1899 the British government bought the empire it had defined for less than a million pounds, establishing the British Protectorate of Nigeria. Frederick Lugard served as the first governor, employing indirect rule to "subdue" the various nations, while George Goldie Taubman established the Royal Niger Company. It was perhaps toward the end of the nineteenth century that the River Ethiope was first navigated by Europeans. Many have gone before me whom I would not claim as kin, and yet I can no longer claim ignorance.

I piece together the foreground that made possible my parents' arrival on West African shores, and I see them in a different light as I consider this. It's not so much that they continued the exploratory line. But surely they longed for fields beyond South Carolina. My mother, who in her hometown of Fairfax must have seemed devout and socially benign and who to me has always seemed less than adventurous, might have seen in West Africa a chance for daring that she could not begin to imagine in her own azalea-strewn front yard. I can imagine her now preparing for her first tour, trying on dresses for my father, considering what would be suitable in the tropics, purchasing her lingerie and cosmetics, and her shoes—those lovely heeled shoes with the back strap and open toe. What sweeps of drama must have entered her head. What an adventure she must have felt this was. How charming to go with a man you loved to a faraway place where you would work and build together. As far as my father is concerned, this connection with the first explorers helps me make sense of his trajectory from high school athlete/rowdy to World War II pilot to Baptist missionary. World War II and its transformations notwithstanding, I don't think my father would ever have gone to seminary and become a pastor in the American South. Part of what both my parents managed in their missionary expedition was a chance for adventure. This never occurred to me as a girl because from my point of view our lives were perfectly normal and routine and I was left to make up my own adventures with my little friends in the back yard where we would imagine long voyages *to America* of all places. My mother's vote for missions was especially brilliant since there were so few ways for an American woman to seek glory in the mid-1940s and 1950s.

According to family legend, my father saved the Ogbomosho Baptist Hospital—that very hospital described in *The Rough Guide*—when he arrived with my mother and older sister, Becky, after several months of language school in Oyo, City of Warriors, about fifty miles southwest of Ogbomosho. There my parents had studied Yoruba by Aladdin lamp in the evenings, learning enough to exchange greetings and buy tomatoes and perhaps a little more than that. Actually, my father learned enough Yoruba to lead devotionals for the hospital staff once my family returned to Ogbomosho, but he couldn't get the intonations right. The men told him this with their stares. So, wisely, he turned things over to Mr. Bolarinwa, the head carpenter. Mother tells stories of shopping in the Oyo market and purchasing Spam for dinner and praying to God daily to deliver her from loneliness. I guess the glory was hard to find at first. More at peace was my sister, riding her tricycle in the shade of citrus trees planted on the Oyo compound by an early missionary. During those first months, my parents would have heard about riots breaking out in Kano, in the Northern region, following a walkout by Northerners of the colonial assembly. Naturally, the North, which had been made dominant through British favoritism, did not wish to be made small merely for the sake of nationhood.

From such beginnings and without my assistance, my family eventually migrated to Ogbomosho and the Baptist Hospital. We were to be like the various tribes of Yoruba, forever wandering and resettling among the savannahs and forests of Western Nigeria.

Begun by Dr. George Green, who arrived in Yoruba land in 1907, the Baptist Hospital occupied the medical compound, adjoining the seminary grounds. At first no more than a one-room clinic—a small mud structure, damp and moldering as I remember it—the original hospital had its cornerstone laid in 1921. These days I long to go sit in that old clinic.

A more modern but less genteel structure than Frances Jones, the larger hospital was built to serve Nigerians and lacked some of the niceties of the nursing home. Patients generally received their food from family members: gari with hot sauce, wrapped in leaves or brought in brightly colored enameled bowls, the kind one could buy in any local market; fried plantain, or dodo; and akara. I never passed the front of the hospital without seeing long lines of people waiting to be admitted. They sat on benches in the shade of the veranda, mothers with babes who sometimes looked too old; young men with wounds tied up in long strips of gauze; children, if they were well, accompanying an elder. Sometimes patients simply sat on the covered concrete walkways, mothers with their backs against the supporting posts, children lying on sleeping mats, sometimes a child who no longer swatted the flies around his face. If I walked along the veranda, a girl my age but wearing poorer clothes might reach out and pick my hand up and inspect it as if I were a tree with white leaves.

Perhaps the new missionaries, Anne and Lloyd Neil, with my sister Becky were served a meal at Frances Jones when they first arrived in Ogbomosho in 1953, before the language tour in Oyo. Perhaps on their way into the compound, they drove past the hospital where patients were waiting, many of them all day, to see a doctor. Perhaps there was the husky smell of mangos on the ground and that evening a sunset like the second coming: feathery wings of rose red magnified against a sky of gold pinions and, near the horizon, a sapphire blue. In any case, I was born at Frances Jones a year later—as my sister says, heavy and loud. And I came to love a country I could not claim, a land I would always be leaving.

A photograph: a baby in her mother's arms, mouth open, wailing. The mother's dress flimsy as gauze, a floral pattern, her arms exposed, smiling into the camera like a queen. A girl beside them, thin and straight, a seriousness on her face as if she might make a mistake.

In retrospect, I think of Becky, who was so social and wanted always to visit someone and who would be going off to boarding school before long, as something like the Igbos of the Eastern region, due to secede from the Federation of Nigeria in 1966 and thus to ignite the Biafran War. It wasn't that Becky was in any way in control. Her personality was simply more extroverted than mine, and going to boarding school was part of the script of a missionary kid's existence. And yet the trajectories of her little life seemed to suggest a breaking up and apart of our family as I watched from behind her.

My parents, on the other hand, were certainly the Hausa aristocracy; they had all the power. And I was the Yoruba baby, robust and appropriating. If I was the minority, I didn't know it.

The business manager's desk my father inherited at Ogbomosho was stacked several feet deep with all manner of accounts. Each patient was issued a statement and many had paid parts or all of their bill. But for months these papers had been laid on the desk with accompanying pound notes or shillings on top, one payment simply placed upon the previous. So while the mission feared that the hospital was badly in debt, it was not. It only needed a good business manager to find the golden egg and it was right there waiting for him. My father boasts that he had the hospital books in order within the year. I have no reason to doubt him; he was a man who could sleep in his clothes and get up the next morning looking like a prince. My father hired a young Muslim man to drive the new hospital truck, though some warned that a Nigerian should not be trusted with the keys. Still and all, the man pledged his honor, my father stood by his decision, and the truck came home every evening.

For such a man as my father, a son is due. And to this end, the Nigerian staff at the hospital prayed: "May Mr. Neil's wife give him a boy." But it was not to be. I came instead and was laden with names like a new wife with jewelry. In addition to my surname—Neil—I was, at birth, bequeathed two sets of first and second names: one Yoruba, one English. My mother named me Miriam Elaine—Miriam after her older sister, Elaine just because she liked it. In a wise move I credit her with, she always called me Elaine, a name which seemed my own. The Yoruba staff, who had been hoping for a boy, were kind enough to offer two names of their own. So I was made Bamidele Funmilayo. My mother always told me that Bamidele means "born away from home," but in my current life, a Nigerian friend assures me that it means "come home with me" or "follow me home" and is spoken with arms outstretched, beckoning. As I write, I prefer this meaning because I consider myself to have been born at home and only later taken away from it. Funmilayo means "she brings joy," ironic given the disappointment of my sex. Of course, my parents claimed always *not* to have been disappointed. They were "happy to have two girls." But given my father's love of sports and my mother's love for my father, this appears unlikely. I was the last best chance for carrying forward the name Neil. Now it would go nowhere like a river that runs underground. And then there were those sweet framed pictures in Becky's and my bedroom, one of a little boy in blue pajamas and another of a little girl in a pink gown, both kneeling in devotion before bedtime. Now if Becky was the pink girl, who was the boy, or who was I? I think for my whole life I have been hoping to make up to my father my failure to be a boy. Either that or I am my father's daughter.

Crossroads

AMONG THE BOOKS I carry in my backpack as I journey home—which is not at all a metaphor but a place, Nigeria, real as an eyeball—Thomas Bowen's *Adventures and Missionary Labours in Several Countries in the Interior of Africa from 1849 to 1856* stands out, and not just because of the long title. It might as well be my great-great-grandfather's autobiography because it was Bowen who began Southern Baptist mission work in Ogbomosho, or Ogbomoshaw, as he spelled it.

I read hastily, delighted by Bowen's observation that "no philosophical ethnologist ever doubted the proper humanity of Africans more sincerely than some of the Africans doubt ours." Of course, Bowen had some misconceptions; he thought Yoruba land was "Central Africa." Still I am mesmerized by the preface, which tells me that when Bowen arrived at Lagos in 1850, the people of what is now Western Nigeria included the Egba, the Ijebu, the Oyo, the Ondo, the Ife, the Ekiti, the Yagba, and the Egbado, to name but a few. I love saying these names; they are like wine in my mouth. These Yoruba people numbered about three million, spreading their influence to far-flung regions. For example, the Fon of Dahomey learned administrative techniques from the Oyo Yoruba and the mysteries of Ifa divination from the Ife Yoruba. Others borrowed artistic skills from Yoruba land. The Yoruba have been a distinctive people for a long time, certainly longer than any people I might claim in the United States. Ignoring the chapters on Sierra Leone and Liberia, I move straight to Bowen's description called "Removal to Ogbomoshaw." In one chapter, he writes about the structure of Yoruba villages in general; in another, he describes the construction of his first house in that city.

> In consequence of frequent wars, all the towns, large and small, are surrounded by clay walls about five feet high. . . . At various convenient distances, the wall is perforated with gates eight or ten feet wide, which are closed at night with heavy shutters. On the inner side of the gate, there is usually a house which we must pass through in entering the town; and here reside the men who remain at the gate day and night.

I know this architecture already, but reading it provides the exquisite joy that comes when a lover recounts to someone within your hearing how he fell in love with you. Within every town, each family—a man, perhaps several wives, children, and sometimes the head man's brothers—occupies its own walled or fenced compound, a flock of houses in a circle or square, some wealthier than others. Generally there is a compound entry, sometimes a room itself. Goats and chickens mill about; there are areas for meeting and cooking and planting and sometimes juju houses. Each wife has her quarters and often there is more than one kitchen.

Of his own compound, Bowen writes:

> On my return to Ogbomoshaw, the chief gave me a beautiful building site near the northern wall, about two hundred yards from the gate to the Ilorrin road. By the end of three months I had completed a comfortable cottage of three rooms, a servants' house, kitchen, etc. and surrounded the whole with a wall five feet high, inclosing a space about forty yards square.

Reading Bowen's account, I become aware for the first time that in building compounds, missionaries weren't "keeping the natives at bay." Instead, they were copying the Yoruba, and for that matter most West Africans, who have for centuries constructed their dwellings in compounds: for safety, for identity, for intimacy. I begin to see Bowen less as a teacher of Christianity and more as a student of Yoruba. After all, he had only one convert after six years in this territory and he was the first white missionary to write an extensive Yoruba grammar.

When in my present life I invite a Nigerian friend to my house, he arrives and remarks about my suburban lot: "What a beautiful compound you have," and thus he increases its value for me one-hundred-fold.

With Bowen as guide, I see the gates to each mission compound. One could not exit the compound just anywhere but had to pass by a sentinel at a small gatehouse. In the case of missionary compounds, gates were symbolic more than actual, since they were seldom closed, and we never had any wars over those walls, though perhaps some angry stares were delivered that I didn't know how to interpret.

When I learn from Bowen how unpopular white people were in West Africa in the mid-nineteenth century, I begin to conjecture that the locals preferred to keep them at a distance. It doesn't surprise me that the chief gave Bowen land at the edge of the city. I can imagine the elder men at night around a fire discussing the newcomer: how odd he smells, how often he eats, but in little bits, how poor he must be since he does not support many wives. Perhaps they discuss offering him another wife, though the woman would not be one of their own daughters. Perhaps they put up with Bowen because they think good trading may follow him. Perhaps times are good and food is plentiful and they feel sorry for this disappearing man.

It was only later that the presumption, the threat of change, the encroachment on tradition, the ostentatiousness of missionary life began to offend.

I read on like a hungry teenager devouring a romance. About the city, Bowen writes: "There is generally . . . a tolerably broad, though seldom straight street, running from each gate to the marketplace, and these wide streets, as the marketplace itself, are commonly shaded with beautiful wide spreading trees." I think about the main drive on the seminary compound: how it was lined with those stately trees I traveled under with Abike, their trunks painted white as if in imitation of a series of gates or posts. I begin to think of Bowen as a father who went before me.

But why did I reverse the order of things, imagining that white missionaries invented compounds? Probably because to the white child on the huge compound of my youth, the city became a village and the compound a small city. The easy intercourse a Nigerian child would enjoy between indigenous compounds or between the family compound and the city was thwarted for me by the success of the mission. Imagine a child born to two parents but she loses one and as a consequence one of her arms shrivels until it is scarcely useful to her. That was my situation living on the missionary compound; my knowledge of my Nigerian compatriots was shriveled like that arm. Still, I sometimes believe that if I were to return to Nigeria today and to settle myself into a Nigerian compound, that arm would come back. It would gain strength from washing clothes and plucking fruit. I would return to my full humanity. Perhaps even my kidneys would be healed.

As I dig through these old books, I dream I am digging in the dirt in Nigeria, collecting bones and buried treasure. All rituals need structure and blood and text.

Some of the litany I remember from the beginning: for example, my parents always saying that Becky and I were the most important thing in the world or their saying I was gifted or their saying that eventually the hospital and seminary would be turned over to Nigerians. I remember learning that *God so loved the world he gave his only begotten son that whosoever believeth in him should not perish but have everlasting life.*

By the time I was born in 1954—the year of the Nigerian constitution that laid the foundation for independence—the first seminary and hospital, built of mud and plaster, were already resettling into the earth. Construction for a new hospital and a new seminary was begun in 1956, when I was two, the year Queen Elizabeth visited the country. My sister went to see the Queen but I did not.

In the streets of Lagos: the Queen's hat, the Queen's gloves, the bouquet of flamingo lilies, the tall buildings like proud young men, the sleek black convertible with the plush white interior, the African guard, the white uniforms, the Muslim robes, the crowded thoroughfares, the market women ignoring it all, the company of dancers festooned with feathers and talismans of shell and gourd, the smell of human sweat and salty air and roasting meat, the spilling foam of warm beer, the chickens crossing the road in advance of the guard, the sky like the flag of all nations.

When the new facilities were complete, two separate but adjacent compounds had been defined with the new hospital encompassing the old hospital and seminary and the new seminary built across the road. I would estimate that the circumference of the double compound was one and a half to two miles, creating a large space in the mind of a young child. The hospital compound included perhaps six mission houses and the seminary about the same. A few of these houses on the seminary side were two-storied, larger than the bungalows I was familiar with. These Victorian structures included wraparound porches up and down and an outdoor stairway, so that in the old days one would mount these stairs at night with a lantern in order to go to bed. I always found these houses so romantic, perhaps because we never lived in one. At the time, they were painted black at the base and then white from there upward to the roof. This detail seems to offer a telling symbolism. My mother says that early on, elaborate candlelight dinners were served in these homes with the missionary women donning evening dresses for the occasion.

In the center of the compounds was a crossroads formed by the intersection of an old local path, expanded through years of use into a road, and a mission-built drive. When an indigenous path like this was incorporated into territories leased to nonnatives, the "squatting" party (in this case, the Southern Baptist mission) was required by the chief to maintain it. So the old path stayed. If one traveled into either compound from this crossroads, one would arrive back at this point of intersection, for each mission drive made a circle. In other words, you couldn't really avoid the crossroads. The result from my standpoint was a kind of lopsided figure eight with the crossroads being that point where the loops met and crossed. The local road, which cut down the middle of the adjoining compounds but also formed a seam between them, was always busy; here one might encounter a woman bearing huge loads on her head. She might acknowledge me with a slight upward tilt of her head, in spite of the load of wood weighing upwards of forty pounds and padded only with a crown of cloth, but she had little interest in me. Her greeting might be translated: "I see you, but you are a small white thing." Occasionally a stray lorry would pass on the local road, and young men walking by, some-

times linking arms, would call out—"smaw gal, let me marri you"—
and then clap and laugh at your silence.

The great challenge of the crossroads was bush dogs. These animals were a threat to my childhood excursions between the hospital
compound where I lived and the seminary compound where I went
to play with Edna Rachel. These trim longtime survivors trotted like
small horses, their heads down and moving side to side in a dull
rhythm. I was not so fearful when Abike was with me, but with only
Becky as protector I was less secure. Once at that crossroads I came
face to face with an orange bush dog. He ascended in front of me, his
ears straight up and a white spot on his chest, his whiskers carrying
a film of dust and dry leaves. The dog was as tall as I, his eyes like an
old person's even though his body was young. But he only swung
his head to the side and then trotted off down the old local path
where he disappeared. Being at the crossroads was like waking from
a dream and discovering you are not where you were when you lay
down to sleep. Or you are not who you thought you were before the
dream. Here I was not a beloved daughter but a curious object. I was
minor when I had thought I was major.

Just near the crossroads, there in the center of the compound,
was a set of apartments for married seminary students. When Abike
stopped to talk with young mothers, I was not privy to the conversation. No one favored me unless another child came up and tagged
me and ran away. I would run to catch him and return the tag. And
so we enjoyed ourselves briefly before I was required with Abike to
continue on to our proper destination.

The crossroads, of course, is powerful in Yoruba land. The trickster divinity Eshu lives at the crossroads, he who is so large he must
sleep in a nutshell. His sport is mischief, so he trips you up, sends you
rolling down the hill. He upsets the balance. But Eshu can be bad
in a good way. He may teach you humility or, if you make proper
sacrifice, he may awaken your own boldness, for he does not mind
contradicting himself. Above all, Eshu represents the variable nature
of life: *no condition is permanent.*

At the crossroads, one can go backward or forward in time, into
the world of spirits or the world of the dead.

Though I was not told about Eshu as a girl, I still met him because he was there in all those uncertain moments in which I met the limits of my own mind and came face to face with my mortality: seeing the bush dogs, the boys who laughed at me, the old woman who had no use for me. I was humbled in the crossroads and this was good, though at the time I thought it was bad.

Looking to that crossroads in Ogbomosho I see I have always been living at the junction of cultures. Wittingly or unwittingly, Bowen was a crossroads figure, a white man on a Yoruba compound. And I am his daughter. Whether I am blonde-haired or not, my bones were made in Africa.

Recently my son, Joel, gave me a small gargoyle as a gift and I placed it in my garden facing the road. These days, I think of the statue as Eshu, the trickster who has been nipping at my heels all these years, trying to get me to turn around and go back. In America we say, "go West, young man," or "go forward," or "go to the moon." But that's all wrong. I have learned in my illness that the future is behind us.

Thus I have returned to my husband and to Joel and our house on Collingswood.

Weeping is necessary labor.

Life is much trouble but it cannot be avoided. This the Yoruba know.

Jesus never said otherwise.

I finish painting the molding in the pink room where I write and fill a vase with flowers.

Better Homes and Gardens

ALTHOUGH I HAVE pictures, I do not recall living in our first little house in Ogbomosho. Originally a seminary classroom building and close to what was then the hospital, it was a small structure, of mud construction with plaster and a tin roof. We could have called it a hut. Still I love that house from pictures of it, with its sweet awnings like eyelids and its simple frame. It looked like the kind of house children draw pictures of. When my parents first moved into this abode, there was no running water and a central room had to be partitioned to create sleeping spaces. A gardener brought enough water during the day for the evening baths and we all used the same water: first Becky and me, then my mother, then my father. Given his fastidiousness, this bathing ritual must have been my father's greatest "sacrifice" in going to Africa. I cannot say what the load meant to the gardener.

The first home in my memory is the bungalow, located on the high point of the compound, the second house on the circle drive away from the hospital proper, the first house on the right-hand side of the road. My father would sometimes carry me on his shoulders between the house and the hospital. My favorite sight on the way was the umbrella tree. I loved its huge leaves and the way they grew in layers down the central trunk. It looked more like a huge weed that forgot to stop growing than like a real tree. I liked its impertinence and thought Nigerians should harvest the leaves and use them during the rains. But they chose banana tree fronds instead, which worked like limp canoes turned upside down.

My first remembered Christmas was in that house, and this is what I recall: waking before dawn and gathering with my mother and sister in the living room around the Christmas tree with those large colored lights, all of us still in our nightclothes and not a sound, the presents stacked like books loosed from their shelves. When suddenly there was a chorus of angels at the front windows singing *Jo-y to de weld* with the most beautiful Nigerian accent. It was the nursing students with my father, but they drowned him out. I remember no gift except that.

The compound road was sandy, two firmly packed tracks with looser sand rising on the edges, not wide enough for cars to pass without pulling out onto the shoulder. Across the road from us stood the oldest house of all on the hospital compound, Rose Cottage, where I first remember getting my hair cut on the screened back porch. Built of mud and plaster like all the older buildings, Rose Cottage gave the impression of a slight narrowing as the walls rose from the ground, like an aging woman whose hips are large but whose bosom has shrunk. Like Frances Jones, Rose Cottage was built half a story or so off the ground and was approached by a huge set of painted steps and clay planters filled with wandering jew. I have pictures of my mother sitting in a floral dress on those steps, me standing in a white baby dress, reaching—I was always reaching—to touch the leaves of that plant.

Rose Cottage served as a domicile for several generations of single missionary nurses. I suppose my mother might have lived at Rose Cottage had she not married my father. This is the story she tells: he and she had met as teenagers in Fairfax, South Carolina, when he moved to town with his family in 1934; his father was the new Baptist minister. This is the story he tells: he was standing in the hotel lobby one day, the new boy in town, when he caught a glimpse of this beautiful girl on the other side of a glassed doorway and fell in love forever. Whoever tells the story, they dated fitfully. My mother was already bound and determined to be a missionary. She was to be class valedictorian, as serious and unstoppable as Bermuda grass. My father, on the other hand, was (pick one): a pretty boy, ne'er-do-well, playboy, goof-off, sportsman, jokester. Suffice it to say he knew how to laugh, which threw down a gulf between them the size of the Grand Canyon.

My father's family was Irish and Scotch. My mother's people were heavily English and German Dutch. This heritage helps to explain to me my father's jocularity and my mother's gravity. And there is more to say on my mother's side. Her father—Benjamin Franklin Thomas I—told her with the regularity of the clock on their mantel that she should "make something" of herself. Those were his words. And "Don't be afraid to be different."

Anne sought her B.A. at Winthrop College, where she studied music, and went to nursing school in New Orleans, where she had patients dying on her nightly, and went to Southern Seminary in Louisville—even though she couldn't take a theology degree; she was just a woman—and was about to be appointed to the mission field with her three degrees, while Lloyd went to Carson Newman College for a year and then rather casually made a switch to business school, stopping along the way to work in a grocery for a year and live at home. Finally, he joined the air force, enlisting with his best friends, the Lightsey boys, for World War II. He was sent to Europe, from where he occasionally wrote to my mother. What would I give for those letters now? He was destined for the Pacific when suddenly the war ended, he more or less unharmed, but his buddies not. They were dead. Lloyd returned, somewhat sobered, to the U.S. He and Anne fell in love again, married rather quickly. My father finished college at the University of Louisville, took a master's of divinity degree, and not long after my sister's birth, was sailing with his young family on the *African Patriot* for the faraway shores of Africa.

There was one little segue. At first, my parents had planned to be missionaries in Colombia, South America, and had spent a year studying Spanish in Costa Rica. But a political crisis in Colombia forced them to go elsewhere. So they were reassigned to Nigeria, making us something like accidental tourists in that country. One begins to see that the spread of Christianity is something like this: how you clean and polish your front room for guests but then they come and all hang out in your kitchen.

In many ways we were the typical southern American family, in our three-bedroom bungalow—I spot the same design in older Raleigh neighborhoods—with our sierra gold station wagon and our swing set and, believe it or not, our cocker spaniel. The house—with some modifications—could have been lifted from the U.S. The building blocks were concrete; the windows were louvered and covered on the outside with both screen and heavy metal latticework; the floors were finished with tile, no carpet; and we had a towering water tank in the back yard. At night, I would fall asleep looking at the faint rectangular pattern of concrete block on the wall. It was the first image I woke to.

I must report that my father, not just Abike, sometimes assisted in my morning routine of anxious dressing. Why it was that he performed this duty rather than my mother I cannot say. It didn't have to do with my father's being more patient; if anything he was less patient than my mother. But I was more likely to cooperate with him. I liked my father immensely for the stories he told and how funny he was. My father actually played with me. But my mother did not share these charms; she was much more businesslike even though my father was the businessman. Even in retirement, my father has something of the Irish leprechaun in him. When my son Joel was little— my father was then a mere sixty-eight—I would spot the two of them in Joel's red wagon, careening down the long paved road in front of my parents' Wake Forest house. In the fantasy life of my girlhood, my mother was the stern captain at the helm of our ship and assisting her is Becky. My father and I meanwhile are playing checkers below deck.

Running about that Ogbomosho bungalow on an average day with my sister at school, my father at work, and my mother sometimes at home or sometimes heading off to teach, wearing her nursing whites with that perky cap, my constellation of human contact was made up of Abike and our cooks and stewards, first Ishola and then Sam and later Abraham. My parents kept sending these young men to school and paying their fees so that they worked themselves out of help almost as soon as they got it. I did not know that I remembered Ishola until recently when I recovered an old photograph, and now I see that his face is older in my memory than my own, with his dark skin and his almost damaging smile—it created such self-doubt in others—and those beautiful wings across his cheeks. Sam was a small man, and Abraham was large and imposing in stature like the Old Testament prophet. Abraham's face was full of drama, but Sam's was like the evening, calm and abiding, like that hymn *Abide with me: fast falls the eventide.* On workdays, all of these men wore European-style short-sleeved shirts that were localized by being cut very large and thus made airy and cool. There was something very graceful and gentlemanly about these men's bearing in their clothes; they foretold the current trend in casual urbane. When in my present life I hunt through slides and find an old picture of Sam looking exactly as I knew him, I cannot hold the tears. All I can think to say to myself—and I say it out loud—is *brother.*

Abraham, on the other hand, kept a certain aloofness. Perhaps it was his changeability that gave him power in my imagination. He could be stern or generous, silent or laughing; I am sure he could be Christian or "pagan." Once he stole some of Mother's silver but then he returned it with great penitence. My parents said they would trust him again and we went on as if nothing had happened. Whether I knew this story at the time or heard about it later I cannot say. What I did know from early memory was that Abraham could disappear. Because sometimes he would be right there, standing, gazing, in front of that huge metal sink below the kitchen window, the one big enough for a bath. And when I would open the fridge only briefly for that tender wand of cool air and turn back, Abraham was gone. And I had not heard the creak and sigh of the screened door.

When he reappeared on Sundays, Abraham wore the agbada gown, popular throughout Yoruba land: a richly embroidered loose tunic that reached to his knees with ballooning sleeves folded back over the shoulders, flowing trousers that sometimes made themselves small at the ankle, backless slippers, and to top it all off, sunglasses and a carved walking stick, this despite the fact that he was only eighteen or nineteen years old. One thing that's true about Nigerians, at least the Yoruba I lived among, is that they are happy to show you they have enough of a thing. The more yards a man can put into an outfit, the better. The tailored look of Americans would be a sign of poverty in traditional Yoruba land. Similarly, if Yoruba parents have many children, they bring all of them to salute you, as Ishola once did on a Christmas Eve, toting his four offspring, all of them handsome and well dressed as if they were on their way to a wedding. And if you dine with Yoruba people, they provide enough food for an entire village, if they have it to give. Nigerians believe in plenty, and having plenty and sharing—or being generous and acting kindly—is a sign of power and goodness, not mere humility.

If you look at traditional Yoruba religious sayings, you can see that largesse is a great virtue in Yoruba land. Those who are generous have the unfailing blessing of Olodumare (God the Creator), and of men always. Thus

The calabash of the kind breaks not.

The dish of the kind splits not.

It is both money and children that flow into the house of the kind.

I guess Ishola and Sam and Abraham and Abike were kind enough because Ishola became the pastor of his own church; Sam studied at the University of Ife and became a pharmacist; Abraham became a great actor, traveling all over the United States and Europe; and after I left her, Abike married a wealthy man.

Depending on the day of the week, a gardener and a laundry man might appear in our yard, though these figures were not so intimate. In fact the laundry man had no patience with me and I suspect now that his manhood was wounded in washing my family's underclothes. I never knew whether to salute him or not, but I loved to encroach on the open door of the little room where he pressed our clothes. Outside was a small, round coal fire built in a pot. There he warmed the old iron. I loved the crackling orange coals, but most of all, I coveted the smell of starched cotton that the iron emitted. It was a smell that put hope in you like milk, so proud it was and so faithful.

Besides all of these workers, other missionaries visited all the time and many Nigerians would call. These included nursing students, church women who visited my mother, Nigerian faculty from the seminary, and occasionally someone famous, like Dr. Ayorinde, general secretary of the Nigerian Baptist Convention and onetime chairman of the Nigerian Broadcasting Corporation, a man more important than my father. Generally, I bowed out during these interviews. One old woman, however, did choose me as an acquaintance. I knew her only as "the groundnut lady," a tall, grayish woman whose blue wrap was tight under her breasts, shortening her blouse and leaving her lean arms exposed. She regularly came to our back door selling groundnuts and popcorn. These were kept separately in two compartments in a wooden and chicken-wire box that she carried on her head. She served her goods in a bit of newspaper, dishing out a handful with a half round of calabash. On each visit, she would arrive and, motioning for me to come, simply remark *pikin,* small child. Then she would reach up for the box and lower it in one long extension of arms. If she came when we were eating lunch, my mother would intervene and refuse the woman's goods, fearing germs, I assume. On luckier visits, when my mother was preoccupied and hadn't energy to refuse me, the woman would serve me a paper of groundnuts, supplementing my diet of guavas with this other native crop.

Certainly it is the case that the master moments of my early life and imagination were lived in the close company of Yoruba language, styles of dress, mannerisms, senses of humor, tones of voice, and in the case of Abraham and the laundry man, tricks of the trade and silences. Yoruba hands attended me and bound my wounds and wiped my nose. Yoruba eyes were upon me.

While living in Ogbomosho, I accompanied my father mowing the lawn.

We are in the garage and it is dark and smells of petrol like the filling station in town. On the floor I see a large green-and-yellow grasshopper jumping away from us. The insect is bigger than my fingers. My father leans over to fill the tank with petrol and it looks like he has ropes under the skin on his arms. This means he is strong. He wears his brown high-top boots and this footgear is why I am with him. Because of my flat feet, I have to wear brown boots every day but Sunday, and so during this one chore my shoes are appropriate. The mower wants to sleep but suddenly it kicks awake. The sound of the engine is like an airplane so I hold my ears. Though I fear that my feet might get sucked under the machine, I walk alongside my father as he strides up and down the yard. Walking beside him, both of us in our brown boots, I am no longer peculiar. Instead, I am like him: strong, capable, fearless, but not unkind.

On another day, my mother watches. Daddy is pushing Becky and me on our swing set after "rest time" and before he goes back to the hospital. He chants a song that makes no sense to me: "Here we go to Sycamore Town." At some point he explains that Sycamore is a small village close to the South Carolina town of Fairfax where my mother was born and he and she fell in love. So while American youth were imagining going to the African wilds of Timbuktu, I was being hastened to the fabulous and unimaginable American outpost of Sycamore.

And again, on some other afternoon, I awaken clogged and damp from naptime. I am all alone with my mother. To ease me back to civility, she offers a special snack: yellow cheese out of a small blue can, a product of Australia, I think. Like the little hot dogs in cans from Denmark, this is a delicacy and constitutes a special show of affection. Mother, sitting in the chaise lounge, cuts the cheese into small wedges which we dish out and eat with our fingers, one wedge at a time, until we empty the can, after which I am ready to return to human time. At moments like this my mother lives a material life and we are together.

As I write I realize that I, like my mother, have lived as an adult very much outside my body with my academic career and books to write and a job to land and tenure to be gotten. My charming Joel once fell in the yard and upset some newly planted flowers, and my first reaction was to straighten the little plants and not the little boy, and his look toward me and his sad little words that came skimming through the air, "You care about the yard more than you do about me." I was trying hard to hold things together, to keep my job and get tenure, so I obsessed about the house and the yard because these I could control and I had lost so much already, and there was little Joel, already eight years old, and how many times had I looked to the book instead of the boy, until my body caught

*up with me and rebelled against American success and forward journeys and
I remembered Africa. Weep with me for our mothers, for ourselves, for our
children.*

During the afternoons of special days, like birthdays, all of the
children and many of the missionaries gather in the yard of the celebrated one. We wear our nice clothes, which for girls means Sunday
dresses—though we might not wear all those petticoats underneath
that make the skirts stand out like a small umbrella—and white socks
and black shoes and everyone's hair is washed. We play games like
drop the handkerchief and here we go round the mulberry bush, neither of which I understand. Tables are set up on the lawns with tablecloths and we dine on cake and Kool-Aid. I suppose these events
were standard American fare. The difference lay in the degree of the
celebration. We had so few events—and no Woolworths, no TV, no
comic books—that birthdays were quite an occasion. You would have
had to be a hardened child not to have felt distinguished when your
time came around.

Part of the drama of compound life in Ogbomosho was tennis in
the afternoon after the workday was over. Here missionaries from the
hospital and seminary compounds along with Nigerian medical in-
terns came together, taking turns at games of singles and doubles.
Some women played with the men, but not my mother, who was
limited equally in sports and frivolity. My father, however, was star
material. One fine day during the summer mission meeting when
Baptist missionaries from all over Nigeria came to Ogbomosho for
ten days of conferences and children attended Vacation Bible School,
my father won the men's singles division of the annual tennis competition. This win became one of many legends in our family that
suggested our distinction, and I later chose my husband in part because he could play tennis.

I always believed that my family was of a slightly higher class
than other missionaries, and in this claiming of distinctive lineage,
I was very Yoruba and very South Carolinian. Our living room was
decorated tastefully and we used real silverware every day. Each meal,
even breakfast, was formally served. Our car was newer; our toys at

Christmas were the best. My father walked as if he were somebody; when my mother spoke, people listened.

And so I lived my early days as if we would never move. I thought we were already home. On rainy afternoons, Becky and I created houses by stretching blankets over a table and playing under it. Or if it were sunny, we made pretend soft drinks by smashing up the multicolored flowers of portulaca in water and exercised our imaginations in the little playhouse that Daddy had built for us in the back yard. I don't mean he built it; the men at the carpenters' shed built it. They also built dressers for us out of mahogany and coffee tables to match the one my mother saw in *Better Homes and Gardens*. These craftsmen had only to look at a picture torn from an American magazine and they could produce an exact copy. They also built a beautiful hardwood dining table big as a raft, whose surface looked like glass it was so glossy.

When I tired of American games, I would move farther out in the yard, past the kept lawn, toward the fence, becoming an eavesdropper upon the life just beyond my reach. On the other side were Yoruba compounds. In my youth, many of the local houses were mud. Like the older mission houses, some were ennobled by a plaster finish, but most were not. Some roofs were tin, others corrugated zinc, others thatch, and some whispered faraway influences: Brazilian-styled windows and doors with arched and ornate moldings and carefully carved shutters. But everything in Ogbomosho was old or looked old, perhaps because of the abundance of dust and rust or because so many items were recycled and seemed to echo a hundred former lives. Everything from newspaper to tin cans to car parts appeared and reappeared in new disguises, becoming cooking pots or a child's toy or packaging for crumbs to be left for babes unborn.

Because the compound was on a slight rise, the land behind my house fell away at an angle, making it difficult for me to see into my Nigerian neighbors' compounds. But nothing interfered with my hearing: goats bleating, radios blaring *All for you, baby, all for you,* women calling out to their men, young girls pounding grain with huge pestles: *Young girl beware. Young girl beware.*

Occasionally, we would visit the night market, driving into town in the Chevrolet, the evening so dark on the road my skin became a forgotten thing and I was merged with the universe. I would lie on the backseat with my head in Becky's lap, looking up at the stars. And then when we arrived at the market, it seemed as if the heavens had fallen because all around were a thousand lights, creating a field of yearning, until you got close and saw a multitude of small oil lamps dotting the women's marketplace. I never bought anything, though I remember plump tomatoes like red hearts on low brown tables and I begged for bread. These brick-shaped loaves made with a Yoruba recipe were not to my parents' taste; they were, said my mother, too heavy and sweet. But I loved this staple that quickly reverted to a tasty dough in one's mouth, and if allowed, I would carry one around, pinching pieces from the middle until all possibility of hunger was satiated.

Widening Circles

WHEN THE OLD seminary tutor Mr. Adegbiti came to call, the greetings began:

E kaaro, se alaafia ni o?
E kaaro, a dupe.
Ile nko?
O wa.
Oga nko?
O wa.
Omo nko?
O wa.

I was a small girl in a Nigerian world; my relationships expanded and I began to know things.

One thing I knew was that my mother did not adore me enough. Every mother should tell a child that she is beautiful and mine did not. Perhaps her parents never told her such a thing. I cannot say. In my present life, my mother might answer to this complaint: *Well, I always* thought *you were beautiful.* But this means little because it was not said at the time. With my father, things were different. He adored me as he ought—I knew this by a look that came into his eyes when I surprised him around some corner—and for that look I was grateful.

And yet my father, who delighted in me, was also sometimes unpredictable, prone to anger and expressions of disapproval, though these were always controlled. Indeed, their very understatedness was part of the pain I felt in disappointing my father. So Daddy had to be courted in a certain way in order that I not meet his quiet but certain disapproval. From my mother I could count on absolute calm, though her calm felt to me like distance. You don't always want calm from your parents. Sometimes you want them to get all worked up; otherwise, how are you going to know you've communicated to them the distress you feel? They should shout occasionally and rail about and forfeit their composure and hold their heads in their hands and weep. Then you know you've gotten through. They see that your world is under threat, that you may not make it, that you're absolutely at the end of your rope, as often I was, even at age four. Instead, my parents appeared invincible to me, and I felt they expected the same grit in me, so we all tried to be strong together. You know: *a chain is only as strong as its weakest link* and so on. In my adult life I want to talk back: *There has to be a place for weakness. Remember: For everything there is a season. . . .*

With end-stage renal disease, you are unable to rid yourself of fluids on your own. You retain water even on your back. You can tell, sitting on the toilet and pressing against your lower spine. Your hands will not close and in the morning your face envelops itself like a cloud turning inward. And yet the Continuous Ambulatory Peritoneal Dialysis (CAPD) I do at home introduces four more pounds of fluid into my abdomen. The treatment works with the aid of your peritoneum and a glucose solution and the process of osmosis; toxins are pulled from your blood into the solution and drained. This is why you need a catheter inserted into your abdomen, so you can "drain" and "fill," the entire process called an "exchange." The form of dialysis is "continuous" and "ambulatory" because you are always full of fluid and when you aren't draining and filling, you aren't hooked up to a machine and can move about. However, my handbook's claim that CAPD "allows you to move freely, just as you normally would," is false advertising.

The catheter includes a hose anchored under your skin so that it just emerges from your waistline, a clear tube about a quarter of an inch in diameter and twelve inches long. At the end of the hose is the "transfer set," a slightly larger, hard plastic piece about the size of a lipstick. It ends with a cap that you unscrew in order to hook your-self up to the bags.

The catheter worries me, even though I tape the set against my pelvis so it won't just hang. Still, what if it got caught on something or was accidentally pulled? And it looks so foreign there against my skin; it is unhuman. How uncouth my body becomes, even to me.

One particularly momentous day, my sister got a new blue bike, a Schwinn that my parents had purchased in Lagos but saved until Becky was ready for it. Up until that time, we had enjoyed our tri-cycles. Hers was green and larger than mine with a huge front wheel and a platform behind the smaller back wheels, so that one could, half standing, lean over to the handlebars and thus push and coast. Mine was smaller and red. The new bike seemed huge but sleek as a yellow-billed egret. The whole family was out for its arrival: Mother and Daddy, Becky and Elaine, maybe even Ginger, the cocker spaniel. Doubtless a few stray onlookers watched lazily, lizards mostly, per-haps a hawk circling overhead, maybe Gary Lynn. Of course, Daddy was the instructor. But Becky couldn't get the hang of the bicycle. Finally, our father threw up his hands as if to say, "why couldn't I have had a boy," and, tossing his head to the side but also half laugh-ing, his knees a little bent as he walked, muttered something like, "my word . . . Ijustdon'tknow." And then he said with a quiet authority that was all the more horrible for its serenity, "We'll just have to put the bike up; she can't ride it." So the elegant cycle went back up in the attic or wherever it had been. Later it was brought back out, but I don't remember that. And then even later it was handed down to me, and I rode it with the determination of a pioneer. I often learned the lessons of life through watching the stumblings of my sister, who, like all first children, was expected to reach near perfection on the second try. By the time I was eight, I knew: not to be clumsy, not to develop ache, not to fail at romance, not to write sad letters home.

Part of my day began to include schoolmates when I was sent to kindergarten at the compound school for MKs. As it happened, our schoolhouse was one and the same as my family's first house on the compound. So I remember that house but not as home. There were about ten of us in that little school which went through fourth grade. I don't know why my mother entered me in kindergarten prematurely; she decided the next year not to send me ahead to first grade and thus I ran through preschool twice. I can't assemble much about this first classroom experience except that I loved crayons and paints. My mother says I was quite an artist, producing fantastic skies in my pictures, not the blue lines at the tops of pages that other students drew but expanses of purple, orange, and red; maybe I drew all sky. I was enticed by the smell of art supplies, the faint, compact odor of crayons and the priestly smell of water colors. I always preferred to make things up rather than copy, so art was more interesting than numbers or letters. I think this preference explains why I teach literature and why I teach as I do, finding in the classroom alternative worlds. Even reading American literature, you can get out of America, or out of the America of malls and trimmed lawns and progress. All good literature, really, is against progress because it asks you to slow down, waste your time, dream.

I knew one British child in kindergarten who was not from our compound. A number of these "foreigners"—white people in Nigeria who were not members of the Southern Baptist mission—entered and exited my young life. Geoffrey's father was the supervisor for Ogbomosho's waterworks. We would sometimes visit the huge reservoir on the outskirts of town, taking a picnic and spreading it on one of those man-made hills that surrounded the water. The reservoir seemed to go on forever, finally blending in with the horizon. Geoffrey's house was close by the waterworks and more affluent than ours, with a great wraparound porch and a super red roof. It was with him that I first caught a glimpse of sexual difference when we went to the bathroom together one day. I never saw or heard about Geoffrey again after that year in Ogbomosho. People simply disappeared on furloughs or at the end of school years, or sometimes during. For the most part, other MKs reappeared like the prodigal son after a furlough year or two, but often something had been lost, some necessary maturing experience between friends. And then some acquaintances like Geoffrey really did just disappear like a dream you can't quite remember. Few explanations were given except, in a general, unspoken way, God's will. It was not until I came to live in the U.S. many years later that I realized it isn't necessarily normal to lose people as easily as the pebbles one puts in one's pocket and forgets to retrieve before the wash.

Of course, my world also included the seriousness of Sunday, that day in which we were to leave our true selves behind and become better people. On Sunday, the aristocracy was in charge in full force. First there were devotionals and prayers at home, led by my father. He would read from *Open Windows,* a Southern Baptist aid to supplication. This little magazine provided a scripture lesson, along with a short meditation, and a list of Southern Baptist missionaries all over the world who had birthdays that day. This last part seemed redundant to me. I thought it enough that my own parents were missionaries; why should we have to pray for everyone else? This was an unfair distribution of labor. Only on the days when my own parents, or someone else in the mission we knew well and loved, had a birthday did this activity seem called for. We had devotionals every morning, but on Sunday this ritual seemed especially trying since there was so much more church to come. And just after prayers, we had to take nivaquine so that we didn't keel over and die of malaria. This bitter pill was truly good enough reason to abandon tropical Africa. My sister tells me I would try to hide my allotment. Perhaps she was dutifully helping to make my bed the day she found half a dozen white lozenges smashed against the concrete block. Maybe this SOS was my first writing.

Then there was Sunday school with other MKs in a classroom on the old seminary grounds. We passed out musical instruments, struck up our little rhythm band, and sang. I would stand in my chair, both to show off my patent leather shoes—though the socks were sagging down and causing me to feel less than Christian—and to be as tall as the other children. We would belt out all the stanzas of "Jesus Loves Me" and "Zacheus Was a Wee Little Man" and "Jesus Loves the Little Children." I could just see Zacheus in that tree and Jesus yelling at him: "Zacheus! You come down! For I'm going to your house today!" I'd seen this sort of action before between Gary Lynn and his mother, Aunt Leslie. As for "Jesus Loves Me," it was a reassuring song because it made me feel as important as I thought I was. We took pennies to Sunday school as an offering so that we would learn to be good stewards, a rather confusing concept to me since some of the Nigerian men who worked in our houses were called stewards and I wondered what giving away pennies had to do with becoming one of them.

Just recently I dreamed of those pennies: I was standing in line in an Amer-ican grocery store, waiting to make a purchase. Beside the cashier was an open box of money and in it coins were stacked neatly in rows. But then I noticed that in the front of the box were three stray Nigerian pennies, those large coins with the hole in the middle—on one side a six-pointed star and on the other an image of the crown and the words Queen Elizabeth the Second. *I longed for those pennies and bargained with the cashier to let me buy them. They were beautiful and shiny in my hands. One had a small imperfection but I loved it anyway.*

After Sunday school there was worship in the old seminary chapel. The sermon was in English rather than Yoruba since many of the seminary and nursing students were from other areas of the country, but the preacher was always a Nigerian. In my entire life in Nigeria, I never saw a white man preach in a Nigerian church. I never saw my father in a Nigerian pulpit. As a little girl, of course, I did not register this significant fact. It seemed perfectly normal to me that Nigerians ran all the churches and everything ended with *Jesu Kristi Oluwa wa.* I did not see my parents as evangelicals. They worked in the hospital. Anyway, in church, I was watching the lizards. These prehistoric beasts—some of them "redheads"—would cling to the blue velvet curtains at the front of the sanctuary, acting out their courting rituals right behind the preacher and just over the head of my terrified mother who was stationed to the right of the pulpit, playing the piano. The curtains were sheered from the lizards' claws, like the palm fronds that were ripped to shreds by nesting weaver birds. My mother tells me she swore she would resign from the mis-sion field if one of those lizards ever fell on her. But of course no lizard ever falls, unless hit by a boy's slingshot. I sat at the back of the chapel, leaning out the open window toward the colossal casuarina trees that circled the chapel, creating a velvety breeze. You had to take what you could get on Sunday because there wasn't that much grace.

Then we ate Sunday dinner on our good china with none of the plates chipped. Though the Nigerian staff generally took Sunday off, Sam or Abraham had prepared the noonday meal ahead of time so we feasted on lukewarm fried chicken and saintly lima beans and rice and gravy and fresh fruit and sometimes coconut cake or banana pudding or chocolate pie. But then came Sunday afternoon rest time, a period of quiet which extended the daily siesta beyond reason. Sunday afternoon was a tough sentence because once freed from rest time you still faced evening worship. Becky and I would try to endure the hour and a half through some negotiation of silence and activity. But sometimes the activity overwhelmed the silence and if Daddy had to tell us twice to be quiet—and even the first time he was cross as a warlord—he would come back the second time with a belt and switch us. Through this Sunday ritual I realized some unavoidable connection between religious training and the threat of punishment. My mind began to be a thing of its own, a little animal moving beyond the boundaries of parental grounds. I might not be allowed to make noise during rest time but I would *think* whatever I chose.

We were surrounded by Nigerian politics in those early days but mostly I heard the words as sounds. One word I remember is the beautiful name Azikiwe, Dr. Nnamdi Azikiwe, said like a short poem: *Ahhh-ZEEK-ee-way,* with the first syllable drawn out and the stress and lifting intonation on the second syllable, and then *ee-way* slowly drifting, like an echo, like *away, away,* over the savannahs and anthills. Azikiwe was an Igbo from the East who had gone to the U.S. for his higher education. America was the land of opportunity for many Nigerians when I was growing up and this was a reason for our being more popular than Mr. Bowen had been or than the British, like Geoffrey's father, who was on his way out with independence looming. During my early life, Azikiwe was a big player in Nigerian politics, like a center forward on a soccer team. I probably heard his name being praised in Abraham's mouth.

Nigeria was drafting its constitution. But each big region was campaigning in its own best interest. There was the National Council of Nigeria and Cameroons in the East, the Action Group in the West where we were, the Northern Peoples' Congress in the North. There was "Zik" in the East, Chief Awolowo in the West, the Sardauna of Sokoto in the North. There were chants of "Life Abundant" by the NCNC, "Life *More* Abundant" by the AG, and "Salaam" by the NPC.

In my own little life, my family had recently spent a furlough year in the U.S. though I do not remember it. My father tells me that when he visited the town of Fairfax, an elder greeted him and offered this advice: *Take all these niggers with you back to Africa.* We were glancing through the U.S. just as the civil rights movement was gaining momentum.

I want to hurry, but narrative is hard work. The crucible of memory melds a thousand paths, but I must separate this path from that, find the source. Or is it truer to say that stories are like children? The more you try to direct them, the more they go their own way. I do not know. I burn with this story. My hair is full of dust. I say the words—Ibadan, Ogbomosho, Shaki, Warri, Abraka— like the names of ancestors. I remember glossy green leaves of orange trees, lizards older than sin, mist above the river, round baskets in the marketplace like huge airy stones, the determined look of cassava unearthed from the ground. These are my gods. Believe me.

In 1957 the three regional premiers met in London with Colonel Secretary Alan Lennox-Boyd to map out Nigeria's independence. The new nation would retain the three regions but also elect a national prime minister. In September, Alhaji Abubakar Tafawa Balewa, "the silver voice of the North," a forty-four-year-old Muslim, took office in Lagos as the new head of state. The Christian Igbo Azikiwe was president. Here were two poems a-dueling, *A bu ba kar, A zik i we.*

Now I see that it is something of a mistake to refer to "Nigeria." British ratification of the regions threatened the hope for unity. Add to that the fact that while many Nigerians were still getting used to an *oyinbo* road in front of their village, the national elite were settling into office chairs still warm from the colonial occupiers. The anticipation of independence in Nigeria was something like the promise of marriage for a young woman: a glowing dream in the beginning. Only later does the bargain become clear.

The meetings continued in London. In November of 1958, Awolowo, our Western leader—the man I had heard that day speaking through the static on the radio—spoke again. This is what he said. This is what haunts me:

> Rarely, in the course of human history, has a nation come to the eve of independence without a shot being fired, without a drop of revolutionary blood being spilled, with . . . hardly a word spoken in anger. . . . We are nationalists, but we are not extremists. . . . [We must create] a system of government which will guarantee the rights of the weakest among us.

Metamorphosis

WHEN I BECAME SICK and in need of a healing for which there is no Western medicine, that's when the dreaming began. And I did not dream merely in sleep. I dreamed wide awake in the daytime. I would take a walk and as I rounded a turn in my Raleigh neighborhood, I would literally pass into another world. My scalp tingled as I flew backward, faster and faster, trees rushing in the other direction until I saw *a yard and a sandbox under a palm, the sand spilling out around the base of the tree. When I look toward the house, I know there is a little girl inside but she does not come out to play. I want to call her, to fix her sandbox. And then I am on a hill looking out at the entire city of Ibadan and it is a ruined place because some catastrophe has occurred and I am helpless to do anything and all around my feet are dead chickens in the unpaved road. It is raining, a downpour. Then I am walking through the forest; I carry a huge walking stick, and when I come to a clearing I see a small river where women are filling basins.*

I convulse at this time travel, and when I get home I vomit in the kitchen sink.

One afternoon in Ogbomosho, we were called from somnambulant play by excited voices in the front yard. By the time I stepped out on the broad green lawn, a small crowd had already congregated.

O story! O yes! So it happened:

A monitor lizard was making its ancient way across our yard. I suppose the entire incident took only a few minutes. But the usually slow pace of the Sunday afternoon seemed stretched out to a near standstill as I watched the creature lumber across the road and ascend into a tree where it perched, unmoving, like a huge ornament. I felt sorry for the large lizard; it seemed embarrassed to have found itself so exposed on the lawn of an American compound, its natural surroundings so clipped and curtailed. It probably came from the large wild lot next to our house, where the umbrella tree lived. Maybe it had a nest in an old termite mound hidden from our view. But why had she come in our direction? Was food in short supply? Sometimes a neighbor's chicken would squeeze through the fence and come onto the compound, but then it would realize its separation from kith and kin and frantically search for a way back home. Unfortunately, the monitor had not the same instinct.

I suppose the adults around me were alarmed. They gesticulated one to the other, running in and out of houses as if something must be done. We had never seen a monitor. I thought it was just a lizard who had eaten too much. Perhaps it was three feet long or so; perhaps it was as long as I was tall. *And here is a missionary aunt, dressed in her nursing whites, next to me, lifting her rifle, taking aim, and firing.* The monitor lizard held for a moment like a great she elephant surprised by the hindleggers' violence, and then she fell to the ground. Other MKs rushed to the monitor's defeat, poking to be sure it was dead, for, if not, they would kill it some more. "Here, wait, I'm going to pick it up," one of them boasted. But he had to use both hands and then kept putting it down and picking it back up so its body was covered with dust and sand by the time they started taking pictures. Our parents decided the monitor should be "tested," so its dead body was put in a huge glass container with formaldehyde and sent off to Ibadan.

Only once again did I see a monitor lizard in Nigeria, in a cage in Joinkrama. And once in my present life, I saw one in a pet store in Raleigh. Sitting motionless in its empty cage, the animal looked at me as if pleading for mercy or death, the same thing.

Whenever she remembers that moment, she sees the nurse's arms lifting the gun, her dress so white it is blinding, her cocked elbow, the deadly gaze, the sorrowful look in the monitor's body as it crumbled to the ground.

She has a dream. She is on the front porch of her house in Ogbomosho, the bungalow with the two broad steps down to the lawn. She is there with a boy, and they are watching an animal approaching them across the lawn. The boy declares that the being is a large insect, a huge spider. But the girl is sure it is not and demands that he let the animal approach. It appears prehistoric, crawling more than walking, its body covered with a tough armor. It comes straight to the house and up the stairs, stopping at her feet. Looking into its face, the girl sees that it is thirsty. She runs toward the kitchen, her *kitchen, for she remembers it as if it were yesterday, but all she can find to hold water is a brightly colored aluminum glass, one of a set that her mother and father received as a wedding gift in the 1940s and deemed appropriate for an African tour. Filling it, she turns around to see that the animal has followed her into the kitchen like a pet. She extends the glass toward the creature, which lifts its thirsty mouth, toppling the glass and creating a shower of water all down its face and throat, a self-baptism. And then, suddenly, the creature begins to transform and she sees that it is the monitor lizard. Its brittle armor turns to a sleek skin that glistens like the finish on the dining room table.*

Later, after she awakens and is fixing her hair in front of the mirror, she looks into her own eyes and thinks: "I am the monitor lizard. I have been looking all these years for a return home and for safety, and there is no road back to the safe place." Perhaps when the monitor was shot from the tree, its spirit came and took up lodging with her and together they have been looking for a safe haven ever since. At least a place to die. "But she should not have trusted me; I was just a girl."

> I was in a country
> once
> that knew me:
> knew me like the rain
> knows the red-eyed dove, like
> the river knows its bed,
> like the sun knows
> the elephant's back.

In Nigeria in those early years, I was learning with my whole body and mind. Every time there was an opening, I took it, whether it was singing about Zacheus or greeting the groundnut lady or visiting the night market or answering Abraham or walking alongside the mower with my father or standing face-to-face with the poor girl at the hospital. But the death of the monitor signaled the beginning of a closing, the beginning of my move away from one sort of being to another. Apparently our compound would not tolerate certain kinds of beauty and power. If we had allowed the monitor to live, for it had never harmed anyone, or if we had allowed a Nigerian who *knew* this animal to take it to safety or even to a useful death, we would have been saying: *There is room in our world for the great lizard.* But instead we said: *We have advanced beyond you. You are only a danger to us.*

I have spent a great deal of time in America acquiring Western knowledge. But all the while I have been moving further from my past and thus my future has shortened itself.

When I did once return to Africa in 1980, I bought a few books, as is my habit. One of these is *A Primary History for Nigeria: Book 3* by J. E. Adetoro, an aquamarine-colored paperback that I purchased in a small local bookshop. Perhaps I hoped to educate myself as I might have been educated had I been born to Yoruba parents and taken my lessons in the village school. The shop itself—Dayspring Books— was in the market, because in Nigeria you can go to the market to purchase books, along with cloth and soap. Within the store, texts were laid out one-deep on a few thin shelves, while outdoors they were hung from a line, held with clothespins, slips of color against a brown background. I bought the book and stacked it with others for years, not really reading it until I began this memoir. The contents interweave three subjects: the early history of Lagos, Nigeria's primary port city; the coming of Europeans and the slave trade; and Nigeria's mission history. If the company one keeps is telling, this trio of subjects bodes badly for me.

One of the stories that is told is that of the famous missionary nurse Mary Slessor. How odd, I think, that my own mother, herself a missionary nurse, did not educate my head to Slessor's story. It seems that I was reared in such a way that I would not have any impression of historical continuity or precedence in Africa. I was being made an American. And hence I experienced Africa out of time. Real time was American or European time. Even white history in Nigeria was silenced; or perhaps I should say white history was especially silenced, perhaps so I would not ever believe that I could *stay* in

Nigeria. I grew up without a sense of the history of my clan, which might explain why, in writing this book, I am surprised to find myself reading about mission history in a Nigerian-authored schoolbook. I had begun to think none of my early life really happened. Certainly, I grew up knowing much less than I might have known of my country, Nigeria. But now Nigeria demands its place, blowing into my life like a storm.

According to Yoruba belief, the city of Ile-Ife, neighbor to Ogbomosho, was the first place in the world to be created. Thus I was born on the Ogbomosho mission compound, a place of proximity with traditional divinities, Eshu being right there in our midst. But I was snatched away from them and dedicated to the Christian deity that had been superimposed there, like the mission road upon the Yoruba paths. Why was I never told as a girl about the legends of Ife? Why was I so poorly educated about the place in which I lived? Could it have been that the adults around me, including my parents, had learned but so quickly forgotten this history, or never learned it at all? Or was there a power in Ife that required constant forgetting in order to resist? And didn't I know anyway, *and didn't I know anyway,* learning indirectly if not directly about the originating claims of Yoruba land? Children know what parents have forgotten. Or children know differently. For sometimes I have lost the facts but remembered anyway. *As in a dream, I am on a path to an old missionary graveyard in Ogbomosho. Here are huge upright stone markers, with some smaller ones, cloistered under a green canopy.*

For anyway and always, Yoruba crept into me, tussling my hair at night, entering my nostrils when I breathed, snuggling in my ears like sandflies. And the agents of my Yoruba training? They were the dark of night, the palm and guava trees, the slant of the earth away from my house, *the gods of noonday,* that absolutely still white moment when life ceases and then with a sudden intake of air begins again, certainly Abike and Ishola and Abraham and all the other Nigerian teachers who ministered to me. This is what comes to me now: Africa should be called the First World, since it is; the United States should be called the Third World, since it is. Perhaps I was being educated to Yoruba land even in the slumber before birth, as Ishola Kunle, my mother's first Yoruba instructor, was coaching her in Oyo about the ways of the marketplace. *Ask the woman for her last price,* he would coax or, *No, Ma, that pineapple is pass ripe.* If so, I have always been, like Henry David Thoreau, regretting that I am not as wise today as the day on which I was born.

In the Shade of the Guava Tree

A DREAM. *I am in a house I do not recognize and then I am setting out candles in a row by the sidewalk. The house is in the U.S. and it is the one I live in with Andy and Joel but it is not familiar. But then the house changes and it is the house in Ogbomosho. I see a young girl, three or four, coming out the front door. She has short blonde hair and is carrying a small wooden box with two drawers, something like a roughly made jewelry box. She holds it close to her chest, and I understand that she is going to bury it in the side yard in the shade of the guava tree. And then I think: "I must remember where she is burying that box because I might need it. I might come back one day, and I should know where it is."*

Into the Forest

IN 1959 WE MOVED to the rain forest of the rivers area, east and south of Ogbomosho—indeed, to the far reaches of the Western region, a land near the basin of the Niger. Always long trips meant the deep dizzy torpor of carsickness and a kind of dampening on and off sleep in the backseat. But one needed such an initiation before reaching Eku, where elephants and hippos once roamed, where the male weaver bird sprouts his long, colorful tail to attract his mate, where cleared land conjures a jungle overnight, and where the gaboon viper keeps watch at your doorstep.

Have you seen the gaboon viper? A more beautiful animal cannot be found. A more deadly animal cannot be found. With diamond head and thick trailing body, decorated in a mosaic of triangles and rectangles, painted ivory, brown, yellow, and pale lavender, he looks like a heavy necklace dropped on the floor of the West African forest. His beauty kills your breath. His venom stops your heart. The Africans say: "If that one stings you, lie down and die."

There are many sorts of vipers, and I came to know several.

We had been to Eku before, for Christmas, spending our time with Aunt Mary Evelyn Fredenburg, a missionary nurse and long-time friend of my mother's. The hospital in Eku was a fledgling compared to Ogbomosho's, though it already looked aged to me with its towering palms and declining tennis court and grease-smeared electric plant: a small, one-room, once-white building, almost hidden beneath a vigorous stand of bamboo. What I did not know at the time and have only recently conjectured is that the Ogbomosho compound was something like the king's seat among missionaries, Ife to the Yoruba. All other compounds were secondary to it, at least during my Nigerian years. In any case, the Eku hospital needed an administrator, so my father and mother, and of course Becky and I, were relocated.

I go slowly over that word now: *re lo ca tion,* forced movement, movement again. I did not know then how often we would move after my first few secure years in Ogbomosho. This is what happened: in 1959 we moved to Eku; in 1960 we moved to Winston-Salem, North Carolina, for a furlough year; in 1961 we moved to Oshogbo, Nigeria, where my parents would serve as house parents for one year at our boarding school for MKs; in 1962 we moved back to Eku, and by the time we got there, I was bound and determined never to move again. We would stay for two years.

Once, on a long trip, my family had stopped on the road for lunch but I was still sleeping in the backseat. When I woke it was because a truck had hit the Chevrolet and I was coasting in it downhill. I remember waking up, still groggy, and looking out over the backseat to see my mother, father, and Becky running for the car, their arms outstretched, the pimento cheese sandwiches bouncing out of the back gate as I slipped forward away from them. The car stopped when it hit a tree but that's not what I remember. What I remember is the slipping away.

Even when I do dialysis exactly as prescribed, I am nauseated half of my life. I have been sick since yesterday. In my journal: *Took a walk late in the afternoon, thought it might jar me into wellness. No luck. Spent the evening lying on the couch, dozing off and on.*

Woke at six a.m. this morning sick to my stomach. Went back to bed, relieved. Woke again at nine a.m., still sick, really just heaving. Back to bed after asking Andy to go to the pharmacy to pick up the nausea medicine my doctor had called in earlier. He went but found no prescription. The doctor had called the wrong pharmacy. Joel dialed the doctor again. Finally had the pills around noon. Slept another two hours before getting up a little after two. Weak and uncertain.

It took eight long hours to travel from Ogbomosho to Eku. Though we were still in the Western region, we were not in Yoruba land. In fact, after independence, the many minority groups of this territory would demand their own separate state, the Midwest region. The Urhobo of Eku were certainly distinct to me. How can I explain it? Yoruba women dress in blue, walk with a casual gait, and lift their arms when they talk. You will think they like you. The Urhobo women of Eku marched to a different drummer, their faces more serious, their backs straighter, their dresses more often oranges and browns, their arms sturdy as sugarcane. As I remember, the compounds and villages around Eku were more humble. The roofs of the houses came down lower.

Moving in 1959, we literally drove into the rains; it was the rainy season, after all, a phenomenon that turned the world emerald, as if we were looking through green glass. It was always the rainy season when we moved, migrating in the "summer" months so that the school year was not interrupted. Always the clouds were sagging like soft gray hills turned upside down. Even though our house in Ogbomosho had been emptied out like an old shoe box, I did not feel any remorse about the move. I had no sense yet that after this every migration would bring us closer to the eventual breakup that would claim us. At the time I believed in nothing so much as the staunchness and invincibility of my family. We were eternal.

Still my mother did lament the condition of certain pieces of furniture when our loads arrived on a huge lorry from Ogbomosho. The bed of the truck was sided but open on the top with numerous canvases arched and stretched over crates, a kind of monstrous camel. Not a single piece of china or crystal was as much as nicked, although the inlaid table received a gash on the top, as if an African civet had tried to take a bite out of it. About such "accidents" as this, my father never scolded but quietly talked to himself as if he was unable to account for some private failure that led to such unhappy outcomes. It was a burden to him to live in an imperfect world.

Weeks before every move, the drums would come out and a corner of the house would be devoted to packing them, which my father would do late into the night. He packed every piece of our china and crystal in a drum, using reams of the *Daily Times*. This was the sort of thing I thought men did. Just as every so often my father collected all the shoes in the house—well, except for my Keds and his tennis shoes—and lined them up in the living room. Then he fetched the shoe-shining equipment and got to work until our shoes shone like hand mirrors in the market, which is quite a lot under tropical sun. There's something very fine about a father shining your shoes. You can go to sleep at night.

I realize now what a telling picture we made, arriving in Eku, the whole moving project a vignette about privilege: makeshift trucks and movers groaning with a load of china and fine glass and mahogany furniture. One of the great trials of missionary women was to teach Nigerian house servants, always male, to handle the family dishware. In our case, we had a set of daily china and a set of in-between china and a set of fine china. In my present life, my sister and I eye the few remaining pieces of this dishware in our parents' house like animals circling a kill.

Perhaps my earliest memory of Eku is of our Christmas visit in 1958. I was four, and at the time Aunt Mary Evelyn lived in her old house not far from the hospital. My sister had filled my head with dreams of Santa Claus, who was on a par with Jesus because he hung around outside your window to catch you being bad. I kept peering out the window of the guest bedroom where we were staying—and you really were looking *out,* the walls were thick mud and plaster— trying to catch a glimpse of his great red figure coming in over the tops of the palms on Christmas Eve at twilight. I believed so hard that I recall as a memory rather than a wish my actual witness of Santa Claus descending through the clouds. Here in the rain forest is where I first heard songs like "I'm Dreaming of a White Christmas" and "Walking in a Winter Wonderland" and "Silver Bells."

Aunt Mary Evelyn's house was something like Rose Cottage in Ogbomosho, the oldest house on the compound, built in 1949, and occupied by single female missionary nurses. Like the cottage in *Snow White and the Seven Dwarfs,* this single-sex dwelling seemed to me even then to exist in a parallel universe, with Aunt Mary Evelyn acting in my life as something of a fairy godmother. You went to her house for

Christmas or she took you to the river or she fed you foods both trivial and bizarre—like homemade pizza—that your mother would never consider serving. Even her dishes seemed part of a fairy tale, a bright, bold assortment of Fiesta tableware that would never have suited in our house. Her cottage in Eku was painted white with dark green shutters and was approached by a circular drive with flower beds in the middle. The kitchen was actually a separate house in the back—no doubt the cook was happy with this arrangement—and sheltering both was a flamboyant tree, that tree that looks as though God painted it green and then tipped over a can of orange paint on top. As is always the case, the house seemed huge to me as a child, but in fact it was rather small among missionary houses.

In my mind, Aunt Mary Evelyn was the linchpin of the Eku hospital. She walked across the compound in a slow swinging gait with her midsection slightly in front of her and her head back, almost as if, even then, she was becoming something of an Urhobo chief; later she was actually so honored. I guess I would say that Eku—as opposed to Ogbomosho, which always seemed to be a male establishment—was a women's compound. Which is why it does not surprise me in my present life when I learn that the first clinic was begun by a nurse, Eleanor Howell, who arrived in Eku on January 1, 1946, accompanied by her husband, a preacher. Perhaps Ogbomosho was male because its roads were open and wide and Eku was female because its paths were meandering and shaded. Ogbomosho was dry and Eku was wet.

Unlike Ogbomosho, the Eku compound had one road that made a great wide circle from one gate to the other, though there was also a stretch of road past our house that connected some newer houses to the older ones. In some ways the Eku compound was a misplaced 1950s American cul-de-sac, replete with outdoor barbecue pits and even, after someone returned from furlough, ornamental aluminum signs that identified each home. Ours said *The Lloyd Neils.* I was mystified. What could it mean: that my sister and mother and I were multiples of my father? That my father himself was more than one? Was Lloyd the subject and Neils the verb? Whatever its meaning, like everything else on the compound, the sign mildewed and faded and began to sag. Before long you could hardly read it, the black mold creeping across the lettering like driver ants.

Our compound at Eku was located on the edge of town, not in the midst of things as in Ogbomosho. Here the fence that edged our front yard was met on the other side not by Nigerian dwellings and pockets of woods and savannah but by a rubber plantation. Rather than hearing the village sounds of radio and taxi and drum and pestle, I heard rubber pods popping—an unpredictable rhythm like distant firecrackers—the wind through the palms before a storm, the hum of the hospital generator. If I had remained in Ogbomosho, I would probably have heard, by way of the Nigerian Broadcasting Company, more of the national celebration as independence approached.

Our house was the first in the new development, which actually put it right in the middle of things. Aunt Mary Evelyn's new house was next door. These one-story ranch-style houses were brand-new when we moved in. The Nigerian building staff wanted to know which one would be "the Manager's house" (that was my father), and they put the best finishing touches on his. Still it would not take long in the rains for moss to collect on the seldom-used front steps and for the roof to streak and mottle, like the fur of a great brown beast.

In Eku I learned to swim in the Ethiope. Trying at first to float on my back, I couldn't tell if I was in the water or looking up at it. Anyway, my feet kept sinking. I had more luck with the dog paddle, heading out from the pier toward my mother or father or Aunt Mary Evelyn, who would grab my hands as I approached and reel me in. Even on Christmas Eve we would swim into the evening at the Ethiope and eat a picnic dinner at dusk before returning to Eku, where I would fall asleep under the Christmas tree.

This is the girl who moved to Eku. She had lived all her life in Ogbomosho, except for one year in the U.S. when she was two, a year she does not remember. She had never seen a television or viewed a film or read an American comic book or seen snow or curled her hair. She kept time by the blossoming four o'clocks at the back stoop and the freckles on her face were like the sand on the ground and she learned to swim like a tadpole made for water.

Here in North Carolina I scoff at the oaks. Who could care for so fruitless a country? The trees are too regular, their shapes too tame and predictable. When I turn to a full-color photograph of the rain forest in the *National Audubon Society Field Guide to African Wildlife,* I'm looking into a mirror. Rather than trees, I see my history in the circular shape of palm branches, like those accordion fans from Taiwan that we bought in the market, the lowest branches dying to gray, the tallest hardwoods encircled with greenery in the upper branches, the dense foliage, the clouds heavy with a week of rains. I touch my face. When I look at another photograph—this one of a palm tree with ferns growing out from the upper trunk where the branches have been trimmed—I think I could die and be satisfied because once I knew a place of such stunning grace that my life has already been fulfilled.

In a poem that is really a letter to my American friends, I once wrote:

The rain forest is a place I went
to and never
left,
a space
in which I hold myself
apart,
that slim decided
separateness
you keep trying
to loosen.

Moving from Ogbomosho to Eku was like moving from Arizona to the Everglades and this is not great enough a contrast. Unless you have been in the great forest, you cannot imagine the height of green, the various layers of it from bush to palm to hardwood, and every sort casting out its limbs and leaves, and the drumming heat of tropical breath, from tender fern to heavy frog to jawing mamba to crowning mahogany. Snails weighting caladium leaves and bossy praying mantises; leaves sagged with young sporangia. The lesser trees seemed to gather together like members of a clan, but in reality they were fighting each other for access to the light. There's a parable here about human nature. Along the road I saw ample evidence of the forest's age and primacy. It didn't so much overtake our efforts at progress as it waited for progress to come to it. And then it peacefully lapped it up. In every village, one could see the skeleton of a half-built concrete structure overtaken by the forest before the owner could collect the rest of his money to finish it. The greenery around Eku was a single huge organism. And still I can see the little emblems: a small, tuberous wildflower that blossomed lavender-pink on the forest floor, slivers of blue glass in the area of the koto, snail tracks.

I recollect only "small small" about my education that year in a dark, vacant missionary house, except for drawing ridiculous images of women that were little more than elongated triangles topped with a circle and arms and long legs like straws. This deformed female may have been a prophecy for my teenage years of dieting. Once, a schoolmate and I decided to expand our palette and create a free-flowing wall mural in one of the empty rooms, but this industry was quickly broken up. I received an early lesson in science from Becky, who told me that the earth turned around in a circle every day. Like all children, I suppose, I found this hard to believe. I thought it should be much windier if it were true. But Becky was adamant in her instruction, so what I began to imagine was that the world circled *around* my house each night, an idea that kept the house and my family stable. I never got up in the dark to check, but now I think that my conjecturing reflects my determination to keep my family firmly grounded in Eku.

The offspring of five missionary families made up our little school. Being in kindergarten, I was among the youngest, and I felt my place, especially in the presence of the "older" Abell boys, David and Ricky, who must have been in the second and third grades and who lived at the very end of the compound, what I considered the wild zone. They seemed to me to live entirely outside the law, forgetting to wear socks with shoes, carrying slingshots, and riding large black bikes. Even

Gary Lynn, who had been my friend in Ogbomosho and had moved, as we had, to Eku, had turned into a young terrorist.

Why do I recall that MK boys were overly violent? One of the earliest bits of gossip I remember was the story of Paul Joiner swinging a cat around by its tail. Did the intense scrutiny of mission life simply reveal more about those boys than might have been revealed in a larger setting? Were they really any worse than my own father growing up in South Carolina and shooting young sparrows to roast on an open fire in the woods?

Perhaps something of the great white hunter mentality had been communicated to my male peers, who found plenty of flora and fauna in Nigeria to exfoliate and extinguish. At the same time, all of us were being urged to take on the mantle of Christ, to turn the other cheek. In other words, the script was terribly confused.

Becky and I undertook one adventure together that year but we did not see it through. Our intention was to spend the night *outside* in the back of the Chevrolet wagon that was always parked in the carport about twenty-five yards from the back door. Becky's friend Connie Gaultney was included in this girls-only experiment. That afternoon, the Abell boys came by to show us how to build a fire. They made a square divided into four sections, which they filled with twigs and leaves. The fire would start but die down quickly. Finally, in disgust, they stalked off, more or less suggesting that outdoor fires weren't meant for girls. We didn't need a fire anyway; we had nothing to roast, no snails and no snakes. Instead, we eagerly anticipated the evening by consuming our dinner of baked beans and hot dogs with the sun still high in the sky. This campy repast was spread outside on the concrete retaining wall that divided the Gaultneys' yard, and we ate hurriedly, trying to urge the night forward.

In the dark car, we huddled together on our pallets spread in the back of the wagon. We had flashlights, but the light only bounced off the windows. We could see nothing outside, and the outside grew enormous. Sounds edged to the car, palm branches creaked, something pinged off the roof and something larger hit the ground. Who knows how long we endured the sounds. Perhaps fifteen minutes?

Perhaps thirty? The last thing I remember is the three of us running for our lives, flashlights zigzagging across the lawn as we sped for the back door.

Becoming a "big girl" with no one like Abike to shelter you was harder than I had thought it would be. You had to make choices that mattered to other people and not just yourself. And then there were temptations that came out of nowhere but possessed you before you knew what your hands were doing. For example, one week the May-halls, a family that included several daughters about Becky's and my age, were visiting, and all of us consorted together to spread talcum powder throughout our bedroom, from the tops of the curtains to the floor. Where this idea came from or what it meant, I cannot recall, unless we were copying the Urhobo devotees of the Mamy Wata. I stood on top of my mahogany dresser, reaching as high as I could, and pitched powder up against the walls and curtains until I was nearly blinded by it. The room looked as if a cloud of thin white paint had burst from the ceiling. We had powder in our eyelashes and under our fingernails and on our tongues. How our parents met this disaster when first they discovered it, I don't remember. What I do remember is that after the Mayhalls left, Becky and I both received spankings for the mess we had made. One night we were naked before our baths and before I knew what was happening we were being spanked in turns for our mischief. My father did the spanking but Mother was in attendance. A punishment is one thing, but a spanking days after the fact is another. In this action, my parents seemed cold and vengeful, and for the first time in my life, I doubted their worthiness as children of God.

On another occasion, I was visiting next door as the Gaultneys' cook was preparing deviled eggs. Without permission I helped myself to one. David was crouched with me under a table in the dining room just before I scored this coup, but he was not as foolhardy as I. As it turned out, eggs were not as free as guavas. My sister learned of the theft and reported me, and after lunch I returned to the Gaultneys' house with my mother and one perfect egg to replace the one I had stolen. I had to recount my crime—though it was well known by that time—and offer Aunt Virginia my apologies, enigmatic Aunt Virginia, whose dark hair and bemused smile might have made me think of the Mona Lisa if the woman in the painting had been drinking coffee from a melamine cup. I thought my mother overzealous in her effort to restore our righteousness. And anyway, shouldn't I apologize to the cook? The ceremony about the whole thing far outweighed the crime and only went to show that my parents were too concerned with appearances. Urhobo youngsters, by the way, are generally free to eat wherever they like, so I was only living by my native rights. But my parents' reputation, which extended to Becky and me, was worth more than gold. In other words, the stolen egg was not a crime against the Gaultneys; it was a crime against the Lloyd Neils.

As the eldest son of the local Baptist preacher, my father had been expected, growing up, to set a good example. In his youth, he failed entirely. But this did not stop him from looking at me with those same preacher's eyes. And it was not just moral worthiness he expected. He wanted me to stand up tall and sprint with the wind and speak politely and make As in math as well as in English. I have to say that his concerns were a mixed blessing because I have often fallen back on the strengths I learned from my father. At the same time, I have often "covered" my weaknesses and imperfections as a way of not disappointing him, and my mother too for that matter.

I covered my diabetes for years, anxious that admitting to such a disease would lessen me in the eyes of others. I covered my brokenness even from myself. Indeed, it was not until I was in my mid-thirties that I realized that mine had not been an entirely happy childhood, that if I were a calabash, I would not hold water. I did not realize until even later that losing Nigeria had nearly cost me my life. One faints after righteousness. In my illness, needles are a daily acquaintance, an iron staff, leaving bruises on my thighs when I hit a vein. And the pricks on my fingers to check blood sugars are as familiar as my freckles, another mapping of my life. But few people know the trouble I'd seen. I have never wanted anyone to think of me: *Ah, poor Elaine, she is marred, she is imperfect; I am sorry for her.* No. Instead, what one hopes for is *Ah, Elaine, lucky girl. She looks so complete.* Or *Ah, the Neils, they are such a lucky family.*

Outside our compound, the nation was being born. It was a hard birth. Not only the Yoruba, Igbo, and Hausa-Fulani, but a myriad of minority groups like the Urhobo were demanding their place in the highlife of independence. The closer the projected day loomed, the clearer it became that the country was divided like that fire David and Ricky built in four squares that started but then fizzled out.

The year for us was short and wet. On rainy afternoons, when there was nothing else to do, I would sit on my mother's bed and sort through her jewelry box—masses of blue and purple beads and matching earrings and rhinestone pins, but no bracelets; my mother never wore bracelets because she thought her hands were too big, like her father's. Or I would empty the button jar in the middle of the bed and sift through the pile of multicolored disks. Or, if my mother was in the room, I would ask about the swatches of fabric in the double-wedding-ring quilt that my grandmother had made in South Carolina from scraps of her eight children's clothes. My mother could identify bits of cloth that came from her own or Aunt Julia's or Aunt Adrienne's girlhood dresses. So this is what my real "aunts" were to me: bits of cloth in a quilt on a high mahogany bed in a concrete house on a slight elevation above the rubber plantation and swamp outside the village of Eku in the rivers area of Nigeria.

Our cocker spaniel coped badly with the rains. For some reason, Ginger took to rooting in the ground, especially around the bases of palm trees. These exercises left her nose bloody, and we ended up putting a muzzle on her as a deterrent. She endured the year, but really, cocker spaniels are not made for the rain forest any more than monitor lizards are meant for pet stores in North Carolina. When we went on furlough, we handed Ginger over to strangers, and I never saw her again. My long-suffering bush cat, Susie, on the other hand, had begun her life of reproduction. When she delivered eight kittens in a box in the garage, I watched from beginning to end and helped bury the dead one. My sister shunned us both in this bloody event. She didn't like cats to begin with so I suppose I could not have expected her to share my vigil. But the new little kittens were magical. In minutes they were lifting their mouths in the air and rooting for milk and mewing and pushing and pulling. I admired them for their life and determination and the way they didn't mind walking all over each other to get to what they wanted. They seemed human to me. I understood and conversed better with them than with any of the humans around me. In fact, it must have been while I was at Eku that I began talking back to the animals and plants that had been addressing me for as long as I remember. It was on the basis of this communion and my affection for David that I would come to love Eku eventually.

> Gecko on my ceiling
> Hawk in the air
> Monkey at the river
> Duiker unaware.

I spoke with nature so much better than with humans. Nature had gusto and took what it needed. People, on the other hand, said what they did not mean and did what they did not wish to do. All around me, adults were urging humility, but they themselves were proud. I was taught not to put myself first, but I could see that everyone longed to be first. Not only that, I was already missing some people and things I would have liked to have kept: Edna Rachel, my friend from Ogbomosho, Abike, our nursemaid, our house near the empty lot where the monitor lizard lived, the guava tree in the side yard. My hunger increased but I didn't really know what for. Still, it seemed to me that I had better look out for myself. The world was becoming a complicated place. Just because you were hungry did not mean you should eat.

Now in my American life, I want to go outside and see a country that is natural in my eyes. I don't want to see my split-level house or jonquils coming up in February or camellias in bloom or robins in the grass. I don't want to see North America. I want to see red-headed lizards in the road, vying for dominance, palm trees overtaken by weaver birds, mud-and-plaster houses with roofs that sound in the rain and dirt roads that look as if they've been traveled forever. Wealth is an elusive thing. Americans have money, a great deal of it compared to Nigerians, who make on average about three hundred dollars a year. Still we have so little that lasts. In fact, because we have so much, we throw away a great deal before it even has time to take on character, including our marriages.

I contracted a bad case of filariasis that year in Eku. My mother had me sleep on a cot in my parents' room for several days, but I felt too ill to enjoy the luxury, my limbs thick but my chest a blank. The sickness, transmitted by tabanid flies, is a rather gruesome one, or rather its effects are. Larvae incubate and then hatch in one's bloodstream, causing enlargement of the extremities, in my case, particularly the legs. These creatures are sometimes detectable under the skin; they might be seen, for example, roaming across your eyeball. This was the first serious illness of my life. I was surprised at my body's failing. After all, I was like my father, swift and strong and lean, and he had never been sick a day in his life. So this was a mistake, this illness. Someone had erred.

Meanwhile, Nigeria grew like a male adolescent whose parts don't all work. This imbalanced growth made the segments jealous, and distrust was planted upon distrust like new hurts upon an old wound. *And the harmattan came on leopard's feet, pounding down from the Sahara plains in wide strides of dust and chilling air; and the villagers stoked their fires while the white people bundled in their thin blankets and threw sweaters over their short-sleeved shirts.* There was planting and harvesting and lovemaking and birthing and suspicion and dread. And the ancestral spirits walked at night and pleaded with the living to wake up. But the music of the market was too loud and the children danced without thought and the parents ate their egusi soup and slept on full stomachs as if they were the dead.

Everyone was eating and everyone was hungry. There was plenty and there was not enough to go around. The country was being born and the umbilical cord was wound around its neck like a python. And the drums pounded: *Beware proud elephant! Beware!* But no one was listening to the old ones. Children are boastful but walk unawares with scorpions at their feet.

God Bless Nigeria, Land That I Love

I THINK ABOUT MYSELF now in those years after Ogbo-mosho; I was like a young goat in a basket tied to the side of a lorry, carried hither and yon. Because after a year in Eku, we were on our way to America for furlough. That's how we said it, never the U.S., always America.

But you can't just bump children along like croquet balls without doing some damage, even if it is the will of God.

As it happened, we left for the U.S. just as Nigeria was approaching its big birth day, sloshing out of Eku in the middle of the rainy season, heading for Lagos. There we departed for England and then boarded the USS *United States* for New York. I had no memory of the land I was returning to.

On ship, I encountered my first film, an American western. Becky held my hand as we inched down the aisle and found seats near the front. These seats were different from any I had ever known. You had to climb in and then they leaned back a bit so your feet were way off the ground and your eyes weren't looking straight ahead but up toward a big white rectangle. The lights went off and we were in pitch dark. I felt like I was drowning as the screen lit up with angry men, hundreds of them on horses, charging in one direction. And then all of a sudden the riders changed. The first riders were dressed and wore hats and carried long guns. But the new riders were hardly dressed at all. Their faces were painted in long stripes of red and yellow; they had big feathers in their flying black hair and they carried long pointed sticks and another bending stick with something like a long rubber band on it. These men made whooping noises like huge birds, but the white riders kept their lips sealed, their heads down.

Then the world changed again and somehow I was with the white riders and we were galloping into those brown-skinned riders. They started falling to the ground, bent over like river weeds. Their horses were falling over too, their legs swinging up into the air as if they had hit a slippery spot. I have no idea what these worlds are or how they fit together, and I am scared out of my wits. Not so much by the fighting, but by my sense of being lost, like I felt in those dreams I sometimes had of falling endlessly into a whirlpool.

I run from the theater, and it is uphill, so I feel I am hardly moving. I can't even see where I am going it's so dark, and there is only one bright light at the back and it blinds me.

Later, when a passenger safety drill is conducted, I find myself separated from my family, lost in the bowels of the ship. Then we arrive in America. We are "home."

I attend first grade in Winston-Salem, North Carolina, in a new school that seems very smart and modern to me. I learn from overhearing my teacher talk with my father that I am smarter than the average bear. I watch *The Flintstones* and *Leave It to Beaver* and see *Peter Pan* on a black-and-white TV on a cold enclosed porch because my parents don't believe in TV. And I eat M&M's and peanut butter and apples and play under large bushes in the yard and learn the smell of cedar and witness plenty of sleet but no snow that year and work on a stamp collection and learn to skate awkwardly after everyone gets skates for Christmas and take my first piano lessons from Miss Mary and hear the story of Pinocchio, which is told to me as a deterrent to lying.

In some ways the year was not so strange as it might have been because we lived with my Aunt Miriam and Uncle Sam and their children, Harriet, Margaret, and Sammy, in a huge, two-story rented house on a corner lot, elevated in the back from the street because the lot was on a hill. In the spring, odd, glossy, almost plastic-looking flowers emerged, which later I would know to be narcissus or daffodils and lily of the valley. Aunt Miriam, for whom I was named, and Uncle Sam were missionaries in Hong Kong, and they had furloughs every sixth year. You can imagine that since our furloughs occurred every fourth year, we seldom ran into the Rankins in the U.S. or anywhere else in the world for that matter. Except this year we did. So all of the parents thought nothing would be finer than for us to double up together. Thus my closest associates were MKs who were also my cousins. We were all normal, I thought, as normal as July. Everyone has furloughs and lives like this. Except that I thought Becky and I were a little *more* normal because we were eversomuch-more even-tempered than the Rankin children, who tended to throw tantrums in the morning about going to school—well, Margaret did, and sometimes Sammy pouted.

One morning I came downstairs for breakfast; I was the last to the table. And as I descended the stairs and approached my extended family, Sammy aimed a question at me: "Who are you for for president, Elaine, Nixon or Kennedy?" I had no idea, but Sammy's knowing tone prompted me to answer surely. "Kennedy!" I announced. "But he's a Catholic," Sammy shot back, as if he had hoped I would say Kennedy so he could leap upon me with this damning news. I didn't know what a Catholic was so I wasn't that impressed or that mortified. "So?" I answered nonchalantly.

Still, I liked Sammy. He had blond hair like mine and I sensed that he didn't take wholeheartedly to this new American scene.

The most significant event of the year was my father's accident. Usually we walked to school by ourselves, that is, without parental supervision, all of us but Harriet going to the elementary school down the hill. Then later my father would come to walk me home since I got out in time for lunch. I would show him my papers for the day, almost always smiley faces, and he would be proud and we would walk home together. It was a fine time we had with my father always showing up, that radiant look of love in his eyes. Until one day, crossing the road to the school, he was hit by a truck coming over the hill. Apparently a glare was in the driver's face and he could not see my father there in the street in plain day. When I got home from school, I was taken by my mother into my parents' bedroom, the only bedroom downstairs in that big old house. We sat on the bed and she told me that Daddy had been in an accident, hit by a truck, and he was in the hospital, but he was going to be okay. His back had been sprained and he had a few broken ribs, but considering the nature of the accident, he was extremely lucky to be alive. This last she did not say. But I could tell that something much worse could have happened because of how my mother sat on the bed with her hands folded; she seemed to be holding herself together so she didn't spill over. When my father came home, he had on a big stiff cast around his chest, which made him stand up straighter than he usually did. After the cast, he had to wear a brace for several months, but I never heard him complain. In fact he joked about it. My father was much more likely to despair over a gash on a piece of furniture than over some physical adjustment like wearing a brace.

The news of my father's accident impressed me. He was the firmest reality of my life but apparently he could just be hit by a truck and—boom—be gone. But we never talked about this feeling; we were so good at regaining our footing and going on as if nothing had happened.

I was neither happy nor sad in Winston-Salem, though I had to adjust to my parents' bedroom being downstairs while I shared an upstairs bedroom with Margaret and Becky. I was conscious of the space between us. Only once that year do I remember being held by my mother at night. Still there was enough novelty in the year to keep me interested and consequently I was fairly obedient. My mother reports that on one occasion I did lose my temper when I heard someone on TV singing "God Bless America." I thought the song unbefitting a Christian nation that would surely want to ask God's blessings on *all* nations—like Nigeria, for instance.

When we visited my grandmothers in South Carolina, I concluded one must prefer Nigeria. The U.S. was a queer country of white abundances and settled weariness and no Africans.

But on the whole, I was now adept at acting as I was expected to act and not as I felt. Thus, I rarely complained about my clothes itching me, I took my turn, I was immensely polite. At night, my mother curled my hair, just on the sides. We went to church where everybody was so white my eyes hurt.

When the year was over, I said good-bye to no one but the Rankins, whom I was not to see again for at least ten years.

And in our absence, in a party of pageantry and palm wine, Nigeria was ushered onto the world stage. In Lagos, they sang:

Yaba is a city,
E.B. second to it.
Lagos so so lovely
Highlife boku n'a de [There is plenty of the highlife].

"In-de-pen-dence de come o," our gardener in Ogbomosho might have said in wonder.

Dislocation and Mother Loss

AFTER COATS AND mittens and leggings, after more borrowed furniture than you could shake a stick at, my parents and sister and I moved back to Nigeria, to the Oshogbo compound and the campus of Newton Memorial School. The city of Oshogbo was only thirty-five miles from Ogbomosho but the compound here was a world apart. It was not dedicated to a hospital for Nigerians or a seminary for Nigerians; instead it existed solely to educate MKs and a few others who applied. It extended from grade 5 to grade 10. My sister would enroll, living in the girls' wing of the dorm. My parents would be house parents for a year. What my role was remained uncertain. Our loads were still packed up in Eku, in storage. So we lived in an apartment in the dorm, using borrowed linens and beds and sofas and chairs. We had just returned from a year of hand-me-down dresses, but I did not feel any doubt about my significance in the world on account of that. I knew I belonged to Nigeria. I knew our things were waiting for us patiently in Eku, like characters in a storybook, waiting to be opened. We needed only to return to claim them. But the detour by Oshogbo was stretching my faith. My only connection to Eku and what I thought of as home was Susie the cat. She did not seem to mind the change of scenery and lounged faithfully on my windowsill at night and came to the back doorstep when I called and let me wind her long body around my neck like a kerchief and mewed obediently whenever I rubbed her and kept down the lizard population in the back yard, not really a back yard but a courtyard formed by the new wing of the dorm.

We were back in the motherland, but now I was sharing my

mother with a cast of extras, and Becky was living separately from us as if she were not my own sister. Like other students, she had to sew name tags onto her clothes so they could be identified after the wash. The four of us were never to live again as a family except on vacations or furloughs. But, of course, I did not realize that at the time. I was seven. In truth, one could also say that we were not to live again as a family after I was five in Eku. That would be more accurate.

What I did realize in Oshogbo was a most curious transformation in my mother. She became a person so separate from me I felt I was viewing her on TV, and this was because she ascended to the position of favorite counselor to the older children in the dorm. Troublesome "older" boys in the ninth and tenth grades sought her sanctuary as if she harbored the Holy Grail. They trusted her more than their own mothers or any of the other staff at the boarding school. Which meant she was always giving her ears to someone besides me. She became a person with whom you made an appointment. The students' need and subsequent devotion ignited her. She had a desk in her bedroom and she counseled them in this inner sanctum. I felt that she was becoming much too intimate with strangers.

In our peculiar new world, my parents acted as if they were not Becky's parents but her house parents. No favoritism was allowed. Thus when it happened one evening that my sister came to dinner without having showered and changed her clothes—because this regimen was always required—my father called her out in front of the rest of the school. I remember how she stood beside the table she shared with five other students, her head down and to the side like a beautiful tall flower that has been plucked in the sun. "Becky, have you had your shower?" my father inquired, knowing she had not because she had on the same dress she had worn all day. "No, sir," Becky replied. "You are dismissed from dinner. Go to your room," he instructed, with a heavy monotone that seemed to make him a possessed person it was so unlike his real voice.

As an act of solidarity and passive resistance I skipped my bath the next evening. But I pretended to bathe. I ran water and threw a few stray bits of dirt from my clothing into the tub and then let the water out and put on clean clothes. I was not discovered and smiled a bitter smile of satisfaction at my misbehavior. But I think I would rather have been caught than not, because going unnoticed, my act of solidarity seemed futile.

As a general rule, my parents thought I could take care of myself while they seemed a bit doubtful about Becky. I tried on occasions like this to show that I might not always manage without their watchful eyes on *me,* but they always missed the signs and I was forced to keep up the facade of self-reliance. My parents believed they were well on their way to divining my inner head: I was gifted, smart, undaunted.

Perhaps it was Becky's living away from us that made me aware of the differences between us. We were both hoping to build collateral with our parents, especially now that we might lose them. I thought the way to do this was just to be myself: what could be better? Becky, on the other hand, intuited that the route to favor lay in being *like* my parents: devoted, long-suffering, and Christian.

Thus my older sister generally gave in to my demands. Once we were offered two little round mirrors encased in plastic, one pink and one green. I wanted the pink one, and a brief battle ensued before Becky allowed me to have it. But Becky was building up something besides capital in pink mirrors in this transaction. She was building up a reputation for self-sacrifice, a reputation I never even considered investing in. In a thousand minor moves, Becky established herself as the loyal daughter, while I, unbeknownst to myself, was crafting the reputation of ambitious, even profligate daughter. Okay. Profligate is an exaggeration. But when you are comparing yourself with a sister like Becky, even normal self-interest looks crass. I didn't have a clue at the time.

Becky's reputation as a "giver" spread beyond my house and into other mission houses. All the aunts and uncles knew about her generosity, so there was really nowhere else for me to stand except under the sign that said "taker." And given my ambition, I tried to fulfill this role to the best of my ability. I just wished someone would bless me for my trouble.

This was what the seven-year-old girl heard every day: the bell at the boarding school rang in the morning to waken her. The bell rang again for breakfast. The bell rang to send her to school. The bell rang again for recess. The bell rang to send her back to her books. The bell rang again for lunch. The bell rang for rest time. The bell rang again to transport her out into the afternoon sun. The bell rang for bath time. The bell rang again for dinner.

The liquid time of Eku was replaced at Newton with the regimen of work. All the time in the day was neatly packed into segments like sandwiches in waxed paper. Ben Franklin reigned supreme at Newton School: we knew about him without ever having heard his name because we knew that *all things are easy to industry* and *a little neglect may breed mischief* and *God helps them that help themselves.*

Nigeria itself was attempting progress. As the industrious Igbo say: *Another time and another time is another word for laziness.* The country had a clean new flag, a white panel between two green ones, that had been hoisted on the racecourse in Lagos on October 1, 1960. The picture books my sister had sometimes studied, of Queen Elizabeth and her family and their corgis, were stored. The feud with the imperialist was over, but now the country had to prove itself. Prime Minister Abubakar Balewa summed things up in his speech to the nation: *Independence is not an end in itself. It is the means whereby we are determined to ensure that Nigeria plays her full part in world affairs. . . .*

. . . but for the seeds of partition, the seeds of partition that were sewn into the birth of the nation as neatly as those patches of cloth were sewn into my mother's South Carolina quilt.

I was one of three pre-Newton girls on the compound that year, sharing a school room, actually a screened porch, attached to the DuValls' house. The DuValls were a large family and always seemed to me like their own little kingdom: Uncle Wallace, the school principal, Aunt Pearl, whose name alone seemed to mark her as specially chosen although one of her legs was shorter than the other from polio, David, two years my senior, Ellen, my peer, Ricky, Kathy, and, later, Becky, the younger set. The thing about the DuValls and Aunt Pearl was that she was *for* her children, no question. While my mother always tried to be judicious and show no favor even to her own, *especially* to her own, Aunt Pearl always voted for her offspring, especially the two eldest, Ellen and David, the two closest to me. This meant that in my relations with this family, I was always outvoted. I had no champion like Aunt Pearl. Even my sister can give witness to this experience, and Becky doesn't exaggerate the way I supposedly do, though I have always believed my witness to life to be a kind of underreporting. How can you exaggerate the need for family and country or the catastrophe of losing either, much less both?

My other schoolmate that year was Vicky Cockrum, who lived with her parents and younger sister on the lower side of the compound, below the boys' wing of the dorm. The Cockrums were not like anyone else. Uncle Buford was an architect and Aunt Virginia said things like *I'll swan . . .*, which must have been Southern Baptist Polite for *I swear*. Then there was Vicky's younger sister, Joyce, who had long beautiful brown hair like a miniature movie star. The Cockrums didn't look like they really figured on coming to Africa. They were used to store-bought clothes and air-conditioning and fancy items for the bath. Aunt Virginia decorated her toilet with those miniature blue glass Victorian slippers that you can now find in antique shops.

Living behind the Cockrums in their own little two-room house enclosed by a tall hedge were their Igbo cook, Mr. Amobi, and his wife, Comfort, and their two daughters and baby son. The older daughter, Nwada, was about my age and she and her younger sister would play with us on Vicky's swing set or in the large sandbox at the edge of the yard. The sandbox was circular, framed by a concrete wall, which was being pushed up by the roots of a huge tree that grew beside it so that the wall sort of leaned out like the waistband of a large man who had eaten too much yam. Sometimes we would all gather around a small concrete box that housed the control to the Cockrums' water supply, for this box was always full of water and tadpoles lived in it. In Oshogbo, my water play had shrunk from the River Ethiope to a two-foot-square box in the Cockrums' back yard.

Sometimes we would go into Nwada's yard, where Comfort would be cooking gari over an open fire, her baby sleeping on her back.

Here we squatted beside her and watched the hypnotizing stir of the pellets in the huge black bowl, indulging in the buttery smell, and eventually begging Comfort for some, which she would give us in our cupped hands and we would lap it up with our tongues.

For once, rather than preferring home, I kept wandering to my neighbors' houses in the afternoon. I am sorry to say that Vicky and Ellen and I sometimes left Nwada behind to engage in ridiculous American girl games. For example, we would dress up in fifties-style prom dresses that for some mysterious reason were available to us and play at make-believe weddings, taking turns being the bride. These dresses were bright yellow and blue and green taffeta with netting and sequins. In these gothic games, someone would stand under the flamboyant tree and act like the preacher while the other two processed outdoors, someone humming the bridal march.

Among the three of us, I considered myself the least pretty and the smartest, but I was not sure which of these was an asset and which a liability. David, Ellen's older brother, occasionally chose one of us girls as his ally; he was a fourth grader and like us was too young for the boarding school. Rather handsome even then with his dark Heathcliff brows, he chose me only once, and so for a few sterling hours I was the favored one.

For the first time in my life, I learned from my cohorts in Oshogbo that I should fear the drums I heard at night. They told me tales of wild Egungun—madmen dressed in wild costumes who danced in the moonlight and looked for small children, presumably white, to terrorize. My parents tried to ease my fears, but the poisonous idea once planted took root and I became fearful of the night.

One day my family left for local leave, headed to Jos. At last the Northern state became a reality for me. In our Chevrolet, we climbed the great Jos Plateau, the first I had seen in Nigeria. Here I witnessed a number of oddities: fewer trees, fewer people, or maybe they were just more spread out; the Nigerian villagers here built round houses; and it was chilly so you had to wear a sweater. I even met an MK who had a horse to ride, a possibility I thought existed only in America. As far as I was concerned, this wasn't really Nigerian country.

But the Northerners who lived in the highlands thought differently. They thought this was the *main* Nigeria. And since the country's political system depended on representation by population, the North kept finding its belief confirmed. So while it seemed to me that people were scarce up here in Jos, the region was so much larger than the West where I lived with the Yoruba, or than the East where the Igbo lived, that the North was the chief state. Even after independence, the Yoruba and Igbo had to fight for their share of British resources, because, of course, the British were still buying and selling in Nigeria and granting or withholding favors.

Americans can think of their own majority and minority populations to get a sense of the struggle Nigeria was in. What if you had three majorities that were really nations unto themselves and several hundred minorities? Good grief. If you were an Igbo in the North or a Hausa in the East, you might have felt like African Americans when they went to the "colored" entrance.

Jealousy abounded.

Aunt Mary Evelyn is fond of saying that she never met a Nigerian child with low self-esteem. So I can imagine what a battle of wills there must have been among the big men in Nigeria in those days.

What I remember from the Jos trip is buying a glass animal at the local Kingsway, a little brown kangaroo, and eating at a restaurant with huge glass windows, looking out at nary a palm.

Back at Newton, we celebrated American holidays, not Nigerian ones, so we had a huge Thanksgiving Banquet each year. Our parents made every effort to make us American children. So Newton School even had a marching band for a while, though there were no half-time shows because there were no systematized sporting events.

Imagine the horns, imagine the brass and cymbals, imagine the flutes, imagine one hundred degrees at midday, imagine the mosquitos, imagine the Nigerians in the nearby woods watching this masquerade, imagine the surprise of hawks veering overhead at the uncertain music winging through the sky.

I became at once more "civilized" and more "barbaric" that year at Newton, living the regimented life of the dormitory timetable but also learning to speak Pidgin English—a habit my mother frowned upon—and going barefoot so regularly that I could run down the gravel drive without a second thought: *De stone no touch mie feet.* I tried to read my Bible, a small New Testament version that had been given to me in Winston-Salem, but I could not find the plot. I thought perhaps the parts in red print would be more interesting than those in black, but the whole book seemed to assume some prior knowledge of the subject, and I finally gave up.

I developed my first crush on a seventh-grade boy named Tim, an African American youngster whose father was with USAID or some other international organization. I didn't think of him as a "Negro"— I don't even know if I knew that word. Once a person arrived at Newton, he or she was just one of us. No one thought to ask why Nigerian youngsters could not also be "one of us." I simply thought of Tim as cute; he seemed neater and more cordial than most of the other "younger" boys in the dorm. But even though I had chosen the most gentlemanly boy, my mother discouraged my affections—I was too young for romance, she said—and after I wrote Tim one missive and received no reply, I gave that up too. Thinking about this first attraction, I wonder if "liking" Tim was as close as I could get to "liking" a Nigerian boy, if I were not, somehow, trying to transgress an absolute taboo. Denied even Tim, I learned to ride Becky's bicycle instead. I rode it in the large oval field in front of the girls' dorm that was created by the circular drive.

I still have a picture of me just at that time, wearing a pair of pink shorts and a little V-necked stretch top with a blue border and blue Keds on my feet and with my hair cut so short I look like a boy except for the huge grin across my face that makes me a girl. Sun bleaches the dry grass in the left side of the picture; it must have been December or January. I am riding into the dappled shade created by a trio of trees that stood a little off-center in the field. Anyone who ever went to Newton knows just the trees I mean. In the background to the left sits the first classroom building. Its roofline from the side—a low, sloping, upside-down V—revives my spirits as I write, though this compound is not a place I particularly loved. Several palms fill out the background, one a young specimen I remember vividly; perhaps it was a special breed because it stood by itself as if someone had planted it intentionally. One large tropical hardwood right behind me looks as if it is rising out of my head. My legs are tanned and sturdy as good books. My palms, grasping the handlebars, have not yet felt empty. The land behind the classroom building crests and falls away, just as I remember it. If you turned left at the gate, you would arrive in town. If you went right, you were on your way to Ogbomosho.

I spent some days catching butterflies with a net and asphyxiating them in a jar until the sport lost its charm from sheer redundancy. The butterflies were too abundant and too easy to catch and died too beautifully.

One evening, I rebelled wholeheartedly, refusing to participate in the exercise of dinner in that huge dining room with my parents and all those older children. My mother gave in, and I was fed in our private living room. But the victory was only bittersweet. I was alone.

By the time I was seven, the four columns buttressing our family mythology were established: Mother was wise; Father—who'd been hit by a truck and only slightly damaged—was strong; Becky—whose left-handedness seemed to spell her fate—was long-suffering; and Elaine was invincible. None of these claims was true, of course, or they were only true in part. Mother was also dispassionate, Father was also impatient, Becky was also politically motivated, and Elaine—who presented a bold exterior—had *No Telephone to Heaven.* She was frighteningly alone and she knew it. Her *true* inner head was a pile of contradictions.

Perhaps my mother would have counseled me with the same stamina and grace she dispensed to the boarding school students had I sought her out. But I never liked to share, especially not my parents. So I pretended I didn't need her. Meanwhile, I was on the threshold of the beginning of envy, watching Ellen and Vicky, whose parents were not expected to take in as many children as mine were.

In my adult life and after my mother and father had retired from the mission field, my mother became quite renowned in the Southeast for her advocacy of women in ministry—in particular, Baptist women.

This was the early 1980s. I had been studying feminist theology at Emory University and now my mother began to study feminist theology and women's studies too. She taught classes at Southeastern Baptist Theological Seminary in Wake Forest, North Carolina, before it was taken over by fundamentalists. She developed a great following among young women my age who were not me.

As I think back on all this, I begin to realize that my chief familial competition was not with my sister so much as with my mother. We have been in a struggle all my life to see who could need the other least, who could let go, who could claim independence from the other, or really who could outdo the other. Our other competitions were elaborations on this theme. One of the reasons I felt I must have a PhD was in order to pass my mother, who had several degrees of her own but none this high. This goal was related to the more fundamental, more primitive goal of walking away from her. According to my mother's story, when she first held me in Frances Jones, I pushed away from her. I have the same memory, only she's the one pushing. Even today when we visit, our sentences joust. Whose story is more important? Whose plot more compelling? That's the question.

I learned to walk on stilts in Oshogbo, which was a very Nigerian thing to do—many festivals and masquerades include the use of stilts. I became amazingly agile with this sport and would walk on stilts all over the compound. It's really not hard, though it seems it would be. Maybe this form of locomotion was preparation for my later life of living in the U.S.: here you are walking in a very artificial manner but you learn to do it and could perhaps walk on stilts for the rest of your life if you had to. That was what boarding school and America were like: artificial, easier to adjust to than you would guess, but resulting in a kind of basic separation from what should be closest to you: your country and your mother.

I have never in my life known where to take my suffering. Certainly I did not think you took it to church. Church was where you went in new clothes and basked in your wholeness, where you showed other people how well you could behave, where you displayed your talent playing the piano. The people my parents came to minister to: they suffered. We, on the other hand, were chosen people in whom the absence of suffering was a sign of goodness.

In my present life, we are interred by a huge snowstorm. Today with sleet and freezing rain, I cannot even go out for a walk. Inactivity weakens me, robs me of will. I nap, and in my dream I sit in a wheelchair in a white room and on the floor I watch a dialysis bag filling with drained solution. The contents look like sticks caught in a stagnant pond.

After nine months in Oshogbo, we moved briefly to Ogbomosho for the summer so that my father could fill in as the hospital administrator. We camped in a vacant house. Our temporary residence was down the hill from our real house, the one we lived in before we went to Eku and then America. I remember deep incisions in the compound road from the heavy rains that fell, sending sheets of water downhill. Sometimes in the morning, the harmattan fog would sit down on that road like a huge brown lion and then around nine o'clock rise up and quietly walk away.

Mother got sick that summer and spent a good deal of time in bed. Sickness was really off-limits in our family, so I think we all ignored her. I had almost no supervision; my father was at the hospital and Becky was up at the Wassons' house, baby-sitting the latest offspring. The Wassons were close family friends—they had arrived in Nigeria in close proximity with my parents and they had sons Becky's and my ages. That summer they were the ones living in our "real" house. Alone, I concocted huge liquid refreshments out of Dutch Baby milk and Milo chocolate powder.

And then one day after Susie had given birth to a healthy set of kittens, she disappeared as quietly as the harmattan fog. Another mother gone.

I am outside in the front yard of the house, in the driveway that is really just a grassy patch depressed by the numerous passings of the car so that two tire tracks have emerged. It is registering to me that I haven't seen Susie for hours, maybe not even all day, maybe not since yesterday, though this seems impossible. I am wearing shorts and a sleeveless shirt and am turning slowly in a circle and crying out her name: Susie, Susie, Suuussseeee, drawing it out before my voice falls into a bellowing silence. I begin to feel that coolness in one's center that is a first sign of fear. I turn to walk to the back yard, my eyes on the overgrown bushes that edge our lot. Any minute, I hope, Susie will pounce out like a lioness, approach me and wind her slender body through my legs, arching her back and mewing all at once, then look up at me and blink her eyes in complete innocence. But already I know she will not come. Already I can feel it is too late. Still I call, wandering around the house like someone newly blind, stumbling over the white rocks that line the gardens in that place, skinning my knee, wiping my hands against my shorts, absolutely forgetful of everything but the fear creeping through me.

"I can't find Susie," I tell my mother when I enter the house, for she has finally regained her senses and is out of bed. It is twilight and the electric bulbs are not yet on and my mother is only a silhouette. But she speaks boldly: "Oh, she's got those babies; she can't be far." When I pull Mother out into the yard, just to see her face because that alone will bring some comfort, she calls with me. The darkness continues to fall, almost as if a great hand has snuffed out the light. When we finally arrive at the washroom and look in the door, we see the little kittens tumbling over one another and crying, so hungry are they and so lonely. There is nothing to do but get some milk and try to feed them, which I do, pushing their noses into the bowl so that their little whiskers are covered in the white liquid. Eventually, they begin to use their tongues. They will not go hungry. But I will, for Susie cannot be replaced.

For several days, I dip the young ones' noses into bowls of milk until they begin lapping without instruction. Secretly, my parents assume that Susie has been carried off by some Nigerian laborers on the compound and has wound up in somebody's soup. Whatever happened, Susie never returns and the summer is over. So my family packs up our meager belongings, drops Becky off at boarding school, and sets out again for Eku, our numbers greatly depleted.

I did not see my parents grieve. Yet how they must have grieved.

The Groves of Eku

THE DRIVE FROM Ogbomosho to Eku was an exhausting seven or eight hours in a car without air-conditioning. After an hour on the road, you felt hungover with some former life that had caught up with you. Thank goodness for those reprieves along the way when we would camp for lunch, either on the road or sometimes at the remnants of a station like the one at Ilara—a drive, for example, lined with trees and that used to lead to a British post. Occasionally, we would stop at Akure in hill country. Here was a government rest house where you could order lunch served on white tablecloths in a dining room. Everything was very proper, and there were even clean restrooms. Then after lunch you could sit on the front porch and look out at the hills. Our route took us through Ilesha and Akure, on to Owo, and then to the famous city of Benin, once a formidable kingdom and home of the exquisite bronzes. Along the way, we left the savannah behind, with its scrubbier trees and dusty roads, and entered again the rain forest, with its booming greens and raucous thunder. We were on the road again, but at least we were going home.

But back in Eku, we were not quite home. "Our" house was still occupied by another missionary family getting ready to go on furlough, so we had to spend several more weeks camping, this time in a house on the old section of the compound.

No house was ever actually owned by a missionary. We moved in and out of these great shells like hermit crabs. I just thought they were ours. So, for example, the house in Eku, which we were going to move back into and which had been new when we moved in three years earlier, was always in my mind the Neil house, regardless of who else lived there or for how long or however much they redesigned it and thus in my mind ruined it.

When, in my adult life, I read Jean Rhys's *Wide Sargasso Sea,* about a decaying aristocracy in a postcolonial world, I think about that house we camped in in Eku before we got home. It was not so grand, but it had once been landscaped and the whole area surrounding the house spoke of a misplaced domesticity, of faded tea parties and lost afternoons. I don't remember any interior lighting in the house except for what entered naturally from the large louvered windows, and even that was muted since it rained every day. We tried getting a kitten to make the place more like home and to replace Susie, but she hadn't been properly weaned and would suck on the ball-like tufts of my bedspread. Mother found this unseemly behavior, and the kitten had to go.

The house was designed exactly like our house in Ogbomosho: you walked into the front parlor, which was flanked on either side by bedrooms and a bath. Behind the parlor and formal dining room was that screened eating porch that I have likened to an African room. It was separated from the formal areas by a partial wall. And to the left of that was the kitchen. On the right side was an extra room or a study, depending on the family's needs. Only, in Eku, you walked into the breakfast area at the back door instead of into the parlor, because all the houses were backwards. Whoever designed the compound believed it more appropriate that the houses face away from the hospital than toward it. So the backs of the houses looked toward the road and the fronts faced a rubber plantation and the rain forest. This meant that the garages opened onto empty front yards where there was no road, not even a driveway. The huge concrete inclines designed for cars simply collected algae and acted as spawning grounds for all manner of organisms.

The yards—themselves expanses of grass and trees leading down to the fence—were spaces largely uninhabited, except by MKs, when we included them in our explorations. During the day, you could spot a man tapping rubber trees just on the other side of the fence. For the most part, we traveled the compound road and met each other across back yards, always entering in the back door, never knocking but yelling "ndo"—spoken like the English word "doe"—which was Urhobo for "hello," "good-bye," and many things between.

Except that someone at some time had planted a garden in the front yard of the abandoned house that my family, absent my sister, lived in that rainy season. There I found an overgrown patio of carefully placed pavers and odd pockets of flowering bushes and a walkway. Much of my life, I have been looking at the ground, looking for evidence, almost as if I have already been where I am now returning. One day I saw a lavender snake like a long curl of hair on that overgrown patio, an initiation for me because in Eku I was to learn how in charge nature was and how little control we humans actually had. The rain forest made all the difference. The house we were in had been built in the early fifties, but it seemed ancient to me in 1962, wet and moss-laden as an old boat. The ghosts of that hidden garden haunted me, perhaps because they suggested that my own footsteps in Nigeria would one day be only a dream.

I had a captivating friend and peer in Eku, David Gaultney; the name is like water over rocks to me. He had been there before when my family was first stationed in Eku. But we were younger then and there had been other MKs around, so our interaction had not been as intimate as it would become now that we had really only ourselves and his two younger brothers, Bruce and Steven. David and I began third grade in the screened back room of that temporary house in the corner of the compound. I remember our books arriving from Calvert School, Baltimore, Maryland, and unpacking them with Mother. The box included rulers and small art prints—of young Abraham Lincoln, Queen Nefertiti, and the Madonna, for example—and pencils and erasers, and the books were sky blue and vanilla. Our two desks faced the louvered windows, looking onto the back yard. We sat in folding wooden-slatted chairs that left imprints on the backs of my legs because in Eku I no longer wore a dress to school as I had in Wake Forest and Oshogbo. I wore shorts. Just outside the back door was a flame tree. Later in the afternoon after class, I would sit at the table in the same room, with my mother, and we would compose letters to Becky. Mother's letters were long and complex, pages and pages of onion-skin paper. The two of them learned to pour their hearts out to each other this way as they had never done in person. I would watch my mother and try to guess what she was feeling and write my own letters with sentences like: "David and I are on Lesson 12 today. We are reading the story of Robin Hood. I have a kitten but she is trying to suck on my bedspread. I can't go to the river because it is raining." Sometimes as my mother was engrossed in her meditations with Becky, I wanted to grab her by the arms and shake her and say *I'm still here,* but I did not.

My first remembered address is from Eku. I wrote it in the left-hand corner of envelopes bearing letters to my sister:

Eku Baptist Hospital
Box 35
Eku via Sapele, Nigeria

How strange and elegant the word *via* seemed to me; in my own system of translations, I determined that it meant "a turn in the road." We took the trip to Sapele about every other month. Via meant close by but after lots of turns.

I read this familiar address from the back of a photograph given to me in my present life by Aunt Mary Evelyn. The photo was taken in 1974. It offers an aerial view of the hospital, showing in the foreground the main road through town and, in the center of the photo, the hospital. At the upper edge, the compound road is barely discernible between the palms. I can almost make out some of our houses. It seems to me that I am viewing an X ray of my body: the roads and pathways like arteries, the buildings vital organs.

My most vivid memory from squatting in that vacant house concerns a certain Sunday. We had gone to church in Eku and returned, as usual, for our noon meal. Mother had left our dinner in a covered pot in the oven. But somehow a mouse had gotten in and dislodged the lid.

"Oh my word, Lloyd, come in here. There's a mouse in the oven.

The lid is off the chicken; it's spoiled. We won't be able to eat it." And my father, who is close at hand, shakes his head and begins deliberately to address the problem.

"Let me see," I venture while holding myself back, not really that eager to look. But Mother swoops me aside. "Let Daddy take care of it."

As was always the case in such an instance, my father had the duty of eliminating the offending creature. Through some means, he captured the mouse and took it out to the side garden, where he flogged it with a broom until it was dead. Whether I went along to beg pardon for the mouse or what my motivation was, I do not recall. I simply didn't think we could afford any more casualties. Whatever the case, the mouse was thoroughly killed, though it was a small small thing, about as big as my palm. When it lay dead, it was smaller still and hardly distinguishable from the garden dirt. Perhaps such conquests were a form of communication between my parents in which my father was saying to my mother, *Don't worry; I will take care of you.* Perhaps the killing of the mouse was a sign of my father's own frustration and loss. Perhaps it was also difficult for my parents to move so often, though they were willing. Perhaps my own father—who I judged to be only slightly lower than the angels—experienced woes I knew not of. Perhaps my mother was often afraid.

I rode Becky's bike, now mine, in spite of the rains. Sometimes I would leave the house, the clouds so heavy they were skimming the treetops. I would get to the other end of the compound, down by the new houses where the rain forest literally leaned over the fence, before Shango began to conjure up bolts and the drops started falling like hail. *Oh no. It's raining; we've got to run,* I would offer to no one, for there was no one there; I was merely dramatizing my dilemma to make it more brilliant. And then I would race all the way back, tilting the bicycle crazily as I pushed down each pedal with all my might, headed into the rain, my face upturned to the downpour. Finally I would burst into the house and run to my mother as if to say: "Look! I rode off and it started to rain and the drops were pelting me but I rode and rode and rode all the way home!" It was glorious whether I said it or not.

I don't know if you've noticed, but children are determined to be happy. In the same situation as an adult—that is, loitering in a mildewing house on the outskirts of Eku in the middle of the rainy season—I would doubtless have been depressed. As it was, I was brimming with my own internal joy. The road was long; the bicycle was swift; I had wings.

Or, on the other hand, I was frightened by the disappearance of Becky and had nearly forgotten myself in our moves and was worried about my mother who had been sick earlier that summer and who seemed at loose ends now. But I was determined to return us to our happy, wholesome selves, and I rode the bike with the intention of recapturing whatever it was we had lost. The feeling I had was like the feeling I'd had those long years before standing with Becky and my father in front of Frances Jones: something was missing even though we still seemed intact.

Finally, we moved home. Six moves in three years, two of them across the Atlantic. The hibiscus my father had planted by the house were in full bloom.

My favorite spot was the screened breezeway connecting the garage and the rest of the house. Here in the evening Fidelis, our cook, served us an enticing dinner of potato fries and bacon, lettuce, and tomato sandwiches, or spoonbread and sliced tomatoes. Fidelis was a quiet man, but he had once boldly announced that my mother had the reputation at the nursing school of making even "stone brains think." We sat at a folding table while the sun set, transforming the lizards on the screen into dark silhouettes. They never moved. In the daytime when it rained, these reptiles would cluster one on top of the other in the far upper corners of the screen, under the eaves. The rain would fall in the space between the garage and the house, a space covered in river rock, the mist floating through the screen, dampening my bangs as I watched the water cascade down in columns, exploding on those round pebbles. Standing there you felt rich and sad and full and empty all at once.

I am surprised now by my affection for those big brown lizards, and the memory of them causes me to believe that our eyes are shaped by habit and what we are told to see. I liked the lizards—they were not ugly to me. I liked them as well as another person might like bluebirds. They were almost members of the family.

During the week, I went to school with David. I thought I was clever, and he was kind enough to accommodate me, so we got along fine. We read books like *Smiling Hill Farm,* an unctuous story of white American homesteaders, and *Mighty Men,* a far more interesting volume surveying the glamorous exploits of people like Hannibal and King Priam and Attila the Hun. It was from *Mighty Men* that I learned about King Arthur and the Knights of the Round Table, the Trojan horse, and Romulus and Remus. I could just see those wee babes suckling that wolf and those men, under cover of night, slipping out of that horse like spirits.

I never thought to ask where the mighty women were. And I never wondered what my connection was with these stories. It seemed perfectly reasonable to learn European history while living on the edges of the Nigerian rain forest and glancing at the headlines of the *Daily Times* every morning.

My most commanding textbook that year was *A Child's History of the World* by V. M. Hillyer. It began with an overview of evolution and then the Stone Age and followed this introduction with stories that led all the way up to the U.S.S.R. I was tantalized by the story of the Parthenon and how the columns were made with a slight bow in order to appear straight. This paradox seemed to explain a great deal. For example, leaving Becky at Newton seemed to make my mother sad, but maybe she wasn't really sad; maybe she just seemed that way. With this rule in mind, I would try to convince myself that whatever I felt or believed I saw that was threatening or out of kilter only *seemed* that way. In someone's eyes—say, the perfect eyes of God—everything was straight and true and had an ending you could believe in.

During most of the school morning, David and I were wards of my mother, at work in the enclosed garage that had been made into a schoolroom. At some point, we crossed into David's yard, and then Aunt Virginia watched us work our math, beginning always with a clean sheet on which we ruled off margins before writing our names in the top-right corner. I always thought my signature more beautiful than David's. He had no interest in curling his letters, and although I respect his preference now, at the time I found it unambitious.

The two of us also occasionally took lessons in Greek mythology from Aunt Alice Gaventa, the mother of the renowned Johnny and Billy Gaventa, older boys who were away at boarding school with our sisters. These were boys you didn't really *see,* even when they were home on vacation. You only *heard of* them. They were already legends. One day David and I were at Aunt Alice's for a lesson. We were sitting at one of those quintessential mahogany tables in that paradigmatic screened room. But I will have to go further back to tell this story.

I knew two white women "gone native" in Nigeria. One lived in a village close to Eku; the other still lives in Oshogbo, Nigeria—the artist Susanne Wenger. This story is about the woman outside of Eku. She was British and she had married a Nigerian man, perhaps after World War II. She had two tall and beautiful daughters though this woman herself was of average height and the very definition of homely. Her body rose like an elongated pyramid, beginning at her swollen, veined feet and the lowest reaches of her skirt, rising through her thick thighs and undecidable waist to her shrunken chest and pinched face. I never saw her smile. On the day in question, she was in Eku with one of her daughters who was sick. Rather than staying at the hospital, however, the daughter was being nursed at the Gaventas' house since Uncle Bill was a doctor and I guess they were friends of the family.

As David and I are taking turns reading the story of Zeus, I hear a noise in the adjoining room. The girl is sick. Immediately, Aunt Alice goes to assist, opening the door just enough to pass through. But a door briefly opened can leave a lasting impression. What I see is the tall gorgeous girl coming out of the bathroom into the bedroom; she is being held up by her shorter, awkward mother. And then the girl falls in a sprawl on the bed. For a moment, her entire back side from the waist down is exposed, her skin like fine sand but her body lifeless.

Everything about this vision is amiss. The mother is herself an enigma. The daughter is beautiful but helpless.

I did not think then of how the daughter was an emblem of the new Nige-

ria, the offspring of West Africa and Britain. I never thought about how we were alike, daughters of two countries or of no country.

In my own body, I was strong and androgynous. I saw no connection between myself and that young woman. I pitied her instead.

Brother

ONCE WE SETTLED IN and I readjusted to the rain forest, life was good.

With David, my days were like silver beads on a long necklace, interchangeable and all the same and every one priceless. He was a long-lost brother whom I loved like the palm trees. I was home. I was back at the river. The whole compound was ours; there were no older MKs to interfere; the only other children were Bruce and Stevie, and they were so young and so pliable we didn't mind them. In fact, they provided ornamentation to our fantasies. I held Becky's memory at arm's length, hoping to stave off any more losses. We played all kinds of exploration games; we spied on people who weren't even there; he was cowboys and I was Indians, or the other way around. David taught me to mount my bicycle by running beside it and jumping on. I became adept at riding full-tilt up a concrete incline on the hospital grounds and literally flying off the other side of the raised walkway. The layout of the nursing school dorms and classroom buildings provided occasion for all kinds of pathways that were lovely to ride along on one's bike. This was a world where a few places—houses and the hospital—gave you access to roads and paths, not the other way around; in other words, for me, the paths were the crucial feature of the landscape and it was just by accident that they actually led anywhere. As far as I can tell, nothing on terra firma is so dear as a path.

Not long after we returned to Eku, we visited Enugu, a prosperous but young town by Nigerian standards over in the Eastern region.

This particular trip held a certain charm because Uncle Wayne Logan had commissioned a trampoline to be made for his son Steven, and I spent most of the weekend bouncing on it. My father inquired about its construction and carried the idea home with him of making one for me. On this trip we also visited an expatriate club that included a swimming pool, a café, and a large pavilion. This was not the sort of place the Neils frequented, living as we did in bush neighborhoods rather than cities like Ibadan and Enugu. We looked on this sort of life as slightly risqué; the European women at the pool smoked cigarettes. Anyway, we went there with the Logans, who must have been more cosmopolitan than we, and one evening we viewed the film *The Magnificent Obsession.* This was my entrée into Hollywood romance and that sweet, bottomless feeling that must be love. So while my father took home the idea of building a trampoline for me, I took home, I am sorry to say, a notion of romantic love as a passion that kills, or at least maims. But I packed this idea back in my sock drawer when we got home; I had little use for it at the time.

Back in Eku, the Gaultney boys and I played track and field with the seriousness of young Olympians, transforming David's back yard into our field:

I slip out the back screened door, careful not to let it slam. One step down and my feet are on the gravel path that runs behind our house and leads to the Gaultneys' yard. Nothing moves but the weaver birds and me, on my way to the afternoon games. I scamper to the tall hedge of variegated aralia that acts as a boundary to our yard and peer out, but no one has spied me, so I sprint, now out in the open, to David's back yard. It is as though he were anticipating me because I don't even have to knock before the door opens and he is beside me.

The Gaultney house looks as though it has been here forever. It wears the aspect of patience, like an elder who has seen many seasons. David and I look at each other for a moment shyly as always we do after a brief hiatus in our activities. Then as if internally we have taken a vote, we are ready to resume our play.

Stevie and Bruce follow us up to the high yard where we will begin our Olympics. We are young gazelles, our swiftness and agility unmatched, never mind the fact that there is no competition but ourselves. It is dry season now so the grass is stubby, the paths arid. You can smell the oily generator plant near the yard and hear the gentle creak of the bamboo by the road. A whole after-noon awaits us.

Our primary events are high jump, long jump, relay, and fifty-yard dash. We race against each other endlessly, and given my height, I often win. Or we face the high jump—a contraption rigged up out of bamboo poles—as though our lives depend on clearance, trying and trying until our bodies roll over in the air above the long reed. We stage relays with Bruce and Stevie up and down the compound road. Stevie's short legs are machinelike in their brief up-and-down insistence as he leans into the air. We give him a large lead before the race begins and he works desperately to retain it. You can see the absolute serious-ness on his small, sweaty face, the strain in his clenched fists. Even if he doesn't win, we declare him a worthy opponent. No one ever really loses.

In my present life, my father tells my husband a story that I over-hear. *Did I ever tell you,* he begins, and for once he has not. *Did I ever tell you about how I would spot Elaine and the boys out in our front yard in Eku? Well, I would look out, and way over yonder I could see Elaine's blonde head above the tall grass. And then if I looked real close and depending on how high the grass was, I could see just the top of David's brown head following her and then they would move a little bit this way or that* (when he says this he raises his hands as if in a Hawaiian dance and brushes them left and right), *and then after a while, why, I would see them come out into a clear-ing and low and behold there were Bruce and Stevie following them, and Elaine was in the lead.* And then his head goes back and he laughs gently at the memory, while my husband does not actually laugh but finds it an amusing, because predictable, story.

Occasionally, out under the sky, David and I would glimpse a jet plane way up above us, about the size of the end of your pencil, its trail of white smoke more visible than the plane itself. Our eyes were fastened to it until there was nothing more to see.

For a while, we constructed mud houses on the concrete wall that divided the Gaultneys' back yard like an equator. We would allow these to bake for several days, until they were dry and hard, and then we would light firecrackers in them and watch them explode. This was an activity David led in. I valued my fingers so I mostly watched

as he took the more dangerous part of striking the matches and lighting the fuses. Running fast and jumping high were one thing; playing with fire was another.

Once for a few weeks we created our own hospital pharmacy.

"Go ask your mother for some empty bottles," David instructed,
acting rather grown up and in charge, smiling for a moment but then
restoring himself to seriousness. "We're going to make a pharmacy."

"All right, but Bruce, you come with me." I always had better success with one of the Gaultney boys along as a sponsor. Mother was
at her desk when we came into the house—and it was hard to get the
boys into my house; their mother forbade them making a nuisance
of themselves. We were in luck because in West Africa you wash bottles out and reuse them forever. It's not like the U.S. where you throw
away enough plastic and Styrofoam and aluminum in a week to sink
a ship. In the storeroom, we found exactly what we needed: everything from small vanilla extract bottles to large pickle jars and everything between. David had already begun to concoct our drugs by
mixing water with food coloring, and back outside but in the shade,
we began diligently filling our jars. We lined the bottles up on a
bench outdoors under a small palm tree. For several weeks our pharmacy sat patiently under that tree. I can still see those bottles so dis-
tinctly. They were pretty sitting there in their blue and yellow and
green wholeness. They sat through the rain, never changing, like a
rainbow captured and held suspended for us. I was humbled by their
beauty.

Sometimes I think that the main thing David and I did in Eku on
those long afternoons, for we finished our lessons before lunch, was
dream. I think our organized play was occasional and the primary
thing we did was linger in states of wonder.

But at some point, American texts began to transform African
dreams. After I started reading Trixie Belden books, I urged the boys
to create a club with me and to imagine that we had a clubhouse and
mysteries to solve and horses to ride. We renamed places on the compound. Now the crossroads where our drives met the compound road
was Sands Junction and the small creek—really an overflow ditch

that ran between the Gaultney and Gaventa houses—was Winding
River and the corroding tennis court was Wheeler Stables. When you
weren't there, America was an exotic place. I rode the blue bike and
David ran like a scout. I adored Trixie's language and tried to imitate
it whenever I could. She produced enticing sentences like:

"Oh, woe, homework on a Friday. It's not fair."

"We've got to prove that he's an imposter."

"I'll sneak into the gallery on Halloween."

I was most consumed by Trixie and her world of riding gear, and
saddle oxford shoes, and two brothers! A few telltale signs connected
us: she too was marked by freckles and short blonde hair. And she
was characterized—by her mother and brothers—as impetuous,
sometimes shortsighted, and overly imaginative. Trixie seemed to
offer a model I could emulate. She was a girl but acted like a boy—
curious, quick, and daring—and for the most part, she was rewarded
in the end. I loved the way she made everything into a clue or a sign,
for I wanted things to *mean* something: for a leaf bent back on itself
to disclose that someone had been looking for me and not merely
that a caterpillar was weaving a cocoon, or for the faint tracks in the
sandy road to be the imprints of a long-lost pet. When I met the
praying mantis on the road, I paid my respects and took his appearance as an omen. I thought of the geckos on the walls and ceiling of
my bedroom at night as messengers who would talk to me if only I
knew how to listen.

On days when it was too rainy for being outdoors, we would
tumble onto the beds in the boys' room at their house and all fall
silent in our consumption of American comic books. We had read all
of these before, but we read them again, always in the hope that we
had missed something. And if we found a particularly funny one, we
would read it aloud to each other, or we would read to Stevie because
he could only look at the pictures. The Gaultneys' house, or I should
say the boys' room, smelled different from our house, mustier, heavier. And I wondered if it was just boys or if families had a smell;
Stevie was probably still in diapers but I didn't think of that. I never
said anything to anyone. The smell was like an intimacy you didn't
speak of.

Once at Easter, a whole slew of folks came from the boarding school to Eku on break, not only our sisters, Becky and Connie, but also the Bond girls, whose parents lived all the way over in Togo, and all of the Failes, the two older children from Newton and their parents and younger siblings from Ghana. We outdid ourselves with an Easter egg hunt that year. For weeks to come, David and Bruce and I were turning up unfound rotten eggs all over the compound. Of course, we took everyone to the river to swim, but the Bond girls had hardly seen water deeper than a bathtub and didn't know what to do with themselves. I was absolutely mystified that there were grown girls walking the planet who didn't know how to swim and would no sooner put their heads under water than spit.

Lessons on the Road

THERE IS A KIND of flow to Nigerian life. You see it in how people live. Once my mother and father and I went to visit the Ebhomielens, who were missionaries themselves, home missionaries appointed by the Nigerian Southern Baptist Home Mission Board. They were stationed not far from us so we saw them on a regular basis while we were in Eku.

At their house for the weekend, I ascertained that the Ebhomielens had achieved a nearly perfect living situation. First, they had their compound which was spacious but not too large and it blended into other compounds so it wasn't as rigidly defined as ours was. Back in Eku, I often longed to walk out of the gate and into the village just like that, as if I knew what I was doing, as if I were kin to a girl my age wearing a yellow-orange blouse and wrap with a pattern of palm nuts in it and a comb boldly stuck in her hair. Of course, I knew that my family was much wealthier than most Nigerians in Eku. But there was something on the Urhobo compound beyond my knowing, and I wanted to get to it. The Ebhomielens were closer to this mystery than I was. And then the Ebhomielens' house was a sort of perfect blend of European-Nigerian design. Their interior rooms were separated not by hard-and-fast doors but by soft, breezy curtains. A child will always prefer curtains to doors because closed doors say "keep out," and no child wants to be on the other side of such a sign. We slept in European beds, but the kitchen was outside. There was nothing fussy about our accommodations. I don't ever recall, for example, being in a Nigerian house where there were knickknacks on display or collections of things like my Hummel figurines and glass animals.

We used hurricane lamps in the evening because there was no electricity. But this was not an inconvenience because the space to be lit was modest, and the lamps produced a warm yellow glow and a somewhat reassuring smell, as when you smell bananas or pineapple ripening in your storeroom.

The Ebhomielens had no children my age; their children were preschoolers. But they were, like most young Nigerians, very beautiful. They looked at you intelligently and you felt your whiteness and your largeness in comparison with them. They did not call me *oyinbo*.

In the morning, we gathered for breakfast in the Ebhomielens' eating quarters, which were under a roof attached to the back of the house on a raised platform that might be compared to a covered deck in the U.S. except that this platform was packed mud. The goats and chickens were right there in the back yard. We ate cereal from a box, which I am sure was for our benefit, with lukewarm milk and pawpaw, separately, because you don't put pawpaw on cereal, and really, I have never enjoyed such a delightful breakfast because there you had the whole world at your doorstep, so much to watch and see and smell, and all your senses engaged. There was a liveliness in the Ebhomielen household due largely to the architecture of the place, such an easy confluence of living beings. Their entire dwelling was like our screened porch, which was the best part of our house because you could smell the rain from there, even feel it, and watch the lizards, and see the rubber trees on one side and the palms on the other. You want to live this way; it's the best. American houses are too tight. In my life in Raleigh, I sit on my front porch in the morning drinking tea in my pajamas. And I fight the winter tooth and nail because it curtails your outdoor activity. I have no use for winter.

The flow of the Ebhomielens' house extended to the market and to their church. Most Nigerian churches in my day could easily be entered by birds, for example, which flew through regularly. Indeed, the flow in Nigeria remains even where it had been banned, for instance in the middle of the streets in the cities where there are signs saying this way or that way or stop or yield. People and animals pretty much ignore them so that cars are displaced by walkers and wranglers. Sometimes this disregard results in a complete standstill instead of much flow, but really the flow has simply been transferred. Now human voices and car horns and cattle sounds mix in a crowded melody above the traffic.

For David and me, outdoors was always preferable, and we moved across that compound observing few boundaries. Every day included some measure of exploration as we pushed at the limits of our known world. If nature and civilization were engaged in a competition on the Eku compound, nature was winning. We ran like wildebeests through the undergrowth in the huge uncleared lot across the road from the Gaventas' house. Instead of stopping for snacks, we ate the heavy air around us. I was still hungry in Eku, but regardless of how much banana pudding I enjoyed after dinner, I grew tall and lean. David's skin turned a golden brown, and our hair shone in the afternoon sun as if we were wearing helmets. Our *ori* must have been vigilant because we never fainted, we were never stung, and no one broke a leg or an arm, even when we climbed those tall trees beside the Gaventas' house. Our worst disaster was driver ants, which would sometimes bite and latch on so tightly that even when you pulled them off their pinchers remained in your skin like a small tattoo.

We should, of course, have been stung often and well on that compound. Sometimes I think I was bitten by the gaboon viper discovered beside my sandbox one day, and the rest of my life has been a brief dreaming before death. There were also, of course, the mambas.

David and I were in my yard one day, engaged on the trampoline. We were trying forward flips when a snake crossed the compound road and was spotted by one of the gardeners. The snake was so long its head reached the other side of the road before its tail was visible and it lay there for a moment like a long stick. But then the mamba pulled itself the way snakes do in order to propel themselves along and in that instant the gardener let out a cry as if he had seen his dead uncle. The call went up in the air and exploded over us like a brief downpour. David and I were caught in midaction. And then several cries came in succession as the lone gardener called out for reinforcements.

By now, David and I were looking down the road in the direction of the cry, but we had not determined on a course of action until we saw two men running toward the hubbub. Then we were off the trampoline and sprinting.

What we saw at first were three gardeners, all in brown clothing, dancing around the tree, all of them leaning forward and then bouncing backward. My eyes were frozen on the men. I could not imagine what was compelling them until at last I followed the direction of their pointing and saw there in the lower limbs of the palm the escaping black mamba.

The men did not speak to us and we did not attempt to interfere but watched as they planned their action. At last one of the men ran off across the grass toward the hospital—a singularly daring thing given the huge snake—while the other two stood watching the tree, talking with one another on and off, swatting flies and mosquitos over their backs, even laughing a bit. I was almost beginning to bore of it all when we heard the third man call out and then saw him loping back. He was leaning to one side because he was carrying a petrol can with one arm. The other two men roused and the excited talk resumed along with the pointing and circling.

The man who had taken charge relieved the running man of the can and began dousing the base of the palm with the smelly liquid. "Make you dress back o," he cautioned to all of us and especially to David and me, "Make you dress back!" At first I could see nothing and perhaps the gardener couldn't either because he sort of leaned in as if looking for the flame and then *whoosh:* the fire leapt up like a cheetah. The man literally fell back and then began to laugh, and all of us laughed with him. As we watched, the flames rose higher up the trunk, until the upper branches were smoking like a dragon. And then I saw the snakes, more than one, winding their way higher into the branches, dancing over the flames among the boot-shaped nests of the weaver birds. At last the tree was an inferno and the snakes were wicks. They began to fall, in long spirals, burning to the ground. In the end we counted four dead snakes. This was unusual because snakes do not as a rule travel in packs.

Just so you know: the black mamba is a steely animal, its skin the dull gray of old gun metal; the largest poisonous snake in Africa, it can grow to twelve feet, all of it gliding along rapidly, its head well off the ground. It likes to strike the face or neck.

For a few days, I avoided walking directly under the large palms on the compound. But after a while I forgot about the snakes, except sometimes at night, just before sleep, I would see those twirling black forms trailing flame as they cascaded endlessly to the ground.

One day my mother and father took David and me over to the town of Agbor for a Christmas party. In Agbor was a mission station with a Baptist school for Nigerian girls run by several aunts who occupied one of those mud-and-plaster houses with the huge front steps you had to climb. It's too bad those aunts didn't have suitors because it would have been so charming for a man in long khakis and holding a hat to climb those stairs straight-backed and handsome in the evening. Bruce and Stevie didn't come along on this adventure and the formality of the situation threw David and me into a somewhat different relation. Going to any aunt's house was always a special occasion; they paid more attention than most families who had their own children. Besides, these aunts had adopted a bush baby, a small animal not much bigger than a kitten. It looked at you with its huge eyes as though it were courting you utterly. I always thought the aunts needed more family than they had (who was going to fill their tree with gifts at Christmas?) so going to see them was a kind of mission outreach on my part.

It wasn't until we were driving back to Eku, however, that the real excitement of the afternoon began. We were caught in a downpour that might have taken Noah by surprise. My father eventually just stopped the car right there in the middle of the Eku-Agbor road. You could hardly see a thing, but the sound of wind and rain was enormous, and if you know the Eku-Agbor road you know that the trees hang over it like a canopy, so we were being whipped about by a thousand branches. It was as though the car had lunged into the ocean so under water were we.

"When will it stop?" I asked my mother, because I could see that my father was occupied with the same question.

"We'll just have to wait and see," she replied, her voice steady but not at all reassuring.

David was looking straight ahead out the windshield, blinking his eyes and refusing to meet my gaze. All I could do was look out the window on my side of the car. Briefly I glimpsed a man on a bicycle wheeling by; he must almost have run into us before he saw the station wagon. All I caught was that instant when he lifted his head from its downward pose just in time to change direction and wheel around us. I felt helpless watching the man, a feeling I often knew when I saw Nigerians in trouble, whether it was a child waiting for a flogging or a teenager turning away from my father after asking for work on the compound when there was none or a mother holding a sick child or a small boy in a hand-me-down blue jacket standing alone and crying. What would happen to them? There was nothing I could do but return my worry to myself.

In and out of seasons, the Eku compound traded with Papa Agbowu, a wealthy man who owned a farm out from Eku where we would drive to purchase eggs. The spacious, well-groomed grounds of his establishment were a place for raising chickens as well as rabbits. After a rain, his neatly clipped grass was as green as the flag and the paths of the farm compound smoothly padded down as if they had been painted across the lawn. The children of the farm workers were robust and cheerful. They knew who they were. Once in my adult life, I dreamed of returning there, and we all had a huge meal spread on a great table under the eaves of a long house.

Papa Agbowu also had a fine bakery in Warri, a town twenty-five miles seaward, where he lived most of the time, and this was where we bought our bread when David and I went with Aunt Virginia and my mother "into town." We also sometimes went to Sapele, where there was a Kingsway and David and I could peruse British magazines for children and actually saw canned vegetables lined up on shelves in the grocery department. Sapele was big enough for billboards and a cinema and maybe even a Bata shoe store, though we never bought Bata shoes.

Once, my father and I went to the Sapele Kingsway alone to buy a framed print for my mother's birthday, a picture of purple violets in a bowl. At such moments, I caught a glimpse of the sweet attentions that linked my parents. Years later in the U.S., my mother told me that when they were first married in Louisville, my father picked a whole bouquet of wild violets for her. My father must have had that moment in mind when he purchased that picture that afternoon. To this day, it graces the space above my parents' bed.

During rest time in the afternoon, I sometimes ventured out of the house and it was as if the white world had been evacuated. During that hour, I shared the compound with the Nigerians. While my parents slept, I might sit in the carport, fingering the corroded lock of an old trunk that was stored there, and watch Lagos, Aunt Mary Evelyn's cook, come outdoors and empty a pail of dishwater onto the roots of the flame tree just outside her door; this tree grew twice as fast as the second one further from the kitchen which never received this gift. Or, in the other direction, I might watch the Gaultneys' husky gardener, leaning over from his waist, moving back and forth with his cutlass, as if keeping time with a great metronome in the sky. Or I might hear our laundry man in the open room at the back of the garage, taking a break from his work, and watch as he pulled a kola nut from his shorts pocket and took a bite of the bitter fruit. Or I heard the carpenters, the buzz of their tools or a plank of wood being dropped, or one calling out impatiently to an apprentice.

Occasionally, while I roamed the yard alone in the hour from one until two, I was witness to the strange process of burial. Sometimes an expired patient's body was not claimed by any family though it lay waiting in the morgue for several days. In those cases, two of the outdoors hospital staff would carry the body covered in a gray cloth on a stretcher to be buried down on the other side of the fence beyond our front yard, and they would walk down the grassy road that ran just by my sandbox and trampoline. I found this a sobering event at the time but I find it sadder now, knowing how significant it is to Nigerians to be buried among their people and near their ancestors and not in the white man's grave.

Surely this somber procession past my trampoline was another example of my Nigerian crossroads; there were so many.

In my present life, I wonder how I will make it through the crossroads of transplant surgery, that twilight of anesthesia, that zone of death and life.

Urhobo Land

THERE ARE FOUR theories about the origins of the Urhobo people who live in Eku. According to the first, the Urhobo have always lived where they live today. The second claims the Urhobo came in several waves from the kingdom of Benin; perhaps some had been slaves. The third argues origins from Ile-Ife, first place of human habitation according to many Nigerians. According to the last tradition, the Urhobo traveled here from North Africa.

Some research suggests that the first settlers date back as far as 812 B.C. Migrations may have occurred up until about A.D. 1370. It seems likely that there were numerous influxes of people, since there are a variety of languages among the Urhobo in modern times. In the Eku Baptist Church, for example, the pastor preached in one dialect which was then translated into another. The sermon was never translated into English, by the way. Almost every large town in our Midwest region constituted a clan. For example, the clan that includes Eku is the Agbon, which numbered 165,000 in 1986. Within the clan are communities defined by the super-extended family. Ideally, this structure includes grandparents, mother, father, children, grandchildren, aunts, uncles, very good friends, and very good neighbors. An *omoni* or brother may be any of these people in the community. Any *ose* or father can discipline any *omo* or child, and any *oni* or mother may take the responsibility of feeding any child. Any *omoni* may visit any other *omoni* unannounced. All the elders of the family are treated with great respect, and all members of an extended family are invested in the well-being of the *omo* or children.

It is clear to me now that just as our compounds were copied from a West African pattern, our mission family was copied from the

Nigerian model. David was my brother, my *omoni*. His mother was my aunt. Aunt Mary Evelyn was like an *oni-rhode* or grandmother.

In my present life, I meet a Nigerian couple at the North Carolina State Fair when I work in a booth for the National Kidney Foundation. We begin to talk, and when I learn they are from Igbo land, I say, "Ah, home of the great Chinua Achebe," and the man replies, "Oh yes, he is my brother!"

Unfortunately though not surprisingly, the extended family model had its limits. Not all Nigerians are brothers. First of all, the country of Nigeria was an imported concept. And as I have already said, the "country" included many hundreds of tribes and nations. Even when members moved away from home, the family "stayed" in its regions. This partition meant that various Nigerian extended families were competing for improvement, including the clans of our newly minted Midwestern state. Many young men and women were coming to the nursing school to improve themselves, to improve their family, and to improve their region. In the afternoons, riding my bike, I saw those students carrying their books and moving across the lawn between their dorms and the classroom buildings. They were primarily Yoruba and Igbo and folks from minority tribes. Sometimes I'd see Urhobo women with babies, making a food sale to a student. You didn't see many Hausa at the nursing school because they were mostly Muslim and had different ideas about improvement.

Though the measures of wealth had changed over the years from piles of yam to English pounds, Nigerians generally like money, and using the *oyinbo* systems to enrich your family might not be seen as crass self-interest but as civic-mindedness. Thinking back, I can see Abraham's theft of mother's silver in this light. One could make an ethical argument—considering our material affluence—that he *should* help himself to our abundance if he were going to distribute it among his kin. I think this notion may constitute the plot of *Robin Hood*. In any case, Nigerians were drawn both ways: toward old gods and new, toward America and Pan-Africanism, toward democracy and socialism, toward the claims of kin and the claims of *oyinbo* government.

More than one census was taken while we were in Eku and all of them were controversial. These counts were extremely important since they determined the revenue going to each region, and also because the North's political domination was based on its reportedly larger population. If the East and West could show that their clans were equal with the North's, this imbalance would be amended. Every time the results came back showing the North's greater numbers, many around us laughed in disbelief and a great controversy ensued.

At such moments, America was invoked as a place of fair representation and the rule of law. So the nursing school students and the Urhobo people of our region were perplexed by reports they began to hear about the civil rights movement in America, which suggested that the land of the free and the home of the brave was also the land of the enslaved and the home of the barbaric. What were our families doing? they asked.

News about the American South fanned over the Eku mission's nursing school. The campus took up one end of the compound, the buildings contemporary in design, with bright red roofs. Someone flying overhead might have read a signal in them. My mother taught in the afternoon, after rest time, and one day I overheard her with Aunt Mary Evelyn talking in chagrined tones about the students' behavior. The pictures on the front of *Time* magazine that made their way onto campus featured Alabama policemen with dogs and bully sticks beating fallen black civil rights activists. The image acted like a match, igniting and then flaming an already smoldering unrest. The students complained of the missionaries' authoritative ways; the notices my father posted at the hospital announcing pay schedules or office hours were pulled from the wall and torn into bits. The idea of autonomy, the history of American racism, the established habits of the Baptist mission, and the ever-present winds of national unrest were mixed together in a spicy soup of anger and resistance. I have to say, I can imagine how hollow the missionaries' explanations for their own home country must have sounded to the students. How do you convince a people who believe in nothing so much as the character of family that you really aren't like your brothers and sisters back home? Not easily.

I cannot say with any certainty how my parents thought about this image problem at the time. But my guess is that they were somewhat mystified that the nursing students could not tell the difference between white racists and white missionaries.

In American time, I dream. I am watching television and on the screen I see a Nigerian man being beaten by two policemen. When I become part of the scene, the time is the early sixties. The British are still in Nigeria. In fact, hundreds of British soldiers on horseback and in red uniforms line the streets. We are on a campus with beautiful lanes lined with teak trees and walkways, buildings, and gardens. But the British are in disarray. And then I see that Nigerian soldiers, who are also present, are in mutiny. All hell breaks loose as the British begin to flee. And then I see dozens of Nigerian men, dressed for war, bearing down on me. British soldiers are falling all about and I do not know whose side I am on or which way to turn.

Left: My father, home from World War II, 1945
Above: My mother, nursing school faculty, Louisville General Hospital, 1948

Abike and me, Ogbomosho, 1955

Playing on water tank, surrounded by onlookers: Becky, her friend Marilyn, and me in wading pool, with Mother standing far right, Ogbomosho, 1955

My father with the Ogbomosho Hospital building and maintenance staff (Mr. Bolarinwa, head carpenter, far left), 1954

Becky and me,
Ogbomosho, 1956

Above: My first re-
membered home,
Ogbomosho, 1958
Right: Arrival in
America, second fur-
lough, Greenville,
SC, 1960

My family with the family of Ishola Kunle, front porch of first remembered home, Ogbomosho, 1958

Me learning to ride Becky's bicycle, Newton Memorial School compound, near Oshogbo, 1961

The Gaultney boys and me (David back left, with Stevie in front of him; Bruce in front of me), back yard of Eku compound, 1962 or 1963

My mother, center, with Aunt Virginia Gaultney, and me to the left, nursing school grounds, Eku compound, 1963

Frances Jones Memorial Convalescent Center (my birthplace), Ogbomosho

New Nigerian flag being raised at a Baptist mission school, 1960

My father handing out Bibles to new converts, Eku Baptist Hospital, 1964

My mother (standing, far right) with church women and Aunt
Lois Norman (sitting, on left) returning from WMU school in a
nearby village, Eku compound, 1964

Egungun, Eku area

Girls' dormitory, Newton Memorial School

Great logs on their way to market, Eku area

Path in rain forest, Eku area

Becky and me after GA
coronation, Ede, near
Oshogbo, 1966

Seventh-grade class, Newton Memorial School (Front row: far left, JoEllen
Norman; third from left, Lee Brothers; far right, Betty Kay Abell. Second
row: far left, Rebecca Russell; second from left, me; fourth from left, Ellen
DuVall; far right, Jan Levrets. Behind class, Uncle Wallace DuVall.)

Holding Molly, thirteenth birthday, family apartment at Newton Memorial
School, 1967

"Older girls" preparing to sing at Valentine's Banquet (fourth from left,
Melba Smith; fifth, me; seventh, Jan Barnes; far right, Lee Brothers), Newton
Memorial School, 1968

Mother, me, and Aunt Mary Evelyn, during the dry season, Ogbomosho, 1970

My mother doing relief work in the former Biafra, after the war, 1971

God's Jewels

THERE WAS NO INDIGENOUS path through the Eku compound as there was in Ogbomosho, but the ninety-nine-year lease to the mission allowed local women to come onto the grounds to harvest clusters of palm nuts from the plumelike crowns of the trees. We would see them arrive with a male assistant who climbed the trunk and cut down the bounty. Then the women carried off the huge "heads" of lipstick-red fruits, their hips waving as they walked away from us, the man carrying home nothing but his cutlass. Those globed red fruits were to my eyes great jewels.

Most of the villagers around Eku were farmers or they were employed in the rubber industry, or they might have worked in lumber, for the great hardwoods grew here—mahogany, iroko, obeche. The women, of course, worked the farms too and prepared food and they sold foodstuffs in the market or housewares or other personal wares. I often wondered why so many women sold the same goods side by side. The beauty of their displays was the opposite of the New Testament's picture of scarcity that gives rise to the fishes and loaves story and makes me wonder if my parents had arrived on the wrong shores. Instead of these women having too little, they seemed to me to have an overabundance—of tomatoes and cassava and red peppers and oranges and limes and dried fish. There was a profusion, an overflow, like the grace you see in a woman carrying a baby on her back, like the wealth of young girls' headdresses, like the radiant dark brown skin of the boys' faces, like the gold earrings in a babe's earlobes, like the delicate carving on the calabash. Africa is not all war and famine, and there needn't ever have been in Africa all famine and death.

The sandy soil around Eku was not good for lima beans and yellow squash, but it was perfect for the oil palms that grew on our compound. The palm nut itself is a trinity: on the outside is the brilliant red skin, inside that a hard nut boiled for palm oil, and inside that the small kernel. Small or not, herein lies the mother lode, the valuable palm kernel oil. To many Urhobo of Eku, prosperity followed a good oil palm crop. The oil was used for cooking and lighting and the kernels were sold. Palm leaves found new life in thatched roofs and sleeping mats. And, of course, the famous palm wine comes from this tree. If the mission had thought ahead, it could have worked the oil palm tree into its salvation story. If it had, we might have outnumbered the Muslims and traditionalists in our region.

The Piano

I HAD MY MOTHER more in Eku than I had had her in Ogbomosho or Oshogbo or anywhere else. She and I were together many a rainy afternoon in that wonderful Eku house that I loved so much; it was large and beautiful and ours. She taught me piano lessons from *John Thompson's Modern Course for the Piano: The Fifth Grade Book.* We covered Bach's "Prelude in C Major" and Brahms's "Waltz in A Flat Major" and Felix Mendelssohn's "On Wings of Song." Sitting with her, our eyes together on that book, we were close. There was not much to distract my mother in Eku. In Ogbomosho, there had been lots of other missionaries for starters, and then everyone came to Ogbomosho for Mission Meeting. People came all year round regardless because we were the middle of the mission. And then in Oshogbo there were all those MKs hankering for her attention. I liked having my mother. I liked her decorating.

Coming to Nigeria on the *African Patriot,* my mother had dreamed of window dressings. She had brought a catalogue on the subject and had in her mind a white fabric with pink roses. She never found that fabric in the Nigerian market, but she did well with what she found. Her colors were always green and blue and sometimes a sash of lavender. Never was our furniture pushed against the wall like so many convicts. Instead, it was melodiously placed in clusters, all areas tipping their hats to the piano, that majesterial piece. And framed prints hung so that they faced you when you stood, not lolling up near the ceiling so that you had to assume the posture of stargazing in order to see them. And there was a jute rug to pull everything together. And the purplish-red crystal candy dish and the soup tureen from Lagos. And in the living room the china sugar dish that mother saw one day at a stall on the side of a village road; she told my father to stop and he did and she purchased it.

I liked our proper habits.

There was the etiquette of dinner, where you never put your elbows on the table or reached for the butter or ate a bite before bowing your head in prayer or before every dish had made its circle and the hostess—that was Mother—began to eat. You never left the table before saying, "I enjoyed my meal. May I be excused please?" And you didn't even say that until you had sat there long enough for your parents to have become a little bored with your presence. And there was the etiquette of language: We said "may I?" and not "can I?" and we knew to say, "He and I would like to go" but also "His mother gave the book to him and me." We rolled our eyes when other people, trying to be ultra-correct, would mistakenly say, "The present is from she and I." My mother and father took their seats at the ends of the dining room table, balancing each other like playmates on a seesaw. But Mother kept the bell that called us to dinner and then called Fidelis to serve us or refill our glasses or clear the table for dessert.

Not long after we moved back to Eku, my parents set out to refurbish the living room. One of the things they did was to cut bird prints out of some handy *National Geographic* magazines, which they framed very handsomely and hung on the walls. My parents had the capacity to take something you might think of as temporary and recycled and make it into something elegant and privileged. The prints were lovely. You would have sworn they came from a fine shop somewhere. These hung on the walls along with the family portraits of Becky and me that had been made on our first furlough. I ignored with great success, by the way, the fact that Becky's portrait was bigger. There was a family story that explained the difference but I ignored that too.

Some nights, between dinner and bedtime, I would comb my daddy's hair while he lay on the couch. This was something of a joke because he never had that much hair. But he found the pastime soothing and I found it entertaining to fit him out with barrettes and hairpins.

In Eku, Daddy had a lovely mahogany coffee table crafted for

Mother, though he fretted that the legs were a darker color than the top, which made it clear that rather than emanating from the mind of God, this table had been produced by human hands and thus was a second remove from the really Real and the truly Good.

Certain objects in our house like that table were to me as people, they were so familiar and so dear. Looking back I realize that our houses changed but the furniture was the same.

Occasionally, I would accompany my mother to some festival or party being held by the nursing students. On these occasions, I would wear a dress and comb my hair and maybe even be so vain as to select a hair band. We would walk out into the night with our flashlights leading the way, past my sandbox and then the little morgue—I would be leaning to the right of the road, away from it—and then onto the nursing school campus. You could hear the music coming from the activities building where we were heading and see students moving toward it in small clusters and the light streaming out the windows. I would hold my mother's hand as we entered, feeling a little timid in this company. Some of the students who had been by the house would speak to me and touch my head, but their real interests lay elsewhere, in each other and in their social life. I joined in a game of charades and then watched the students perform skits. As a people, Nigerians love acting, and they are very good at it because many of their traditional festivities include rituals of acting. A Nigerian pretending to cry is a glorious thing. He is so very very convincing, your heart goes out to him; you nearly weep yourself.

At home before bedtime, my mother would sometimes play the piano or I would play my favorite hymns, "Make Me a Blessing," or "This Is My Father's World," or "Fairest Lord Jesus." We now drew the water for our baths directly from a hot water heater, operated by a pilot light, that was rigged up above the tub. This always gave our toilet a slightly gaseous smell, a smell I wish I could re-create in my present life. Later, my parents would read *Heidi* to me, a story I loved about a little lost girl who takes to the Alps like butter to toast. I admired her optimism, the way she lit up the old Uncle, and, of course, there was that nice detail about the young goatherd who became her fast friend. I had no clue about human sexuality, but it was clear to

me that there was nothing in the world more necessary or more enticing for a girl than a friendship with a nice boy. At the time it did
not occur to me that I also liked the book because it was about an
itinerant girl who finally found a home. I still own the drawings I
made in school that year of Heidi in front of her Alpine cottage: in
the background, huge pointed mountains of purple, green, orange,
and pink; in the foreground, the little house, a representative goat
and a cat—though there was none in the book that I remember—as
well as a stack of hay and a palm tree. I did not recognize any errors
in this assemblage and no one pointed them out to me.

My parents also read aloud *Pippi Longstocking,* the story of an
iconoclastic youngster who pretty much did and said whatever she
wanted. Pippi was fond of herself. Faced with scornful adults, she
simply walked around them as if they were mud puddles in the road.
I longed for such carelessness and indifference to public opinion.
How sweet it would be to lay courtesy aside and just say what you
meant. It was not that I had anything particularly mean or vindictive
to say. I simply had my own opinion, but I was always having to
shape my opinions to conform with parental approval. I remember
once my father asked me if I wanted to help him with some chore
and I said, "No, I would not like to." What came out of his mouth was
something like, "Well, I should think you would want to say yes even
if you don't feel like it." In other words: you should want to be a person who at least *says* she's agreeable. What I was told as a child was
that God knew my thoughts; so why did we spend so much time trying to cover them up? This was one of many mysteries to me.

At Christmas time, Becky came home for several weeks and preparation began for the biggest celebration of the year. Dad would pull
the artificial tree—which had to be assembled bit by bit—from the
attic. Then the lights were strung up with the seriousness of dressing
a bride. Then finally the ornaments were brought out and every year
I broke at least one on the concrete floor. "Elainski!" my father would
declare, because he still called me that, but I was bold with Christmas and just ignored him. At last the tinsel was unpacked. It could
not be thrown on the tree in handfuls but instead had to be placed,
silver string by silver string, so that it didn't clump. And before we

could finish, Mother was already placing presents under the tree. I would shake these daily, trying to decipher the contents, which I never could. But Becky always guessed, and much to Mother's chagrin, she generally notified me ahead of time about my gifts. On Christmas morning, Becky would arise first and scout out the situation and then she would coax me into going out for a look, but she had already reported most everything by now. There was, however, that one Christmas when Becky missed the trampoline since it was out in the yard. After all the other gifts were opened that morning, my father found some pretense for getting me to the back door and when I looked out there was the trampoline in its square perfection with a huge red bow on the side.

As far as interior gifts, I wish now that my parents had been investing in African art as Christmas presents for us, but alas: we received white American baby dolls and paper cutouts of Colonial American families. Once I received a ukulele and another time a miniature sewing machine and once a tea set.

In all truth, I loved the little tea set, almost as much as the trampoline. Even with a miniature tea set, which is too small for actual use, you are learning to *desire* tea, tea with sugar and cream. Nowadays, I believe that the purpose of tea is not so much the hot sweet liquid but the sound of the cups against the saucers and the spoons against the cups. The clinking sound is a comfort and a joy because you know the china is fine and breakable but it is not broken; it has merely sounded and now you're having your tea.

Sometimes for Christmas we would receive special candies, and rather than eating mine I would hoard it in my top dresser drawer. My sister found this disgusting, not because the candy might attract bugs but because I would retrieve it months later when her portion was only a memory. I also practiced leaving my money at home when we went shopping in Lagos or Ibadan and then "borrowing" from my father. Becky found this behavior even more morally degraded than hoarding candy. But to my way of thinking, if I was smart enough to invent this plot and my father was gullible enough, or loved me enough, to fall for it, it was just Becky's tough luck that she hadn't thought of it first.

Even today, when I play Christmas carols on the piano—and it's only when I hear them on the piano, our one constant instrument in Nigeria, and especially the minor chords of "What Child Is This"—I am in a dark African night with only candles and lamps, waiting for the arrival of angels. I am entirely at peace and full of hope. At the sound of that hymn, the firmament bursts into a multitude of the heavenly hosts. I am surrounded by fireflies and the still sense that we are all clustered like babes in the hands of God. My ears hum with the sweet sound of that hymn accompanied by drums. Even though Christmas itself had to be something of a letdown, I forgave everyone just because of the taste of that sweet anticipation that came with the music. The world could not be evil with a song like this.

For unto you a child is born. And unto you a gift is given. . . .

Those early Christmases were promises of things unseen but more believed than anthills and rain. Christmases with Nigerians at night in church were moments of absolute forgiveness and grace for all our sins. We sang in every language we knew; like newborns, we weren't even aware that we were in language. We were children of God and our differences were like an eyelash they were so thin and I knew that I had no privilege here. I was one of many and we were alike and for once I was any Nigerian.

Straining the Calabash

NIGERIANS CELEBRATED Boxing Day, the day after Christmas, and on the Eku compound you could hear the firecrackers going off at night in the village. We made very little of Boxing Day or New Year's, but we celebrated Becky's birthday on January 4, just before she had to head back to boarding school. The day before she left, everyone would be somber as children who have been corrected in public. At the dinner table, Becky would look positively sick, and Mother would be fighting back tears. The morning my sister left, everyone on the compound turned out of their houses as if they were on fire and the older kids boarded a van to be carried back up-country to Oshogbo. David and I would play outdoors a little later into the evening on those days in order to avoid the sadness that still clung to the walls of our homes like an illness.

Now I think of so many Nigerian youngsters sent to board at British and American schools. How their families missed them.

With kidney failure, I spend many days in bed, getting up only for dialysis. Too weary with the illness, with the circle of drain and fill, drain and fill, drain and fill. Weary with my face of optimism, reconstructing myself every day as if I were whole and well. I feel as if I am literally putting myself together each morning, like my father reconstructed that Christmas tree from pieces once a year. The routine habits of life become very odd when you slow down this much. You look at your hair curler or your lipstick and wonder where you found them or what they are for.

The thing about being on dialysis is always the urge to lie down, to rest. You are endlessly anemic, losing protein, weary in your muscles. Your body pulls toward the bed. Just as you are finally dressed—after hours of nausea, and dialysis, and dressing, and eating if you can bear it—your body remembers its one true desire: sleep. Lethargy is my middle name. My first is redundancy. I am a circling sleeper. Now in my dreams, I am losing my eyesight: I am in a bathroom, looking in a mirror, but I can hardly see, and I cannot tell if I am sleeping or waking or somehow caught between the two.

Deep in the Country

ONE DAY WE LEFT FOR Joinkrama, a group of villages in the East, on the other side of the Niger. We would drive to Asaba, where we would board a ferry—for there wasn't yet a bridge over the great river. As soon as we were on board I would need to go to the bathroom and this made the ferry ride interminable. Finally we made it to the opposite bank and to Onitsha, the great market city. I remember as if it were yesterday those noble river vessels: huge canoes with thatched roofs that crowded the shore. The market women of Ogbomosho would have looked like beginners in Onitsha because Onitsha's market women had been there forever. They were licensed to sell. They had been selling since long before the observations of Mungo Park and Richard Lander. They were God's original. The brown-rusted tin roofs of thousands of market stalls went on and on, *titi laelae.* In the market proper were umbrellas, standing like mushrooms, over open stalls. I remember especially those that peaked with a little minaret on top and the large umbrellas made of various colors, each color like a slice of pie. People wearing cloth, people selling cloth, bolts of cloth standing one next to the other like encyclopedias. There were enough white enamel basins in Onitsha to catch all the water in the sky.

From Onitsha, we traveled to Owerri and then Ahoada, not far from Port Harcourt. We were now without a doubt in the Rivers region, where Aunt Jo Scaggs lived. When we stopped at her house, just a low, unpainted cottage, hardly distinguishable from its neighbors, she served us squash, that rather horrible, unnaturally orange drink made from concentrate. She didn't have any ice, but she didn't seem to notice. Aunt Jo was in that select category of *real* missionaries who were issued Land Rovers and spoke native languages and lived among Nigerians. I was amazed and looked back at her as we drove away. But she was on her haunches speaking with some Igbo youngsters. It occurred to me that she did not think I was any more special than they were.

You didn't finish getting to Joinkrama by road, however; after all, the name of the community meant *carver of paddles.* What you did was park your car at Mbiama and then load yourself and your bags onto a canoe-taxi to head upstream to the Baptist mission. We were going to visit the Normans, a family with a daughter my age, JoEllen. At Joinkrama there was still one of those big brown colonial trading posts, a relic from days gone by.

The amazing thing about JoEllen was the way she just wandered all through the forest, from village to village, as if she were an African. For some reason, there was no fence around the Joinkrama compound, perhaps because the river rose occasionally all the way up to the houses, which were built on stilts, so fences seemed superfluous. I mean, in weather like that you could glide in your canoe *over* the fence posts. So JoEllen was not hemmed in as I had been in Ogbomosho and Eku. There weren't any real roads here because there weren't any cars, just broad and not-so-broad paths. "Playing," for JoEllen, who had a couple of younger brothers but no MK peers, was wandering around the territory. As we walked between villages, the paths narrowed so that if you held your arms out at forty-five-degree angles, they were in the grasses and bush. The foliage in Joinkrama was densely packed like the leaves of a cabbage. Around a curve, I nearly ran into a tall stone—almost like a column, it was just off the path— and it seemed to have a face in it but I couldn't be sure because my attention was suddenly diverted by a cage on stilts, and in the cage was a monitor lizard, dark with yellow spots. And then the bush ceased and we were in a clearing, the ground absolutely flat and swept, smoke rising from cooking fires.

Back in the Norman household, Aunt Lois, JoEllen's mother, had been trying to get her to learn French. She had ordered a set of records that spoke to you in French and then you were supposed to mimic the words and thus learn the language. But the real foreign language

JoEllen and her brothers were learning was Pidgin English. "You no feet swem" was the sort of sentence you might hear coming from the boys, which meant, of course, you're a terrible swimmer. Russell, the youngest, spoke only in Pidgin and other missionary parents were afraid he might be mentally handicapped for life.

No one would think the mission compound at Joinkrama was a city unto itself. It was just a clearing in the forest like the Joinkrama villages except that the hospital and the houses were concrete block painted white; as soon as you left the clearing you were engulfed. There were just these few white people, the Normans and the Moores, and one or two single missionary nurses like Aunt Aletha Fuller, and then all of these villages without Star Lager beer or BP Pass All or a local photographer. Occasionally in this area, you might hear the jingle of a bicycle bell, but that was pretty much the extent of the traffic. And yet I didn't notice that anything was missing. JoEllen and Joinkrama seemed to me to have everything you could need, except maybe David.

Back in Eku, I found the Gaultney boys waiting like stationed guards. I realize now that David was my first love and he spoiled me for life. He was generous and he admired me and I didn't have to be as generous but I admired him too. I liked the way he smiled out of one corner of his mouth and the way his brown eyes gathered in the noonday sun but twinkled at me and the way, when he walked, he leaned to one side as if he were listening to some distant music, and his olive brown skin, so unlike mine, which was fair and freckled, and his somewhat rumpled look. Once when we were playing, he imagined himself at a Western saloon, and leaning across the "bar," ordered a beer, which he then, with a wink, amended to a "root beer." I thought he was so cosmopolitan. It was one of a million secrets we shared. I never loved anyone else as I loved David.

Our favorite activity was going to the river. Looking back, I think the Ethiope was the laughter of divinities. It was cold enough to have been spent snow instead of tropical water. Coming into view, it appeared as if the upper currents were racing the bottom ones, as if it were overtaking itself. It was absolutely transparent. But because of the surrounding vegetation and the river grass, it looked—at an angle—green, green like the green mamba or perhaps a few shades darker, green like the glossy leaves of palm trees.

Always I was stunned to see that any earthly thing could be so constantly *new,* so fresh, so gorgeous as the Ethiope. Nothing you could tell me about Jehovah was equal to the proof of divinity provided by the mere existence of so lovely a river. And so I worshiped it.

But entering that effulgent church was a challenge. Sometimes David and I would let ourselves down slowly into the cold stream, using one of the ladders descending from the piers. I would dwell on the indigo smell of the damp earth nearby to distract myself. On other occasions, when we were feeling daring, we would take off from the car at a clip and run straight down the longest pier and veer out over the water, taking on the river all at once. This was the wiser approach, believe me; the other was torturous, especially when you reached the regions of your private affairs. But however one entered, in swimming the cold Ethiope, it was only hard at the beginning.

David and I loved to cross the river against the current, pull ourselves up on a tree on the opposite shore, and launch ourselves with a rope swing out over the water. Your feet would skim the surface back and forth and you could lean back and let the top of your head tunnel through the water. Sometimes when the swing was high in its arc, you would let go and fall into the current, your feet going so far down they might touch the green weeds that grew on the riverbed. Occasionally a boy from Abraka would join us—though we might not speak—and he would climb farther up in the tree than we did, and rather than swing out on the rope, he would dive straight down into the water. We might have said to him: *Brother, like the lizard that fell from the top of the iroko tree without hurting itself, you deserve praise,* but we did not. I think we felt tongueless in the presence of such a feat. Our own courage was exposed as timidity.

I remember everything at the river: the thatched dressing rooms without roofing where we sometimes changed into our swimming clothes under the willing sky, the minnows with the little bright spot on their backs that you could capture in the shallows, the bottle caps we threw into the water in order to dive for them, the way I would soap up my hair and then dive so that the white foam splayed out behind me.

During my years at Eku, a new high dive was constructed at the Abraka landing. Already a set of interlocking piers and a low diving board graced the shore, and now this skyscraper was added. It probably was not that high, but it looked high to me, especially standing at the tip end of the board, looking down to the bottom of the river. I don't know whose idea this board was, but its construction coincided with the arrival at the Eku hospital of a new missionary couple: Uncle Jack and Aunt Barbara Tolar. Uncle Jack was a skilled diver and could turn flips this way and that before entering the river. The rumor was that he had performed for Vice President Johnson. Uncle Jack's prowess, like the Urhobo boy's diving, raised the stakes for David and me. Jumping off the board was one thing, but diving was another. One day, I was determined to master this feat, so I told my dad to watch as I ascended the ladder. But once up there, I had second and third thoughts. I lifted my arms obediently, making a little arrow out of the palms of my hands, and leaned over, but nothing happened. My father stood patiently, holding his towel, his long, thin legs slightly bent at the knees the way they always were. The sun started to set and his body turned dark against the light as if he were a statue. But then he called out and clapped—as an encouragement and a push—and became my father again. Finally, after what seemed hours, I leaned over and fell into the water head first like a dead person. I was so elated, I required my father to drive us back to Eku to fetch Mother so we could drive back to the river for me to perform for her.

An easier piece of equipment than the high dive was the red raft stationed in the middle of the river, kept in place by a huge chain attached to a log on the river bottom. We spent a good deal of time swimming out to it and then diving off. You could get under the raft because it floated on large drums. I have pictures taken of me standing on that raft, my legs long and lean, my hair short and slicked back from the river water, a girlish manner in the casual sway of my body.

I had not yet learned to be looked at. I was not yet posing. In her black one-piece bathing suit, my mother would swim upstream to the raft as a form of exercise and then she would hold on and kick her legs but always with her head aloft. She would sometimes swim across the river, though I never remember my sister doing so; it might even have been my mother who swam with me the first time I attempted that crossing.

One day a snake swam to our shore from the other side of the river and wound up taking refuge beneath that red raft. The snake was milky-colored in pinks and creams and amazingly swift. We exited the river like a covey of birds lifting from a field.

Sometimes during the Christmas season, the British would visit "our" landing, but they ignored our river etiquette. The men were loud and wore very brief swimming suits. Not only that, their stomachs were large as beach balls. They wore gaudy gold wristwatches and drank beer and said Bloody this and Bloody that. I can't even remember the women; there was no room for them in my vision after I had taken in those men. Always I thought of the British in Nigeria as foreigners, whereas we Southern Baptist Americans belonged.

Perhaps such a foreign presence spurred David and Bruce and me one afternoon to "hike" up the edge of the river, in the shallows, to the landing that lay above us. It surprises me now that our parents let us undertake this venture since it took us well out of their viewing area. In any case, we set out, pulling ourselves against that determined spring. Moving upstream like that required determination: you had to keep your head down, charting the floor of the river rather than looking ahead:

At that moment I was whole, amazed at the beauty of the river, its greenery and sand like small compounds underwater, its brilliant sleek fish with the electric colors of blue and yellow and orange. I have never felt less alone than I did then, in the river, headed upstream. Just above my head, a canopy of overhanging trees, perhaps a family of monkeys, red-capped mangabeys, watching my movement, those swift noisy foragers who love the oil palm nut.

The landing, once we reached it, was already fully occupied with villagers doing their laundry or washing their cassava or retrieving water for the evening or bathing. Here a long log fallen into the river served as the diving board. Such a log becomes an object of love for all children, its reliability something to marvel at, its smooth dark sides a solace and the little eddies of water it creates a guarantee of graciousness. In these eddies small children splashed while older children dove from the log into the deep water. We swam to a small sandbar on the opposite bank where grew a hollow reed which we plucked for breathing underwater. As soon as we heard a parent's voice calling, we raced our way back to the standard landing.

I experienced my first orgasm in the Ethiope, lying on an innertube in a small inlet where the current pressed gently against my body. It felt as if a spirit were stirring between my legs and then there flowered between them a feeling as red and frilled and elegant as the flower of the gloriosa lily.

On the way home, David and I rode in the back of the station wagon with the gate up but the glass down. We would pass the farm planted in corn, and on rare and wonderful evenings my father would stop and buy a roasted ear. The kernels were so hard and blackened you could really only suck on them, which was why, I guess, my father thought the purchase less than worthwhile, but the smell was so enticing, the corn seemed a delicacy. My fingertips would be shriveled from swimming, and the evening air gave me goose bumps. Passing back through the villages, we saw the orange moon come up and inhaled the sweet and enticing smell of dinners cooked outside on open fires, a smell so pungent and flavorful I felt honored to have it pass through my nostrils. It was a high smoky smell—sweet, really, of pepper and onion and palm oil. At this hour there were no children running by the car, waving and calling out to us. They were instead gathered with their clan, waiting for the soup to pass. You might catch a glimpse of a lonely figure with a load returning from the farm or an old man still sitting in the open air of an evening under a canopy of hibiscus.

As much as I loved the river, I always felt a sense of homecoming when we got close to the compound. A large tree stuck out into the tarmac at a slight bend in the road before you could see the compound fence. Every child who ever lived at Eku and approached it from this direction will remember this tree and how it inserted itself into your line of vision. Of course, roads in Nigeria were built like this, following established paths and accommodating the landscape. Once around that tree, I could see the beginning of the compound fence and that meant soon we would see the sign I cherished, *Eku Baptist Hospital.* The car would slow down like an animal finding its way home and then turn in through the gate. Finally, I would hear the crunch of tires on gravel as we eased into our drive. By now, my hair would be dry except for the very back. On these evenings, I didn't have to bathe. I would eat like a soldier home from war and fall into bed still drowning into the pull of the river.

> The wind in the palm
> like a mother's voice drifts
> over her pink and yellow curtains,
> opens the drawers, and lies down to sleep.

> She dreams of the river and her father. He calls her
> fish and she swims
> with the pleasure of forgetting who she is.
> Sand in her teeth like diamonds.

It must be that David and I were friends in that short moment between early childhood and adolescence when you don't yet think about gender but are already charmed by it. It is perhaps the only real time in which males and females are absolutely true to each other. I was won over by his loyalty to his brothers and his constant availability in our collaborations. He was quietly *there,* which was all I needed, and with very little of that chilling bravado I had seen emanating from some other MK boys. I guess we were young trees, growing still in the shade of elders and before the distinctive marks of our genus were upon us. I was destined to dream of him for a long time yet.

O Blessed Water

ON THAT TRIP TO West Africa with Andy in 1980, we made our pilgrimage to Eku to visit Aunt Mary Evelyn, who was still there. When we reached the gate of the compound, I got out of the car, took off my sandals, and walked alone the beloved road. There was the excess of sand in a curve where I often lost control of my bike, zigzagging until I found my balance. There was the place where the black mamba palm had burned. There was our back yard where the trampoline had crouched. Standing in Aunt Mary Evelyn's new house, I waited for the rain, and then I watched it as it fell, huge strips of it falling straight down, bathing all of those thousands of palms and the whole known world, an absolute engulfment of water.

One day during that visit, we drove up nearly as far as Obiaruku, parked the car, and floated down the Ethiope on tubes. As we pushed ourselves into the current, Andy looked at my mother and father and said, half in jest, "now I know why I married Elaine."

On our last day in the area, we went to the river at Abraka. I came with a jar, to collect sand. But not from the shore. I wanted sand from the center of the Ethiope's bed. I asked a young Nigerian boy if he would dive for me and he did. It took him only one attempt before he was surfacing, his hand with the jar appearing first as if he were passing off a baton.

In my life now I disdain most American waters. Pools are lethargic and smell of chloride. Lakes are opaque and dusky. The ocean is boisterous and threatening. Still the beaches of the Atlantic are my favorite place in America because from there you look out over the ocean knowing this water touches the shores of West Africa. O blessed water! O lucky shores!

Fellowship

IN EKU, I DID NOT think of myself as American or as white or as Nigerian or even as an MK. Most days I didn't even think of myself as a girl. I simply thought of myself as Elaine. I guess those other names were flexing in me, sometimes competing, sometimes overlapping each other. I knew that I was gifted because my mother said so over and over.

Once I went with my father to an associational church. All churches were members of an association, of course, but you thought of the church in town as major and self-supporting while "associational church" meant minor, a beginner. We drove in the station wagon, parking on the side of the road, as was our manner. Walking the path to the church, my father and I carried boxes of plates and cups for the sacraments, along with one of my mother's beautiful tablecloths from China. When I spied the church building, I could see it was not complete. It was a light gray shell: concrete walls and a roof and openings for windows and a door but no actual door yet, no shutters. Anyone could come into this church, including the local wildlife. Standing on the steps was the young minister, in black pants and a pressed white shirt and a long slender tie and brown sandals. He was holding his hands together, cradling them. But when he saw my father, he sprang to life, lifting the boxes from my arms, trying as well to take my father's load.

There was, of course, a baptistry in the church behind the pulpit with a river painted in it and palm trees on the shores and on either side of the baptistry a little semiprivate room. To one of these we three headed—it was not time for church yet and no one else had arrived. The pastor and my father began unpacking the serving pieces, the young man as if they were sacred relics even though the little cups were only plastic. Sometimes with an older Yoruba or Urhobo man you sensed a deep knowing and stoical sadness from his face. This man, still young, was serious but also expectant, almost smiling. Later, talking with my father, he held his chin with his right hand, the elbow cupped by his left, and I could see the tips of his fingers, almost the color of mine. Because we had no grape juice at home, we filled the cups with Coca-Cola, and this was the blood of Jesus to all who came to the Lord's table that day.

When we were engaged in "fellowship" on the mission compounds, we sometimes let go of religion. "Fellowship" was a word we used often and it covered everything from an extended toilet stop in someone's house when we were traveling from place to place to extravagant holiday meals to weekend suppers together. These repasts were followed by Forty-two, a game that was apparently reserved for adults and older children, so I didn't learn to play until I was fifteen or so. I found the dominos tantalizing in their shiny blackness with the little white dots and loved the sound they made bouncing off one another when they were being shuffled. It was a sound like teacups clinking, a fine, rich sound reserved for people who had finished a tasty dinner and had nothing better to do than satisfy themselves further, or for a young girl falling asleep on the couch in the secure presence of her parents.

After the Tolars came to Eku, the fellowship of tennis picked up at Eku because Uncle Jack was as good at tennis as he was at diving, and Aunt Barbara played because Uncle Jack thought she should and because she was always trying to lose weight. Aunt Barbara was very young and tall and beautiful and I could not see that she needed any improvement. But Uncle Jack, who was then a true American, thought everything could be improved, including his wife. Later Uncle Jack became more African and so there was hope for him.

One night in Eku when the older children were home on holiday, we received the entire compound at our house for dinner. We sat outside in the back yard, our chairs clustered in an arc of candlelight. Uncle Curt and Aunt Betty Abell had engineered a set of candleholders; they were emptied tuna tins nailed to slender wooden poles and topped with clear glass globes that you could get in the market. Mother, however, had engineered dinner, and the entrée was her famous lemon butter chicken, which my father had cooked on the grill. Chickens in Nigeria tended to be smaller than the pumped-up poultry we consume in the U.S. and the small pieces smothered in Mother's special sauce and cooked outdoors were the choicest bits of bird I have ever tasted.

Late that night, as our missionary family was preparing to depart and everyone was picking up something to take inside, I offered to blow out the candles. Perhaps I thought being gifted meant being quick to volunteer. But the wicks didn't want to give up their light so I had to lean right over them and blow hard to quench the flame. As I was attempting to snuff the fourth candle, I caught a pungent smell, sweet and rotten at once, and when I looked up, I saw little sparks at the tips of my hair. I have often been reckless in stepping up to tasks I was not ready for. I left the rest of the candles alone.

In a journal entry written during my separation from Andy and as I was declining into kidney failure, I wrote:

It's 5:40 p.m. I just came in from the cold and have fixed a cup of Earl Grey tea. Joel is in his room doing chemistry, listening to James Taylor: I've seen fire and I've seen rain. I look out my apartment window, which faces west, to see a beautiful pink and blue sunset. Some gray—really blue-gray—clouds scuttle in the foreground. There's a strong wind blowing leaves from the trees. Something about the sudden frenzy of air, the dark tree line against the sky, the extravagant sunset, reminds me of Nigeria. I realize that I prefer a sad sense of Africa to any sense of America.

For a very long time I have resisted intimate friendships: when people leave or if I move, I make no effort to stay in touch, even when I receive numerous letters from those I once kept company with. Why is this? Is it because I moved so often as a girl: after a while, you expect to lose people? Or am I seeking to rekindle a greater loss, to remember a more primary interruption?

I conceived Joel in West Africa, thinking a child could save me. Perhaps I hoped in creating him to bring a piece of Nigeria to America, to plant him in this soil, to synthesize in him what I could not synthesize in myself. But it was not to be. I could not heal myself through him. He could not be my medicine. He should not have to be. And perhaps instead I have only re-created my own loss in him, requiring him to live through this breakup.

You cannot know me because I do not even know myself. I have been gone from home too long. Of course I stage a coup in my marriage; of course I invite my own civil war. I will not tolerate this pretense of wholeness any longer.

On Sundays when I was not following my father, I walked with my mother and Aunt Virginia and the Gaultney boys into town to the Eku Baptist Church. (David's father also went to the villages.) Here I couldn't help but notice that I was white, but mostly I thought of myself as out of luck. These services ranged from an hour and a half to two hours. My only real pleasure lay in looking out the door near the front pew where I was parked, watching the younger Nigerian children who remained with better luck outside. In the farther distance, young boys, pagans I suppose, ran by with a soccer ball.

The music at church was highlife in a box. The choir, wearing robes and mortarboards, would sway, all in one direction and then back, but not enthusiastically. There may have been shaky-shakies, like maracas, and a drum, along with the pump organ, but the choir director slowed the time, as if he thought solemnity was the correct European attitude in a church. Sometimes everyone knew the words to a song and no one had to hold a book, so all would clap—but not like Americans, who hold their hands in front and gently bounce one off the other; instead, they moved their whole arms. Still, this was church and no one was going to fly.

For a few weeks, my mother tried to get me involved in the Sunday evening "Training Union" that met in the rooms of the local school across the soccer field behind the Eku church. I don't know why David wasn't invited along—maybe his mother wasn't as ambitious as mine. But there we were among a classroom of Urhobo children, mostly boys. These children were not like the ones I saw on the road when we drove to Abraka, dressed simply in a long shirt or an old dress faded and torn at the waist or in no clothes at all. The boys in Training Union were dressed neatly in khaki shorts and button-up shirts and the girls had on newer dresses—even if they were short-waisted—and their hair was neatly plaited with maybe a bright orna-ment and they smelled sweet with cologne. I volunteered to keep attendance, which was a stupendously naive thing for me to do since I hardly knew anyone's name. I didn't realize what a poor fit I was in Eku proper until this experience. I had become too Americanized to feel comfortable trying to pass as a Urhobo girl, even if we were sharing the Word of God. And none of the young people in atten-dance was especially sympathetic to my plight.

At evening church, the sanctuary would be lit with Aladdin lamps. These attracted moths that circled over our heads, casting huge shad-ows against the walls and falling like sacrificial angels into the smol-dering wicks. Dante could have written it.

When the service was over, we walked back down the main road with our flashlights in front, passed through the compound gates, and made our way up the long drive to our house, or maybe I am making this up. In any case, everyone sometime should be allowed to walk in safety with nothing but a flashlight down a Nigerian road at night. I remember arriving home, where I would take off my sandals, shake the insects from my hair, and once again become my own oddly native self.

At some point, I began to understand that a text had been divined for me: the Gospel of Matthew, chapter 25, verses 14 through 30. Here Jesus tells the story about a man going on a trip who leaves his ser-vants in charge of his money. To the first, he gives five talents, to the second, two talents, and to the last, one. In the man's absence, the first servant manages to double the money, and likewise the second. But the last servant, out of fear, merely buries the money, and when the master returns, he can do nothing but return the original sum. I think he was banished or worse. Since no one informed me that "tal-ent" means lots and lots of money, I thought the scripture was about being gifted. What that parable meant was that some of us have been given many "talents," and from them much is expected. Since I was often told by my mother that I was very talented and could do anything in the world I wanted, it came to seem that I was the one in the family with the biggest lot. This divination led to my dreaming of greatness—nothing ordinary like becoming a doctor or an athlete or a teacher but instead a kind of gauzy fame, like the effect filmmakers achieve with tricks of the camera.

In Nigeria, our houses were just there waiting for us to bring them to life. Our mission community was just there waiting to take us in and give us a place and an identity. Nigerians who had rejected the British by and large welcomed Americans. My father—a business-man—signified the possibility for beneficial relations. By the time we arrived, the Nigerian Baptist Church was so large that we were less a threat than a means to enablement. There was clearly so much to be done in the world; I assumed that at some point I would know how to fulfill my destiny.

Instead I came, eventually, to America and was a foreigner no one recognized as such. I didn't realize that I would have to create community and family and hearth and home in this country that was sup-posedly mine. I often attempted greatness, but it was very hard with-out a village behind me. I had never seen my mother clean a toilet or mop a floor, but when I was in graduate school I did both between reading assignments in the historical Jesus and poststructuralism. In my youth I thought I was destined for a brilliant life. I had no idea that most of what I claimed as a girl was tentative, like a nickname you have for a while but when you move, no one calls you that cog-nomen even though you wish they would. And then all of your glory is gone.

The Fall

I AM UP AT DAWN, even before my father, which is early indeed. I am dressed, slipping out the back door which I have to unlock, something I have never done. A chill runs down my back, though it is not cold, not even cool. But fog covers everything as far as I can see. I pick up my bicycle from its place of abandonment on the gravel path and glide off with only that brief crunch of tires on gravel and then I am on the grass, pedaling hard because there's an incline up to the compound road. When I reach it, I stop momentarily to look about. It's as though I am surrounded by ghosts because the fog is thicker in some places than in others and I seem to be moving in and out of these bodies of white mist. I hear nothing but my own breathing. And now for some reason I am sweating, though moments earlier I was shivering. I ride down the compound road toward the tennis court, my bike noiseless on the packed sand. Perhaps everyone is dead. Perhaps only I am left here. I approach a pile of concrete blocks and for some reason I stop the bike and climb the blocks. Now I am up in the air, above the earth, and I can barely see the ground below. Perhaps this is something like death: you are still thinking but everything is changing. At some point, you will not be able to return to where you were before you were here.

My waking became disjointed.

There came a day, for example, when I passed, like Alice, through the looking-glass. I was walking down the hallway in our house, toward the full-length mirror that was hung to the left of the bathroom, between my own and my parents' room. It was just after lunch and before rest time. The mirror itself was somewhat imperfect so that my image waved and shifted as I approached. I walked all the way up to the glass and stopped. And in the twinkling of an eye, I was not myself; I passed through the mirror to the other side and saw that there was nothing there. Or rather, I saw that I was in two places. There was the me that faced the mirror, who was composed and distinct and unaware. And there was another me outside of me, in front of and behind the image in the mirror, who could look at the composed but now naive me and say things like, "Who are you?" or, "Why are you over there?" This split made my head light. I wanted the outside me to get back inside so that I would be the way I was before. I didn't want to think about myself thinking about myself. I felt as I did the time I stood at the compound fence with my mother during an Eku festival and a Masquerade charged me, as if I had left my body and was watching something happen to someone else.

During the same period, I learned about eternity, the most disquieting concept I had ever encountered. Try as I might—and I tried very hard—I could not fathom it. I would fall asleep poised in some patch of well-being when a demon would edge up to my right ear and begin to whisper, *e-teerr-nity,* over and over. I would start awake, screaming for my mother until she came to my bedside in her nightgown, her body pungent from the bath and a generous dose of Yardley talcum powder. Pulling me to her, and shaking me slightly, she would then hold me close, and her sensuousness drew me back into the living world and then into the comfort of sleep. During the day, this bad spirit would lurk around my trampoline, and when I was alone at rest time, it came looking for me as if I owed it money. All I could do at such moments was to pull myself up and run down the path or ride my bike recklessly over to the carpenters' shed where Mr. Atigari, the chief carpenter, was still working. I would yell out to him and make human contact and thus enter again the stream of life.

I often wondered why others were not scared out of their wits by eternity—not that I feared hell. I feared heaven. Perhaps my fear had to do with a growing awareness of the contingency of my world. I could see that my sister had fallen off the edge of our secure domain and landed in boarding school far away. Add to that the fact that we were headed before long for America. To me, eternity seemed like damnation: having to live life forward forever and ever. Circling back seemed like a far better idea, as when we traveled to the river and then back home to sleep and then to waking. Or to America and back.

Late in our tour at Eku, other families appeared on the compound. They came to relieve Uncle Bill Gaventa, who kept finding himself the only doctor at the hospital. First came the Pitmans and then the Normans, or it may have been the other way around. Both families, however, had a daughter David's and my age, so our little classroom was suddenly multiplying; where there had been two of us, now there were three and four. You might think this amplification of playmates would be a welcome change, but I don't remember it that way, even though I had a good history with JoEllen. Instead, the delicate balance David and I maintained, in which he and I were cocaptains and Bruce and Stevie were our footmen, was spoiled. A crowd of people is never as friendly as the boy next door.

For one thing, having other girls around meant I had to think more about myself *as a girl,* which was a subject I'd been avoiding. Now I saw that one might prefer to be petite or to have dimples or to pull one's hair back in a ponytail. All these choices complicated my outlook.

One afternoon, I was with David and the younger boys along the side of his house where a tree grew that produced huge leaves. The stems of these, once they fell and dried, were almost like African drumsticks. We used them in all sorts of play. But then Julie Pitman-of-the-long-dark-hair strode up. She was not so interested in the sticks; she had another agenda. Standing in her blue jeans with her weight on one leg and her hips slanted provocatively, she asked David who his girlfriend was. This was a frightening question and one I had never even imagined. David and I were simply friends, very close friends, like cousins. David said nothing for a long time but Julie kept insisting: he must have a girlfriend. Apparently, having a girlfriend or boyfriend was a requirement like breathing air. These were not avoidable categories. So she proposed an answer: *Is it Elaine?* And then after pacing a bit and ignoring Julie further until she was fairly hitting him with the question, he whispered in a low voice, as if his answer was coming to him from a distance or maybe he was just making it up: *It used to be.*

I wanted the ground to open and Julie to fall in it because you cannot get back in front of a sentence like that any more than you can take back hitting someone in the face. You have done it or it has been done to you and you will never be the same.

It seems fitting now as I look back that Shell Oil arrived in our neighborhood at about the same time as these missionary outsiders. Seismographers even came onto our compound to explore the possibility of oil deposits. My parents just laughed since this was before we even knew there was oil in the region. They should have known; major oil finds had been made a year or two earlier at Ughelli in the western delta, about forty-five miles from Eku, twenty-five miles as the crow flies. Production was due to start in the Greater Ughelli area in June of 1965, when the trans-Niger pipeline system linking the Midwest fields to the Bonny Terminal was completed. By 1966 the area would be producing 300,000 barrels per day, approximately 15 million tons a year. We began to witness trucks and rigs moving down the Eku-Abraka road like columns of war. To the left and right of the one-lane highway, vast expanses of land were cleared, the smaller trees looking as if they had been chewed by a towering predator. Now stretches of the shadowy drive were fully exposed to the sun. Rigs were erected at some distance from the road, though we could see one at least on our drive back from Abraka. Returning from swimming in the evening, you could spot oil flares emitting black smoke and flames on the seaward horizon.

Bearing down on the country at the end of our tour was the 1964 election. If you had drawn a line connecting all the political camps in Nigeria at that moment, it would have gone up and down, north and south, east and west until basically you crossed out the country. But the overpowering division that arose took the shape of Muslims in the North against Christians in the South. (Remember, the South included the West, Midwest, and Eastern states.) The elections of 1964 were destined for failure. Literature alleging "Igbo domination" began to appear, not because the Igbo ruled by numbers—the Hausa-Fulani of the North had the numbers—but because the Igbo had traveled hither and yon, picking up all kinds of government posts. Several members of the election commission threatened to, and some actually did, boycott the polls.

Between all the stories I heard and the life I lived, a rift was developing. I

*was assured that God was in control, but at night when eternity snuggled up to
me, I felt wildly out of control. I had seen beggars in Lagos right out in front
of Kingsway whose legs at the knees bent backwards and who walked along the
street on their hands. I had seen the great mamba, whose spirit still clung to it
in death and refused to admit defeat; I had seen Egungun dancing toward me
fearlessly with uplifted cutlass; I had seen the yawning face of death in the
draped and heavy bodies of expired patients carried to a wet grave in the rubber plantation at the end of our drive. I had seen the space between my mother
and my sister open up like a reinjured wound when they were forced to part. I
had seen my own blonde self split in two at the mirror. And still I had witnessed the yellow hibiscus big as a hand, a golden spot hanging on a bush, only
slightly denser than air, a swan's back so soft, its stamen pure electric.*

New spirits were being born that would rob the River Ethiope—
today there is a hotel at the landing where I swam; during the Biafran
War people were killed on the banks of that river; the oil has brought
prosperity to very few.

Certainly, a case could be made that even today I do not know
what the cost has been to anyone but myself. Though in the present
as I write this, some awareness comes to me. In the local paper I read:
*More than 100 charred bodies, many of them children in school uniforms, lay
scattered among burned palm and rubber trees Tuesday after a damaged gasoline pipeline exploded in southern Nigeria, killing villagers scavenging fuel
with buckets and chamber pots.* The story goes on to say that *absolute poverty in the region means many people remain willing to risk death for fuel.* The
puncture in the pipeline may have been created by militant activists
who are trying to *force the government and oil companies to give compen-
sation to communities for land use and . . . pollution. In other cases, villagers
collect the gushing fuel to make a crude mixture of oil and gasoline for cheap
generators and other motors. Nigeria is the world's sixth largest oil exporter.
. . .* This explosion occurred just a few miles from Eku in the village
of Adeje.

One night, after falling asleep to one of my parents reading, I
was awakened by a pulsing sensation in my hair. Still trailing dreams,
I shook my head to discover a baby bat flapping unhappily on my

pillow. I didn't wait to call my father; I ran to him. We all came back to view the baby bat fluttering on my pillow, but my mother left as quickly as she came, calling out to my father in her retreat to "get rid of that thing." The poor animal was, of course, efficiently disposed of. This was a routine I knew by heart. Certain creatures were not to intrude upon us regardless of how much they belonged: these included snakes, roaches, mice, monitor lizards, and now bats. I have to admit that I was myself fairly unhappy to have had a bat in my hair. The thing was too odd and too otherworldly even for me to concoct a story of its victimization. Now, however, I view the bat as I do the monitor lizard, its disturbance of my sleep that night a harkening to many rude awakenings still in wait.

In my life in West Africa, I faced the same crises and anxieties that attend most growings up. But I hardly knew what was going on around me. I held a multitude of things in my heart and they multiplied down endless compound paths. But I had little understanding of the vast trade winds that had brought the Lloyd Neils to the Gulf of Guinea. I looked in the mirror with my own blue eyes, fearing the shadow that was myself, but not discerning the greater shadow that hung over us all like night.

Because the truth is, we had been here before. For generations, white people had been coming to these shores in search of treasure, and the treasure had been human beings. I have known for a long time that West African slaves were brought in putrid boats to the American South, but never before had I seen how closely my Nigerian and American neighborhoods were linked, not until I began to write. Here is how I discovered that intimacy:

Looking at a book, my eyes fall upon a second picture of the River Ethiope and in the center of the picture I see those mighty logs: two or three huge trunks, trimmed of branches and roots, almost perfect cylinders attached parallel in sets of two or three for the trip downriver. I recognize the way the logs are tied together as they make their heavy and inevitable way to market. Their destination: Sapele. But Sapele brings Warri to my mind, because it was equidistant from Eku and because we took turns going to either city to shop. And as I continue to read about the region I make a discovery: Warri was a slave trading station in the eighteenth and early nineteenth centuries. My parents certainly were following in the paths of early explorers and traders. When I look at a map of Africa and the Americas in Kwamena-Poh's African History in Maps, *I recognize an awful symmetry that rewrites my family history. A heavy black line connects the Nigerian coast with Charleston, South Carolina, the arrows pointing like the hand of God from Africa to America. What this means, the map key tells me, is that Africans were being exported from West Africa through the West Indies and finally into the American South. My mother's family goes back several generations in South Carolina and her great-grandparents were slaveholding landowners.*

My mother grew up with "Aunt Hale," an ex-slave who worked for her family. She remembers also "Aunt Fibbie," another ex-slave and mulatto who was a close associate of her grandmother, Mary Rebecca Harter Deer. Indeed, my mother has long suspected that Aunt Fibbie and Mary Rebecca were half sisters. Rebecca's two brothers were killed eight miles from the family's home-town of Fairfax—my great-grandmother could hear the shots—at the Battle of River Bridge, during the Civil War. They were defending slavery, of course. Did my great-great-grandfather purchase slaves from the Nigerian coast? Could Aunt Fibbie have had Yoruba or Urhobo ancestry? Am I a part of her extended family?

I venture to say that my family's first contact with Nigeria was by boat but not the African Patriot, *the freighter my parents and sister boarded on their way to "the field" when they were first appointed. Contact may have begun much earlier, with West African men and women and children working my family's land.*

And I think this history is why my mother was compelled at an early age to become a missionary and why she ended up in Africa.

During the summer of 1964, we began to prepare for furlough. Every day one of my friends would ask how many more days it was until I went to America, and I would answer cavalierly, "fourteen," "thirteen," "twelve." I was anxious and excited. My faith in David had been shaken. Maybe something better lay around the corner. But I wasn't sure.

One afternoon on the way home from Abraka, I overheard my mother talking in excited tones with Aunt Mary Evelyn about something called *the Beatles*. She had seen the latest copy of *Time* magazine which featured a cover story on the British band. I didn't gain much information from the conversation except a general sense of amazement and superciliousness. The only detail I remember is my mother saying something like, "Their hair is longer than Elaine's!" And then she guffawed nervously as still she does when confronted by something in popular culture that she does not understand. I was alarmed by her alarm. America was going to be a place full of mysteries.

One evening in preparation for this transcontinental journey, I sat on the floor in the living room, in the middle of the big jute rug, and studied a Sears catalog. Trying to get a picture of myself in America, my eyes come to rest on a girl like me. Except that she was not me; she was better. Her blonde hair was neatly combed and fell to her shoulders where it turned back up in a perfect half circle, like the letter C on its back. She wore a navy blue hair band and her blue eyes were not so large as mine, but her nose was more obedient and not freckled and her lips seemed redder and her upper teeth did not protrude. The clothes she wore were both familiar and impossible: a crisp white shirt buttoned to the very top, tucked into a pleated navy blue skirt. I did not think I was going to pass.

A few days before we left, housecleaning and packing began in earnest. My sister, home from boarding school, was helping my mother go through my things. But she should not have been so bold. When I discovered that she had dispensed with some of my least prized but nonetheless most familiar possessions, I was overcome with grief. With my mother trailing behind, I undertook a hasty reconnaissance effort down to the koto. But the cherished items were too soiled to retrieve. So I left them there to rot among the orange peel and old shoes.

Sometime that summer, my father drove the sierra gold Chevrolet station wagon down by the back steps where he washed and waxed it and took pictures of it and then sold it off to the highest bidder. We went swimming at the river the day before we left. After that I remember standing with Aunt Barbara and my mother on that tiny bridge over a ditch—this was one of those features of the landscape that David and I imbued with great significance—and Aunt Barbara said to mother, *I'm not going to come down and say good-bye tomorrow; I don't say good-bye.*

On the following morning, an unfamiliar van drove into our back yard. David was standing by our house, looking sideways into the middle distance. I got into the transport without giving him a hug or even a proper good-bye, closed the door, and looked straight ahead, determined to take on the dark continent of America.

Those brief years in Eku were for me a moment of fragile peace between losing my sister and losing everything. Those brief years in the life of the young republic were a moment of fragile peace between independence and civil war. That sweet time was always getting away from me, which is perhaps why in my imagination I stretch out those years like the first book of Virginia Woolf's *To the Lighthouse,* which is really only an evening and a day.

Bamidele

IN A DREAM, *I am on the front porch at the Gaultneys' house. I imagine that if I dig in the ground around the shrubs to the left of the steps I will find something I left, presumably a toy, but maybe a piece of jewelry, something that will show I had been there and thus attest to my history in Eku and with David. The bushes are large and shiny and multicolored: green and red and yellow. My hands are full of dirt. But then I begin to find what I am looking for, at first some little plastic human figures—a policeman, a Santa Claus, a young girl. And then I uncover a handful of pulls like the sort you have on a dresser or wardrobe or jewelry box, little brass pulls. And then, unbelievably, I find a cluster of Nigerian stamps, beautiful stamps in the shapes of triangles and rectangles, depicting rain forest and river and elephants and birds. And emblazoned on the stamps, my very own name: Bamidele, Bamidele, Bamidele. Follow me home.*

American Shrines

ANYONE WHO THINKS MK life is about the trauma of landing in Africa without prior knowledge of culture and country doesn't know anything about MK life. West Africa will take you in. The trauma is coming to America, which will not. It was an American songster who asked how it feels to be without a home. To be on your own. Like a rolling stone.

My primary impression of the U.S. in 1964 was that it was new. The first thing I did when I got off the airplane in Greenville, South Carolina, after the obligatory hugs and kisses among all sorts of relatives whose names I forgot as soon as I heard them, was to walk up to the first gum machine I could find in the airport and insert the shiny American penny I had gotten from Daddy into the slot. The gum ball was so much richer than the ones I had chewed in Nigeria. It was fresher, too. The gums I had known were something like the pieces of candy I had stored in my dresser among socks and slips: flavors and smells had commingled and transferred. That gum had known another life. But American gum had never been anywhere. It had no history. At the time, I thought this was good.

In America there was no dust; everything was clean. The hymnals in the Baptist church were so new it was hard to separate the pages because they had never been turned before. The Sunday school classroom I attended was so shiny I thought the paint must still be wet and so I avoided touching the walls with my dress. Suburban houses appeared to me like something that had been delivered whole; certainly the furnishings had never been packed into drums and crates to bounce around in the back of a lorry. And people bought snacks at the grocery that were wrapped separately in cellophane. I thought these were a sign of great wealth and spiritual wholeness. There were no watermarks on the tables in my aunt's house, no nicked edges of tables, no cracked and mended vases.

Television became my frame of reference, confirming for me that nothing in America had any depth. In Easley, South Carolina, I saw films for the first time without my parents—Elvis flicks and once the James Bond film *Goldfinger* when I convinced my mother, more out of ignorance than connivance, that it was a comedy for children. This was before ratings, and my mother would not have known Elvis from Bond from Yogi Bear anyway. As it turned out, the Bond film did not harm me, but it didn't entertain me either; I simply had no idea how to understand it. Visiting my Grandmother Neil in Landrum, I watched in admiration as my cousin Susan tore her hair out and sacrificed it to her Beatles shrine, which was her entire bedroom. I think she must have slept in the hallway on a mat out of respect for those icons.

My impressions about the newness and slickness of America in 1964 are not entirely accurate of course; not everything was new. I saw the small dying towns in lower South Carolina on my way to visit Grandmother Thomas. But it is still true that compared with Yoruba land, the country of American immigrants is like a young teenager trying desperately to impress.

The towns that had surrounded me in my childhood were ancient. The dust that filled my nostrils had been kicked up by millions of heels, made into houses that had crumbled and been remade into the pottery of the marketplace and the sculpture of ritual and worship. As a matter of fact, not only did Nigeria smell old while America smelled new, *I* smelled like Nigeria. My new acquaintances sniffed out my foreignness in the time it takes to flounce a skirt. I was made out of the land in which I was conceived, out of the air my mother breathed in the market and the water she drank and the tropical fruits that passed through her lips. I was born hearing the toads outside after the rains, the shift in the night as the pineapple grew, the buzzing of insects in the pushing grass, the hi-fi in town, the lorry on the road.

For the short time that I was in the U.S. in 1964–65, I did my best to pass. In actuality I did a little better than my best. I had always made As and Bs in school and that seemed plenty good. But suddenly I was hearing about the possibility of making *straight* As, and though I was bored with school, finding it less than challenging, I sometimes found it necessary to "borrow" an answer from a neighbor. This scheme worked beautifully; before long I was a straight A student. Perhaps in an effort to square myself with God, I decided to declare my faith in Jesus and get baptized. On school days, my eyes would wander onto a neighbor's paper and then on Sunday I would rededicate myself to God. After a while, my mother started holding onto me while we sang "Just As I Am," so that I wouldn't go forward again. This was an interesting hymn for my confessions since I was becoming just the opposite of who I was. I was becoming a great success and losing my soul in the process. So much change came so quickly, moving from an African to an American stage in a matter of days. It's hard to hold up under that kind of pressure and remember who you are. Maybe in cheating I was trying to get caught, trying to say, *Someone, please, take notice!*

One day that year I wrote a little story called "Being Homesick" that I still have.

> "Mother, Mother," I called as soon as I got home.
> "Yes," answered Mother.
> I asked questioningly: "Where have you put all my things?"
> "They are packed," she murmured.
> "What, packed?" I shouted.
> "Didn't you know we were going to move?" my mother asked.
> "Why no," I exclaimed.
> "Well, we are. Tomorrow we go to the airport and get on a plane. From there we go to America!"
> I didn't want to move, although I knew we had to. Slowly and with a heavy heart I began to get things ready for moving.
> The next day we were on our way. I didn't like planes at all. When we got to New York it was extremely different from Nigeria. On the following day we came to Greenville. How I longed to be back in our happy home in Nigeria. But soon I discovered many interesting and

exciting things in America. I feel almost at home now. Even so, I am eagerly looking forward to returning to the home that is so dear to me.

Reading the story now, I notice that I "shouted" and "exclaimed." I guess I only did so in the story. Still, I'm surprised by the clarity and passion of that last sentence. I don't remember being that clear about where I belonged and what I loved when I was ten years old. In my adult life, before kidney failure, I had forgotten that sentence entirely.

The story is signed *Elaine Neil* and dated *Nov. 10, 1964.*

All my life in the U.S., I have felt *almost at home* but never really home.

In my front yard in Raleigh, I encourage myself by growing a few tropicals: a single red hibiscus and some flaming love in a pot and a palm tree, which, like the other two plants, I take indoors in the winter. But sometimes on a summer day, I lower my face into the hibiscus so that I am very close to it. I caress its leaves—they are a little prickly, like a fine sandpaper—and when I am up close like that, I am truly home, coming around that last bend on the Eku-Abraka road and spotting the compound fence and then the sign that says *Eku Baptist Hospital.* But when I back up and gain a proper perspective, I can see the aggressive azaleas under the pines and the rhododendron, which is becoming gigantic, and the mums bursting out in their flames of white white white. My little bit of Africa shrinks and I am still on dialysis, still waiting, still split at the root.

In Easley, watching TV, I ate bag after bag of greasy potato chips and miraculously premade, though not very good, chocolate chip cookies and little white doughnut holes—all of this on Saturday morning before my parents even got up, thus ruining myself before the day began and feeling slightly sick until Sunday morning. My hunger was enormous. No wonder I needed confession. So many things were available so easily in America. You could go to the store every day instead of every other month. You didn't even have to get dressed up in your better clothes. The choices at the candy aisle had expanded since last you were there. In America you didn't have to wait several weeks for Uncle Jerry Gaultney to work up a batch of fudge or Christmas when your mother made coconut macaroons. And every Saturday, you could go and stand in the toy section of the general store and stare at all the Barbie dolls and Barbie clothes, and now Skipper, who was even better because she was your age. Almost every Saturday you would buy something to add to your collection, like a set of Barbie accessories—handbags and shoes smaller than a fingernail— or a cheerleading outfit for Skipper, spending your own allowance, or if you were smart enough to leave your money at home, appealing to your father, who would buy it for you while smiling at your duplicity. I still had no idea who paid the rent.

I watched *Gilligan's Island* on Friday night, and I dreamed desperately of watching *Bonanza* every single Sunday night; but we were usually at church so I only saw it occasionally when we didn't go. I loved those men. I was ready for them. On Saturday mornings, there were cartoons: *Daffy Duck, Mighty Mouse, The Flintstones, Bullwinkle, Yogi Bear,* and *Huckleberry Hound.* I had never been so entertained, or should I say, so stupefied.

I could tell I wasn't an American. For the first time in my life I felt outside, but I was outside among my own majority. I was on the other side of an invisible wall. The girls at school—like the twins with the cute haircuts and the clothes that didn't wrinkle and the socks that stayed up and who made Bs and Cs in school but were wildly loved anyway—seemed to have emerged from TV land, they were so perfect. And I thought if I could just get beyond that wall, into the land of perfect hair and cute skirts, then everything would be lovely. The off-white Naugahyde couch in the living room was my flying carpet and the television was my crystal ball. But I never managed liftoff.

My foreignness would not leave me alone. Sometimes I would throw caution to the wind and go native, abandoning the electric box. I made an evergreen tree in the back yard into my best friend and gave it a name and decorated it with hats and scarves in the wintertime and danced around it like a witch. In such a mood, I would reject the image of the twins and join another tomboy in my neighborhood

for a foray into the woods where we would catch minnows and tadpoles and salamanders, bringing them home to grow up. My sister
hated these creatures and was happy the day a dog wandered onto
our carport and scattered my animal compound, setting the salamanders free and leaving the water-dependent creatures to die a slow
death. At least one of the tadpoles had matured into a young frog.
Perhaps he had a better fate. I had named him Fingerling, after the
thumb-sized hero of a British novel for children that I had read in
Eku. The day of his disappearance—or the day of his liberation, depending on your perspective—I came home and my mother told me
what had happened. I sat in her lap in the shrunken dining area of
that small brick house on Cedar Street in one of those standardized
brown chairs that went with what I thought of as our false dining
room set and wept as if my father had died. I was slightly overweight
and sweaty in the way children are at age ten. Every year seemed to
end this way: with monumental losses that others treated as minor.
But I did not have the words to explain this to my mother.

On our last trip to Fairfax to visit my Grandmother Thomas, I
carried a little tin box into which I put some treasures from that year:
trinkets from gum-ball machines, some coins I had saved, a bracelet,
and a picture of myself. And I planted the box under a small tree in
the side yard. It wasn't an easy task because it was summer and hot;
and the dirt in that yard was very sandy. As soon as you'd dig a little,
the surrounding sand would cave in and you'd have to start all over
again. Besides I was digging with a kitchen spoon; it was all I could
find. I often faced difficult challenges in my young life, setting out
with all the wrong tools or perhaps I should say all the wrong expec-
tations. What my parents and Nigeria gave me were a potent sense of
human need, a love for the sounds and smells of the market, a jealous attachment to tropical nature, a taste for the genteel life, and a
huge but generalized ambition *to do* something worthy. As you can
see, this list doesn't exactly add up. I felt that so much was expected
of me but I had little opportunity in Nigeria actually to practice a skill
or prove myself. I was told I was an excellent swimmer; my father
joked about my swimming in the Olympics. But unlike Nigerian or
American children, I had no teams, no venues in which to find out

what really I could do. I learned almost nothing about money; we seemed to have what we needed. The message I received was simply: *Make something remarkable of your talents and everything you need will be added unto you.* I was like a princess set down to a sumptuous banquet but without even a spoon like the one I used that afternoon in my grandmother's side yard to bury my treasure. Nothing I have ever done has seemed large enough for what I thought was expected of me as a girl.

I knew I was ready when the season came to leave Easley. I never regretted departing the U.S., not once, not even a little bit. America was like a dress you try on at a store, thinking it looks nice on you or it would in a certain light. But when you get home, you realize it is wrong; it won't do at all. And if by chance you still have to wear it on one occasion, you stand against the wall with your arms crossed over your chest and look away when it appears that a boy might come talk to you—because if you meet his eyes he will see that you don't know what to do in your dress. It's better to lose someone before you have him because anyway he will probably change his mind. So you sip punch and talk lightheartedly with other girls at the refreshment table—the servers—and you laugh too much. And finally you slip out, knowing that nothing can be worse than when the best you can hope for is that no one noticed you, not even your parents.

Miracles

SOMETIMES NOW *I dream of flying. I hover over the Cockrums'*
yard in Oshogbo, sweeping down over the tadpole box, or I am at Eku, coast-
ing in the air of that deep front yard. I am bodied but light and my legs extend
behind me long and thin and brown. Someone tells me to stop flying, to come
down, but I ignore him, raising my wings and lifting up, high up, so that all I
see is the palm trees, thousands of them, below me, looking now like a pattern
on cloth in green and mustard and brown. I fly out over the Bight of Biafra
and see the boundary where water meets sand and then the trees, thick in their
greenness. I dive down to an inlet where I see a village on stilts out in the water,
connected by a crisscrossing of walkways.

I am healed in these dreams or perhaps this is a premonition of another life
awaiting me. It makes no difference now.

Many a Winding Turn

So we left Easley for Nigeria but not for the home of Eku. Instead we coasted back to Oshogbo and Newton School, where I, like Becky, would be a boarding student. Once again my parents would be house parents: my father would be the school's business manager, my mother would teach health classes and return to her position as chief counselor. But the school had grown and now there were two dorms, one for girls and one for boys. My parents would be house parents in the boys' dorm, living in an apartment that Becky and I would share with them on holidays. Our neighbors were the DuValls and Ellen was my closest peer.

She turns into the long curtain, wrapping it around her, and then she unwinds and does it again. She is a tall girl, as tall as I am, and thinner. Her brown hair is thick and glossy and deep brown, like a kola nut in the sun. Her skin is smooth and tan and every feature of her body is perfectly symmetrical. She has no scars. You might say she is pretty.

I am sitting on the top bunk on the bare mattress in a room on the younger girls' hall, looking down at her in her bliss. Everyone at Newton is younger or older; younger means fifth through seventh grades, older means eighth through tenth. The girl is talking; I am listening and the room is not ours. It is no one's yet. In fact we are conjecturing whose room it will be in five days, the day school begins and the roommate list is posted. Until then, no one knows but the adults, including our parents, who, as always, control our destiny.

The girl is Ellen DuVall. I am myself, more or less, having recently returned from the U.S. I don't understand yet that this association with America is supposed to mean I am hip; I am not. Though I am shedding two pounds a day now that I have returned to the tropics,

I am still a little chubby and I forgot to bring back any Beatles records to show off.

In the "summer," which is quickly being eclipsed by "fall," my family shares the compound with the DuValls and my future house parents, Uncle Bill and Aunt Novella Bender, and their children, and some single women missionaries who will be our teachers. Just as Eku was Aunt Mary Evelyn's compound, Oshogbo belongs to the DuValls. They are the one permanent feature at Newton since Uncle Wallace is the principal. Unlike my family, which resides in an apartment, Ellen's large family has its own house, always the same house.

Watching Ellen in the empty dorm room, I could tell she knew her territory. In front of me, twirling in the curtain, she knew everything and I knew nothing. She was a boarding school veteran, having attended Newton the year before along with David Gaultney who had come for the first time. I could tell Ellen liked him though I continued to harbor the belief that no one shared with David such a relationship as I. In any case, he was on furlough now with his family and I still had not seen him since that day I rode off in that stranger's van without saying a proper good-bye. I would not see him for two more years and by then the world would have turned around and broken in half.

The way I felt watching Ellen was as if someone had taken my place. Someone had come during my absence in the U.S. and taken up the position of the favored daughter, the favored girl. From that moment on, I was not sure of my place. Because when I was the favored daughter at Eku—and this favored status fell to me partly because I was the baby in the family, partly because my father saw his likeness in me, partly because I was the only daughter with my sister away at school, partly because I was the only MK girl on the compound most of those two years, partly because I was David's closest friend—it was not because I was pretty. It was because I was myself. But now it seemed to me that being the favorite would require me to be someone else. I had hoped to return to Nigeria as it was, but I found I was in Nigeria as it had not been or I found myself in a different Nigeria or I found myself different in Nigeria. I found myself in boarding school, or rather, I lost myself.

Ellen knew the important things, such as who had "liked" whom last year. "Liked" was a euphemism for "dated," a term that inflated the reality of the situation, like teasing your hair might make you look sophisticated, but still you were only a girl. Just as the other compounds I knew were bound by a fence, Newton Memorial School compound was a delimited space, self-contained, and more isolated than either Eku or Ogbomosho, positioned two miles from the outskirts of Oshogbo. Perhaps our parents didn't want us escaping into town. Or perhaps this area two miles out of Oshogbo was as close as the town fathers wanted us to get to their compounds. The town of Oshogbo had a healthy self-image. In any case, going on a date at Newton, even in the advanced position of a tenth grader, was like shopping with your mother—a little dull. The boys would leave their dorm and walk over to yours, all in a group. When they arrived, a "younger" girl messenger would run down the hall and tell you he was here and sometimes she would report on what he was wearing or how he looked. Then you would walk out where he was waiting, carrying your smile in your pocket so you didn't look too pleased, and you would saunter with him across the lawn—at this point about two feet apart—and head to the chapel where the lights would go off and you would watch a movie like *The Hunchback of Notre Dame,* which I must have seen fifty times before I finally left Newton for good, or some old newsreel that was so plotless you lost interest even in your date's hands. There were no choices about entertainment. The whole school attended every event. The only question was whether or not you had a "date," and this question was as relevant when you were in the fifth grade as when you were in the tenth.

After the movie, you found one of numerous concrete park benches scattered across the campus—that is, if you were at least in the eighth grade; otherwise, you had to sit inside where there was a light directly over your head. In either case, you found a place to sit with your date, maybe for half an hour or more. You talked or kissed if you were lucky. A few people doubtless did more. Then the boy walked the girl back to her dorm and said good night and maybe there was one more kiss in the hallway. Someone would be watching so it felt very dangerous and clearly performative. Like correspondence school where you wrote everything down instead of discussing subjects the way you do in a regular classroom, dating at Newton was largely an exercise in silence. This curtailment of sexual expression intensified the experience more than any outward exercise would have and left us exhausted just thinking about it. No wonder when we heard songs like "Love Child" or "Just Call Me Angel of the Morning" or "House of the Rising Sun" on the turntable—and we played these over and over at high volumes in our rooms—we sang along with such zest. Most of us didn't know what the lyrics were about, or at least I didn't.

Romantic competition was stiff at Newton. Consider one of your own middle-grade classes and imagine a random selection of about ten students from it; then ask yourself how many truly "datable" people you would have. Not many. But we had to make do even if we were in a class of twelve girls and one boy and he was less than you hoped for. I was feeling the winds of this competition as Ellen talked so blithely, so securely about boarding school—Ellen who would never be without a date in her life, wrapped like a young goddess in the curtain in the room of all these ghosts of girls who had occupied it in the past and might occupy it in the future. Ellen talked about "liking" and she talked about "banquets": the yearly Thanksgiving and Valentine's Banquets. Any girl at Newton who had any sense or who mattered at all could recite in a heartbeat who went with whom to each of these events the year before. Our bathetic history was made this way, for example: 1963 was the year Ellen went to the Thanksgiving Banquet with so-and-so. And Susan went with so-and-so, and Connie went with whatshisname, and Brenda went with . . . Not to have a date was not to have a history. There might as well have been a separate table for those who went alone, a table for the nameless ones. They know who they are and they remember. No one else remembers them, except maybe in pity.

Watching Ellen so lost in her happiness because she was ready and she knew how to be liked, I thought: *I better get prepared for this game. This is a new sort of competition, not like racing David in his back yard. I don't know how to gain an advantage.* I didn't know how to flirt or act coy and indifferent. If I wanted something, you could read it in my face. And I didn't know how to get my hair to behave. How was I going to become a princess like the one dancing down there before my own eyes? This was a conundrum Trixie Belden could not help solve. In fact, we were in a new novel now and the heroine wasn't Trixie at all but her friend Honey, the rich sweet placid dark-haired beauty who lived up the road from Trixie and had none of her flaws. She was the one things happened to, not the one who stirred things up; the one people loved even when she suffered—in fact, especially when she suffered—not the one who brought trouble on herself and then was despised because she suffered. Who did she think she was anyway?

I knew how to pack for boarding school because I had seen Becky do it. Now, like her, I had name tags. Every August, I would head back to school with lots of newly made dresses and new underwear; my mother packed those things. What I packed myself were the prize mementos from home that I was going to take to the girls' dorm to shore up my identity: stuffed animals and my August Angel statuette and a jewelry box and a photograph of my parents, which I took even though my parents were right there in front of me.

You didn't take your Barbie doll to Newton; that was passé (we were so grown up), even though I had gotten my Barbie equipment only the year before in Easley. And you didn't come to Newton at all unless you had a Bible and a flashlight, which you kept with you in bed between the hardwood frame and the mattress, and a thermos for carrying drinking water to your room. Water, a light, the Word of God, and a picture of your parents. What more could you need?

The Sunday afternoon before school was to begin, we all moved into the dorm, my sister and I shuttling across campus while everyone else came from places as near as Ogbomosho and as far away as Ghana.

Once a student, I tried to act like everyone else. Even when I saw my parents. For example, somewhere between the boys' dorm and the girls' dorm, somewhere on that path that ran diagonally between the two dwellings, a path that provided no shelter from the bright afternoon sun because all the trees had been cut down in that space, somewhere there was a dividing line, like the Mason Dixon line, and once I crossed that line, I was not a daughter but a boarding school student. Often I encountered my parents on this path during the school year as they were walking one direction and I the other. We spoke cordially, hailing each other like boats in a channel, but we did not touch in that white open space.

There were some but not many exceptions to the rule of behaving like a boarding school student, not like your mother's child. All the girls took piano and I did get to practice every school day at home in the boys' dorm in my family's living room. This meant I could fix peanut butter and crackers and have some Coca-Cola from our private refrigerator. For three years I made this traversal between not being my parents' daughter and being my parents' daughter, moving between a living room that I shared with twenty-five or thirty other girls, where everything was stacked and squared, and the gracefully appointed living room in our apartment, with the newly re-covered lavender couch and the mission chairs with the new striped cushions and the long low Sapele-wood table in front of the window, and mother's collection of blue and green glass all sparkly in the sun, and the radio on the square wood-inlaid table from which my parents listened to the BBC and the Voice of America, and the record player on which in the evenings and on Sundays they heard the music of Chopin and Debussy and Grieg and Mendelssohn.

Perhaps I should explain why my parents kept getting reassigned: from Ogbomosho to Eku to Oshogbo to Eku to Oshogbo. It was not because they were hard to get along with and people wanted to get rid of them. It was exactly the other way around. They were very popular. My father was a capable businessman, a steady, efficient, funny sort of guy. My mother was thought of as an effective teacher, a wise counselor, a superior intellect, an altogether solid *and* charismatic leader. Furthermore, they were willing to go where the mission asked them to go. Some missionaries were less flexible and stayed in one place forever. Not the Neils. I have long come to recognize that it was because my parents were so *good* that I got so little of them after a certain age. And it was because they were so sweet (hear that as African "sweet") that I missed them so much.

That first year at Newton I tried to call them back to me.

In the morning, the boys were served their breakfast first. They were like the big animals, the elephants and hippos at the water. The girls ate second, so we were something like the zebras, I guess. I imagine this arrangement was considered necessary since it took the girls longer in the morning with their toilet. We all had to take our hair out of rollers and style it and the older girls had to put on makeup. Since my parents were the boys' house parents, they ate with them in the cafeteria which was in the center of the girls' dorm, for this was the only cafeteria, and we all ate there. Often in the morning, while the boys were eating, one would need to get from one side of the girls' dorm to the other. There were doors opening onto the front of the dorm at either side of the cafeteria, so you would simply go outdoors and then re-enter on the other side. But often I would get to the door just as my father was beginning to pray:

Oh Lord, thank you for this new day, for the opportunities in it, bless the members of our mission family today, bless all the missionaries around the world who have birthdays today, bless the leaders of the Nigerian peoples as they meet in Lagos this week to discuss the future direction of the country, be with our own Convention as it meets this month in Ibadan, help these young people today at Newton School in their work and play, let them know what is right and good for them to do, let them know that you are with them. Oh Lord, make us ever mindful of your presence with us. Thank you now for this food, bless it to the nourishment of our bodies and our bodies to your service, for we pray in the name of Jesus Christ our Lord, Amen. His prayer is long and drawn out and I am sure the boys do not appreciate it. But to me the prayer is poetry because I have heard this sort of thing tumbling out of my father's mouth all my life. This morning, however, I am relegated to some domestic duty—like cleaning the music room—while my father and mother preside over the boys' breakfast. Apparently, my prayer time no longer coincides with my parents'. It's as if they're on Eastern time and I'm on Central. So I linger while my father prays, loving the sound of it. As soon as the prayer is over, however, the boys sprint to the cafeteria line, so I continue on my way to the music room. Once there, I dust the windowsill and the top of the piano and I arrange the magazines, which are in disarray. I even dust the leaves of the philodendron because Aunt Novella has instructed me to do so. I sweep the floor and arrange the cushions on the divan. But as I finish my task and face the return to my room, via the outside detour around the cafeteria, I realize that I do not feel well. My head is swimming, or at least if I focus hard enough, I can imagine that it is swimming. I have a pain in my abdomen, or I might have a pain in my abdomen if I concentrate. Yes. I think it is the case that I do not feel well. I will need to tell my mother, because she is the campus nurse. But I am shy about entering the cafeteria even though this is my very own mother because I will have to pass in front of the eyes of all those boys gathered there in their maleness for breakfast. Some of them like George Faile are very big, and it seems to me I am better off if I just stay out of their way. I'm like a young cub separated from its mother. But unfortunately my mother does not know that this is a bad thing. She has forgotten her instincts. I must go and remind her. So I walk a thin line between all those boys at table, finally making it up to my parents, whose table is the farthest away. This is the very table where I sat with them years earlier when my sister was a boarder, taking my Flintstones vitamins and drinking my orange juice and eating my eggs in their very shadow. But now they sit there without me. My mother sees me coming but she does not smile. Instead she greets me with a firmly cheerful *Well, good morning* as though it is a surprise to see me. When I just stand there for a moment, she puts her arm around my waist but still she does not inquire *What do you need?* or *How are you?* because to ask would be to invite an answer. So finally, when I see that she is not going to help me unless I prompt her, I say in a low and faltering voice, *I don't feel good.* I cannot say, "Let me come home." Where was that? Or "Let me eat breakfast with you." It never even occurred to me that I wanted to say any of those things. In a world in which you plan all your life to leave your parents just when you need them the most, and this is the will of God and the Foreign Mission Board and everyone else in the world who has any authority, how are you going to imagine that you need to go home?

"You don't feel good? Well, you look fine."

And she raises one palm to my forehead.

"You don't have any fever. What doesn't feel well?"

This whole setup, is what I should have screamed. But instead I venture, "My stomach."

"You probably just need to eat some breakfast. Why don't you see how you feel after you eat. Sometimes in the morning I feel a little sick to my stomach when I first get up. It's because you're hungry. I bet you'll feel fine by the time you get down to Aunt Jamie's classroom."

My father is privy to this interview but he is of no help. When it is over, he looks at me and smiles and gives me a half hug, because he is still sitting down, and says something benign like *Do good work today,* as though he has not heard anything I have said or picked up on any of the pain I am sure is written all over my face.

I have failed. They do not see how impossible this is, being here but not being here as their daughter. It's as though half of my body has been erased by some great cartoon artist in the sky and no one notices I'm only half present.

Even the few times I did pass as ill and made it to the infirmary, I wasn't sick enough to command such attention as my mother's. I only got Aunt Novella, who could manage aspirin and an occasional pat on the head. I think she actually liked me. But I was going for my mother, so my plan didn't work. I couldn't make myself sufficiently ill. I had to go to school.

In the afternoons, I got to watch my father from a distance, with Uncle Wallace, leading the boys in their exercises. My father was a sports legend to me. He had grown up a local hero, a football and baseball star in South Carolina in the 1930s. He was trim, accurate, fleet, and golden. Later he was an artillery gunner flying B-52s in World War II. He flew nine missions over Germany. And, of course, once, in an age long past, he had spent his afternoons taking me to the river. But Aunt Mary Jane was my coach. At least I liked her. She taught all of us English and every year she taught us over and over again *to read and follow directions.* Aunt Mary Jane was strict and elegant, tall with beautiful brown wavy hair and a kind of willowy aspect to her person. When she wasn't leading us in deep knee bends, she wore lovely flowing dresses and flat slipperlike shoes, and she had a self-satisfied laugh. She really did not try to please you but stood for what she believed and let the chips fall where they may. There was a myth surrounding Aunt Mary Jane and this was that she drank Coca-Cola and ate bacon, lettuce, and tomato sandwiches for breakfast. As an eleven-year-old, I thought she was courageous and distinctive, and I loved her for being herself, something I was quickly forgetting how to do.

I cannot to this day conjure my mother on that sports field, not even as a spectator. I wonder what she was doing in the boys' dorm on those long afternoons. She didn't have to fix dinner or prepare lessons—well, not many. She taught health to the eighth graders but not even every day of the week. I wish she had been keeping a journal or writing a novel. Later, when Becky went to the U.S., she might have been writing to her. But I wonder about those hours now. I have never wondered about them before and it strikes me how little I know about her life then. Maybe she was becoming a feminist. A copy of *The Feminine Mystique* sat on the bookshelf in our apartment hallway. I know she read it and other books as well. She and Uncle Wallace had a kind of book club going, I think, recommending "must-reads" to one another in this American outback.

My parents, I am sure, thought they had eased the difficulty of my going to boarding school by becoming house parents at Newton. Unlike the other children and unlike Becky in earlier years, I did not have to tell them good-bye and travel for hours to Newton where I would not see them for weeks and in some cases even months. But their half presence also made it impossible for me to fantasize that they really *wanted* to be with me if they could or for me to look forward to their visits. They were already there; they just weren't there for me in any intimate way. Our family's common ground at Newton made it *appear* that we were not separated. But this was mostly appearance. Once in my adult life, describing how my family lived and ate separately while I was in boarding school, my therapist, startled, looked up at me: *They did that on purpose?* he asked.

At Newton, when I wasn't courting illness, I would no more have failed to show up for dinner than I would have stood up at my desk in the middle of the school day and begun undressing. Here, we stopped borrowing our patterns from the Nigerians and turned to the British. We were punctual and organized and correct. It never occurred to me that a person might decline this regimen. In my four years at Newton Memorial School, I never remember a student simply refusing to show up when it was time to be counted. We were there like enlisted men.

Eventually I experienced my first banquet, going with some boy who was not anything like David, not equal and friendly and comfortable all at once. Dating at Newton so exaggerated male and female difference that boys and girls could hardly find a regular meeting place. I never went alone to any of our banquets, but I also seldom had my first choice of dates. There were so few really likable boys—well, likable enough to want to romance; even the boys who were considered the best seemed to me a little suspect. They were all right for playing frisbee with after dinner or Ping-Pong in the empty classroom building in the evening or capture the flag on Saturday. But few had a hand I wanted to hold. Still I had to participate in dating because the first thing a girl had to have at Newton in order to be anyone at all was a boy.

Unable to tell that my sickness was really homesickness, my parents continued to believe I was strong. At staff meetings every year to determine roommates, they always volunteered me to board with the "hardest" cases, the girl no one else could get along with or the new girl no one had ever seen. This was part of our mythology along with the notion that Becky was responsible but not especially courageous. This last wasn't true of course. The truth was that my sister was on the front lines while I was still behind in the bush. And I watched her take the first blows and learned from her mistakes. Only later in life, when I rushed into marriage before she, did this pattern change. I should have stayed in line, but the men around me were so convincing and I was so startled by my own potency that for once I went where Becky had not. I followed by having the first pregnancy and the first child, a son, and so the first grandchild and the first boy for two generations. But I did not give him the name Neil. I knew that name was reserved for Becky and didn't want to add insult to injury. I took from my family only Houston, my father's middle name, the one he would joke about when Becky and I were little, coming into our room early in the morning and late at night, half-singing: *Lloyd Houston Neil, the most beautiful name in the whole wide world and the most beautiful name of all is* Houston. And he would smile slyly, holding back some mystery in his face, and then bend his knees and lean forward in the middle. Then he held his hands out and laughed as he looked at us one at a time. I took Houston and it came true: Joel Houston Orr is beautiful, and he tells stories like my father but is slow to anger and is musically gifted and self-indulgent. When he was young and Andy and I would banish him to his room for some mischief, we could hear him whistling through the walls, transported by his own imagination. I have tried all his life to shake the effervescence out of him but have failed. Joel is very like a Yoruba.

An observer would have said I was very enthusiastic about everything at Newton, always eager to get started, to be in the middle of whatever activity was at hand and to lead it. But it is often a mistake to take a child's behavior at face value.

We had a new set of monkey bars behind our classroom buildings, and I was often on these, not merely swinging from one bar to the next all down the line but standing on the steps and then throwing myself out into the air to catch myself midway down the bars. I would try this stunt over and over, each time attempting to reach the next bar, until I would land flat on my back on the hard ground, my breath completely knocked out of me. Did I enjoy this sort of thing? I don't think so. I think, instead, this throwing myself into the air was a secret message I was trying to send to God or someone to catch me for I was falling. Or perhaps I undertook this exercise out of pride. Even though I was stumbling in boarding school, I was determined that no one should see me daunted, and so I would keep trying for the hardest things in order to show my certainty.

Boarding school was like swimming underwater and only underwater. You couldn't come up for air. And after a while you adjusted to this world where relationships are distorted and you can't judge distance. You actually forget how it feels to breathe.

So I practiced the notion that the most important thing in the world is not who you are or what you do but what boy you attract. And I threw myself into the air, hoping for the arms of Jesus. And I learned to treat my parents as though they were copies of themselves and their primary mission was to be house parents. All the while something else was brewing. Just after we returned from Christmas break, a coup occurred, igniting what would become the Biafran War. It was January 1966. Historians would call this the "first" coup.

Detention

KIDNEY FAILURE IS your body's own breakup or break-in. Your energy dissipates, but poisons, like marauders, take up every residence that was left, and they will not be easily moved. Furthermore, you are yourself detained, not a prisoner of war but a prisoner of medicine. Even if I go to the beach for the weekend—carrying all the loads of dialysis, my personal iron staff—still I have to come back to my room every few hours for an "exchange." And when it's not the mere fact of dialysis detaining me, it's the illness, the nausea.

In the morning, I am too exhausted to rise, too nauseated to sleep, and thus I awaken to a state of stagnant frenzy, the joy that petaled my youth a distant curve in the air.

Finally in the bathroom, I lean over the toilet.

The day begun, I now have to do dialysis, four times today, as every day, and it's already 9:30.

This is my waking, my sleeping.

Not a Grove but an Island

NEWTON WAS A TRUE island, the only of the three compounds I lived on that went by an American rather than a Nigerian name. This compound housed the mission architects and the boarding school. The only residents—except for Mr. Amobi and his family, who lived in that small cottage—were Americans. No Nigerian student ever attended Newton, although some African American students occasionally did, like Tim, the boy I fell in love with in second grade. And once an Indian girl came, but she stayed only a semester, long enough for me to taste some of the exotic snacks she kept in her room and ate instead of shepherd's pie and fried okra. Perhaps because the architects lived on this compound, it was the most beautifully designed of all the mission compounds. The entrance boasted a stone marker with the artistically crafted words *Newton Memorial School.* Here the roads were not mere dirt but light gray gravel, edged with white painted stones. As one entered the compound, one's eyes were met with pulchritudinous shrubs—some beaded, some flowered, all lush and overflowing. Benches dotted the landscape, and about a quarter of a mile into the compound, the drive forked, creating a circle. The entire campus suggested serenity, the way pictures of families suggest wholeness.

Perhaps because of the way I saw it expand over the years, the Newton compound seemed to start in the center, with the girls' dorm, and then to grow outward, clearing the land and absorbing it. Newton had no mud houses, no age. It had no wildness left, or very little. There was the remnant of a cocoa farm in a few trees that survived across from the classroom buildings. These few specimens were gathered in one spot like escapees. Cocoa was then a major export crop for Nigeria, though like the oil palm trees in Eku, these trees were not especially preferred by Americans. Still Ellen and I visited them often on holiday, watching for a pod to mature into a ripe yellow-orange. We would then pluck it, sometimes a difficult task in itself with bare hands and no knife. And then we would strike the pod against the tree multiple times until it cracked open across the center lengthwise. Inside were the coveted seeds, about the size of a medium olive, and these were covered with a milky sweet, sticky substance that clung to each one. We would take our prize to the other side of the schoolroom buildings, back where no one could see us, and sit with our legs against the bare cool concrete and our backs against the stone wall. There we would take turns "eating" the seeds, one by one, as with a box of fine chocolates, until every last one was gone. What you really did was suck on each one long and hard and then throw the seed away. It would be a while before we would harvest another pod. At such times and released from boarding school competitions, Ellen and I were friends.

The field in front of the girls' dorm, the one created by that circular drive, stamps my early memory like an often repeated prayer. This was the circle in which I had learned to ride the blue bike. Now I jumped rope with a few other girls in the brief and therefore coveted few minutes between dinner and devotionals or I played frisbee during the same time with some of the younger boys. By now, most of the girls my age were combing their hair after dinner or painting their nails.

Apparently, I was hanging out with the underclass girls, though I didn't know it until a member of that class informed me: "I like you," she said, "because even though you're popular, you play with us." "Us" meant Anita and Jennifer and Deborah. Deborah was the most underclass girl ever to appear at Newton School. Eventually, she made up a story about how she was adopted and we didn't know her real family; she was actually the daughter of gypsies. I didn't yet realize the cost of playing with outcasts.

In any case, the evening from 6:30 to 7:00 was the most winsome time of the day, with the sun setting and dusk gathering under the ferns in the palms and a defined breeze and the smell of fire coming from a distance where farmers were clearing land; a smoothness was in the air like the sides of eggs. Nothing bad could happen in that time; the minutes were too short for envy and malice. You had only enough time to feel your arms free of chores and your mind relieved of duty.

The girls' dorm, originally the only dorm, was a comely structure, symmetrical, firm, and graceful all at once. In the center was the living room and dining hall approached by those broad high steps. Then on either side of this center, set back a ways, were the wings which extended in each direction before turning back out, so that the whole thing if you were facing it was a "double u," a W, with two little courtyards. In the middle of each of these grassed yards was one huge single shrub, a plant that grew up and around as large as a small tree, which bloomed profusely all year with little pastel flowers and then orange balls, attracting a swarm of butterflies. The wings themselves—or halls, as we called them—were fronted with huge screened windows, creating a kind of veranda from which you could observe the compound. The girls' dorm, like all the Newton school structures—the classrooms and chapel and boys' dorm—was built with huge granite stone and concrete block. The concrete was painted a light salmon pink with darker trim. The combination was entrancing though it is only now in pictures that I recognize how lovely and expensive it was. Running up the front walls of the dorm were huge philodendrons with leaves bigger than a human head. The flower beds were packed and professionally arranged with canna lilies and giant elephant's ear and African daisies, and in pots on the porch were flamingo lilies.

The athletic field where we had PE in the afternoon was located behind the girls' dorm. It included a tennis court and a basketball court and a soccer field that was also a football field and a baseball park and a track. Here, in our designated playground, sports were more strictly monitored than they were in the front of the dorm, where we were playing for free.

I realize now that during the holidays when I lived with my parents in the boys' dorm, I searched that compound for a clue to my existence. I followed the lead of every path and turned over rocks and sampled every fruit and read the sky in the afternoon and examined the bark of trees, and yet I found no answer to my questions: Why is it that suddenly my power has gone? How is it that other people now hold such sway over me? And when did my parents become such strangers? Even when they were within full view, I wasn't sure where they were.

In my memory, I am on the compound headed away from the girls' dorm toward the boys' dorm, down the new road that was cut when it was added, and suddenly I remember the kapok or silk-cotton tree. It was the only such tree on the compound, the only one of its kind in my life that I knew well. The pods rained down on the road and popped open, leaving multiple small masses of white silk strewn all around, the open pods little purses spilling over. Walking, I would pick up a pod and finger the silk as I meandered along. In my mind, I am now on the road on the side of the boys' dorm, continuing around to the front. There's really nothing here but a barren expanse of cleared land. So I circle and come back up and I'm in the little courtyard area by my family's apartment. I once planted my own small flower bed around one of the palms outside my mother's window, the smallest palm. I put in coleus and some caladiums and maybe some annuals like begonias—nothing very fancy. The little garden did well for at least a season.

I wander now back over toward the girls' dorm and that circular drive with the field in the middle. I can well recall standing up in the girls' dorm on those screened verandas and watching for the first cars of returning students to crest the hill at the entrance and pull around that drive. I remember a number of singular comings and goings unfolding on that drive like silent movies. I remember, for example, that first year at Newton, watching as my old friend Edna Rachel stood waiting there with her sister Susan because their mother was gravely ill and they had to leave suddenly for the U.S. I did not tell Edna Rachel good-bye, and I never saw her again, or even wrote to her. I had grown away from her after leaving Ogbomosho seven years earlier. I don't remember that we boarding school students were called to those screened halls to witness such occasions, but I do remember being there as though the scene were choreographed, and all the girls in the school stood on that veranda and watched these events as if we, in the shadows, were an audience, while those in the driveway were cast in scripts. I also remember standing there on another day when the Barnes girls arrived, Jan and Gwen. It was evening, just before dinner; a car drove up, and in a moment these girls from America stepped out. School was already in session but that didn't matter; they were coming to join us in their short straight shifts which ended before their fingertips and their fishnet hose. I could see them from the window forty feet away. They wore little pumps with short stacked heels and white lipstick, which I saw when they came up close. I don't think anyone really spoke to these girls for days. But looking out from that screened veranda and seeing those little pumps, I thought, "I am sunk."

I even remember watching events from that hallway-veranda that I didn't actually see. For example, the Levrets girls, Susan and Jan—who were first cousins of Helen of Troy—arrived in Nigeria the year I was on furlough. Their beauty and romantic prowess made them just a little lower than the gods, and by the time I arrived, also newly from America (but there was no comparison really, since I hadn't grown up in the U.S., and that was a difference you could not overcome), they were already legends in their own time. So I conjectured their arrival on the driveway. I imagined I had seen them step from their car like Jackie Kennedy, one after the other, their legs extended first and then their bowed brown heads and white arms. When they stood up, the theater darkened and the spotlights descended on them and music began playing, something like "My Girl." Their hair was flipped and they almost smiled but they looked at no one directly as they appeared to float forward. I made all this up, of course. I have no idea how they arrived at Newton. In any case, they never lost their charm. They never went out of fashion. When I would stand in the cafeteria line next to one of them, I would peer out of the corner of my eye, trying to decipher her power. It was in the turn of their ankles and the way they held their arms lightly crossed and the way they did not speak but left you guessing and the soft curve of their breasts and the thickness of their hair and their thin wrists. It was in all these things. Yet none of these revealed the whole secret. They even made Ellen look awkward, with her height, like mine, and her more chiseled edges. Susan and Jan had such great success so early in their femininity that they had cornered the market. On our little island between the savannahs and the rain forest, no one else came close.

Burning Love

IN THE DORM, I was so afraid of the dark I could not fall asleep. I convinced Aunt Novella to keep the light shining in the hallway outside my door all night long. It shone nightly for a year, for me. Still I was afraid. Our bunk beds were constructed with open shelving at the head, and there was a space—perhaps three feet—between that open headboard and the wall. The light did not shine that far into the room, and the top of my head felt exposed to an impenetrable darkness.

During the day, I learned to conjugate all the irregular verbs. And I read a long poem titled *Lorna Doone* that made a world I recognized because it was green and filled with longing. I also played jacks during rest time and then went back to school for one hour in the afternoon where I learned medieval history. We staged a play and I was the director, of course, and I learned the word *endeavor* and made everyone say it a lot. The queen said: "I have endeavored to be your faithful servant" to her husband. And the knight said: "I shall endeavor to do my best" to the queen. Even the cobbler on the street said he would endeavor to fix your shoes and the shepherd told his father he would endeavor to watch the sheep and not fall asleep. I also staged and performed in my own adaptation of *Swan Lake*—my family had seen the ballet in New York on furlough—but I had to be the prince because no one else would. This was a girls-only cast and of course the really consummate girls wouldn't be in it at all. Betty Kay Abell was the princess, though I hardly remember her anywhere else that year except in *Swan Lake;* she was like a chameleon the way she always faded into the curtains. Now that I look back, I think Betty Kay was just a lot wiser than I. She knew how to keep out of danger. And I consider my poor sister in the audience. How did she endure my misplaced ambition?

At Newton I learned to fix my hair, more properly than I had in Easley when I was trying desperately to be an American girl and over-did it, employing hair bands and several barrettes simultaneously in an effort to simulate the cute girls' hair. I didn't know that trying wasn't supposed to show; as with magic, the trick of good looks must remain hidden.

The juju was hours of dedication on a daily basis, and on Saturday almost the entire day, in order to have "good" hair. After you had deep-cleaned your room—that meant dusting and washing every shelf and louvered window and sweeping under your mattress and scouring the toilet and the shower and sweeping everywhere and straightening everything; after that—you washed your hair. And then you sat down in front of the mirror on the little vanity (only the girls had these mirrors) and rolled your hair, but only after applying Dippity-Do. You might even tape your bangs. Then you put a scarf around your head—this was the only part of the procedure that had Nigerian roots (no pun intended)—and you got ready to sit around for the rest of the day and do nothing so your rollers didn't fall out and your head didn't sweat and your hair curled. My hair has always been wispy and fine, so this effort could not be foreshortened, not if I wanted the kind of metallic, even outcome we all hoped for. The style could not be amended just because you didn't have the basic goods to work with. There was no such thing as considering the individual girl and what would look good on her. Instead you looked at an American magazine like *Redbook* (probably two years old) and then you willed yourself into the form. Around five o'clock, you took your hair down and if you were smart you got an older girl to come to your room and help you comb it out and then tease it and then comb it out and then tease it at the top and put a little bow right in the center above the bangs. And then you went to dinner and pretended the style was natural. You always look this way. I'm not sure what the few African American girls in attendance did with their time or their hair during these ceremonies.

Also on Saturdays, after all that cleaning and after rest time, during which we were supposed to write a letter to our parents, we lined up in the dorm to collect our allowance of three shillings. I didn't really have to write to my parents, but I probably should have. I might have told them how I actually felt. But I still collected my allowance, lining up like all the other MKs to receive my allotment in a little manila envelope. My father, being the business manager, conducted this affair, and every Saturday when I opened my envelope, there was a note from him on a little yellow slip of paper. He always told me he loved me or he loved me very much, and this expression was followed by a line of exclamation marks. And it was true. He loved me immensely. I was just too close for him to see how far away I was. Looking back, that passing of notes seems hugely telling. My father told me he loved me in secret, as if such expressions were not allowed in public. Today I still own these little yellow dispatches.

One Friday night I chose my favorite dress, really a matching skirt and blouse, that my mother had bought for me in Easley; it wasn't homemade. The fabric was a light blue and lavender and green floral print, very light and fine so that from a distance the effect was a blend of pastels. It buttoned up the front with a little round yoke and short sleeves that turned up; the whole ensemble had a kind of soft but structured shape. The waist was gathered so that the skirt flared; this was becoming because even if I didn't have any breasts, I had a nice small waist and the flare of the fabric accentuated it. This Friday night, our entertainment was planned in the living room of the boys' dorm—not my family's private living room but the large diamond-shaped room near the boys' wings. As always, my mother had transformed this once shamelessly ugly sitting room into a lovely space. Whoever had arranged it before her had simply thrown all the sofas and love seats and chairs against the wall so that if you sat down, you looked across a great gulf to a person thirty feet away. In other words you felt like you were in the waiting room of a jail. But my mother had created cluster seating in each of the four corners and put planters with abounding philodendrons in the center.

As I entered the living room that evening, I pondered where to sit. This was always a loaded question because in boarding school any move you make is watched and interpreted and, if you're not careful, reenacted. So I waited a moment at the threshold, fresh and expectant in my favorite dress. The room was a blur with other students moving about, and then my eyes fell on Dan, sitting right at the front all by himself in a little green love seat. His eyes met mine and he motioned to me to come and sit with him. As I made my way over to where he was, smiling at me, his hand on the seat beside him because he was saving it, all the other students evaporated and I could hear music; it must have been *Close your eyes and I'll kiss you.* When I sat down, my skirt levitated for a moment before settling around me. This was better than I had hoped for because Dan was a seventh grader and not even an MK so he was "new" and he was absolutely the cutest boy in the school, playful and funny and not at all mean. Every girl would have liked to sit by Dan.

Who knows what the entertainment was that evening. It could have been Aunt Joan Amis, accompanied by my mother, singing from some opera or other, or it could have been a visiting dentist lecturing on oral hygiene; it didn't matter. I paid no attention. All of my focus was sideways, toward Dan, not that I looked at him, but all of my senses were heightened in his direction as if there were fine wires strung between us. Every time he moved, my temperature rose. I noticed his shoes and the hair on his legs and his hand, which was still on the couch between us, and I could smell him, warm and Old Spicy after his shower. I wondered if Dan had planned to invite me or was it the way I looked standing in the threshold of the room that made his mind up? I never knew. When the evening was over, we walked under the stars of the sloping sky, the long way back to my dorm.

But my luck with Dan did not last. Before long he was dating Martha Alice Logan, a ninth grader, and their romance bubbled for the rest of the year despite the fact that he was a "younger" kid and she an "older" kid so they were often separated when our social events were tiered by age as often they were. She was, as they say, robbing the cradle.

On Sunday evenings, we had church services on campus. I remember my father speaking one evening after that first coup. I remember the wavering in his voice as he recounted how as a young man he had not taken advantage of an opportunity to study the violin and how since then he had wished he had because he loved its sound. And then he talked about Nigeria because it was a young nation full of opportunity and I did not see the connection at the time. He prayed for Nigeria and this part I understood because I loved Nigeria as I loved my own body. And we sang "Great is thy faithfulness oh God my Father."

Of course, the coup had always been coming, the way a disease has a long foreground. There was the aquiline nose of the white outsider, the better to look down upon you with, the tripartition of the country, the rise of the new ruling class, the lining of pockets, a deep knowing of injustice.

Actually we had our own worries in the West before that first coup. There were two parties in our region now and two leaders—Awo and Akintola—and each was throbbing for power. My parents, I suppose, heard of Nigerians being stopped by thugs on the road and quizzed about their loyalties and then finished off if they made the wrong choice. We never drove anywhere after dark. "Operation Wetie" began, code name for wet with petrol and burn. Day and night were no longer two halves of a whole. Instead, during the day, the market in Oshogbo was held as usual; children went to school, and men and women went to the farm. But at night, folks stayed close to home. There was burning and plunder throughout Yoruba land like a horrible masquerade turned against the participants. My mother says that in the evening we could see smoke from Oshogbo rising above the tree line, so perhaps on those evenings when I was jumping rope, it was not just grass burning to clear farmland that I smelled. On the road in front of Newton, adolescent boys marched back and forth waving green branches and scaring my mother, who was sure they were going to come onto the compound and molest us. But they had bigger enemies than the Southern Baptist Convention, and what the green branches actually meant was *bring us peace*. Historically, Oshogbo was a town of peace. On our Saturday trips to shop, you could see where rioters had been as sometimes you see the path of a tornado. Here a shop was burned but next to it another shop was perfectly intact. Always transistor radios serenaded.

So it was in the night, while our Western region was burning, that five military majors and one captain, almost all Igbos, convinced junior officers, even Northerners, to strike against the government. Out with the elite who fiddled while Rome burned. Only ten Nigerians were killed in that first coup, but that is like saying only one person died when Kennedy was shot, because only Yoruba and Hausa leaders were killed and the North would never forgive the Igbo plotters. You may wish to chastise your leaders but you don't want someone else killing them for you. *And so as Sir Abubakar Tafawa Balewa, the silver voice of the North, sank down, an old antagonism flamed.*

The coup did not stand; that's a Nigerian way of putting it. Major-General John Aguiyi-Ironsi ("Johnny Ironside") was tipped off in Lagos and managed to pull off a counter coup. One of the men to help him was Yakubu Gowon, who would later lead the Federal side of Nigeria's civil war. In the West we read in the *Daily Times* that most folks were relieved. The corrupt fellows had been brought low and yet order had been restored. Ironsi, an Igbo, became the new head of state. This detail would become troublesome later.

At the back of our apartment in the boys' dorm, a laundry building had been erected, a huge two-storied brown structure, the only building on that compound that was not beautified with granite stone and a salmon exterior. Above the laundry itself was an airy attic where some of my family's things were stored. You could walk straight up to it and I would visit the attic often on those afternoons after piano practice, for this was where my new cat Molly had been moved to deliver her kittens. The attic smelled of planed wood. These visits were like a reunion with my younger self in the guava tree, for I was alone but not far from home, free from judgment and happy in the suspension of human conflict. Molly was beautiful with long gray and white and brown fur and a becoming face and an enchanting manner. She acted as I wished to act: pleased with herself and unconcerned with outside opinion. From up in the attic of the laundry, we two and the kittens could look out and see most of the boys' dorm and the new tennis court up the hill to your left and on the other side the fence and the forest. I could see our carport beside the apartment where our new Peugeot sedan was parked along with Dad's new silver bicycle before it was stolen. I could see the flower beds my mother had planted full of marigolds and jungle geranium, also called burning love.

Up in that storeroom over the laundry room, I could see my father coming and going from the apartment and hear the whir of the car engine and the conversation Mother was having with someone at the doorstep and see the curtains in Becky's bedroom blowing slightly with the afternoon breeze—this was the room where she had posted the United States Declaration of Independence and the Bill of Rights in a mahogany frame over her bed, because in her maturity she had decided to become interested in American politics. I could hear Mr. Muli downstairs talking loudly and see the laundry outside drying in the sun, mostly the boys' jeans—upside down and inside out—and shorts and open shirts. From the second floor of the laundry room, I could see the sandpile between the dorm and the laundry. Occasionally the younger boys played king of the mountain on it. But it always reminded me of the white sand at the bottom of the Ethiope. It was as if a stray current from that river had been deposited here and the water had dried up leaving only the sand.

No one was in the attic but me and Molly and the fat kittens skimming over the big brown floor. But at some point I had to leave the attic and go back to the girls' dorm in order to shower for dinner and then devotionals and then study hall and then thirty minutes to curl my hair and prepare for bed and then lights out.

In the year 2000, I am less and less human; I'm some hybrid between fish and human or human and machine. Friends ask me less and less how I am because I have no good news. I do not begrudge them. The living are skeptical of the dying. We smell.

In a dream, I am at the river but the water is not cold and the current is too tame. I swim upstream and am just reaching out for a branch to hold me when the current increases and I am sent downriver. Suddenly everything is unnatural. Police officers patrol the shore. The river becomes narrower rather than wider. And then the shores are concrete and all the foliage is cut down. The river is merely a channel now. I flow with it into an American city where the channel divides into four smaller ones, all paved with concrete. I try to head back upstream but even after trying every channel I cannot find the way back to the river as it was: unhindered, cold, wide, and green.

Trials and Errors

AFTER THAT FIRST COUP, a new contest was going on in me, though it seemed to be going on between me and my peers.

I was taken by surprise the day during social studies when Uncle Wallace came into our classroom and distributed the ballots. We had already voted once: for king, queen, princess, and prince of the Valentine's Banquet. I had almost forgotten about the whole thing. But now Uncle Wallace was back, telling us we had to vote again because there had been a tie in the princess category. Whether it was a four-way tie or a two-way tie with a couple of other names thrown in to ease the pain of losing, I don't know, but the name Elaine appeared on a half sheet of paper along with Ellen and Jan and Darlene. One of us would be crowned princess. Jan had already been voted princess the year before—she and her sister Susan were the ones who walked across the campus to the tune of "My Girl" and whose hair flipped so perfectly you were prepared to pull out your own—so I thought she should step aside or be deemed ineligible but there she was. We had to vote in this runoff.

I had never been in a situation where I had to decide to vote for myself or for someone else. And I wasn't given much time to reflect on the complexities of this dilemma. I smelled a budding blue envy. While I had never wanted to be a princess, now that someone *else* might be elected, now that it *was* a competition, I was interested. And yet I thought it must be unchristian to vote for yourself; well, at least, if you were a girl, it must be unchristian. If you were a boy, it might be okay. So I pondered the issue in the brief moment I had and I compromised; I voted for Darlene. I figured she wouldn't win anyway so a vote for her wasn't really a vote against myself. This way, I would gain points for being charitable and not lose points by being too self-interested.

I have regretted the decision for the rest of my life.

The Valentine's Banquet arrived and we were still in the dark about who would be victorious. That evening the girls dressed up in long formal gowns that our mothers had made for us, and looking back at pictures, I see how lovely my dresses were and how lovingly my mother made them. We spent the entire day getting ready, amplifying and exaggerating the sorts of things we did every Saturday, like curling our hair and painting our nails. The older girls had been dieting for weeks and doubtless had eaten nothing that day. And of course they shaved their legs and put lotion on them and then sat in their rooms soaking up their sexuality. The week or so before this event, the boys had been cornering us between class or after study hall to ask if we would like to sit with them at the banquet. You didn't get asked *to go* with someone because we were already there, being on the compound. Some girls had not been asked and you were grateful not to be in that category.

On the night of the banquet, the dining room was festooned with cupids and hearts and all sorts of predictable Valentine paraphernalia. Every girl's hair was a solid sheet of hair spray. We were served by the kitchen staff, who wore their best work attire, though they were still barefoot, hence soundless in the room. I suspect, however, that they were not so much in the dark as we. I think now how horrible all this was: the country between coups, though we didn't know about the second one yet, and those men with so much to lose watching us in this indecorous celebration. One must remember that the fight of our parents' lives was to mold us as we would have been molded in their own country. They could not see the impossibility of this endeavor since America was not *our* own country. At least it was not mine. Our brief lives at Newton were anesthesia before surgery, because our parents were trying to get us out of the country, or, more accurately, get the country out of us, not just literally, but spiritually and psychologically. Newton was the beginning of our departure for America, our real land of opportunity.

On February 14, 1966, I was sweating my future in my beautiful sashed dress. The banquet was really preliminary to the main event which was the crowning of the royal family. For the coronation, we walked down to the classroom building, where the festivities were to continue in the very same room in which on Sunday night we held worship services. It was perplexing to have these events in the same room as if they were of the same significance: God and my father praying about the coup and Valentine's Day.

By this point in the evening, I was beginning to feel a tight clutching in my stomach; I would rather have been praying. Because I wanted to back up into a world in which no one voted for a Valentine's princess. I wanted to get back to someplace in time—say the river—in which this sort of competition did not exist.

Finally, the moment of truth arrived and Uncle Wallace, who always presided in this sort of thing, stood up. As his voice came to me across that room, I realized we were going forward and there was no way out.

"Prince Dan," he exclaimed, and there was only one Dan, the one I had sat with that night in my pretty print dress. And then, with a smile on his face, "Princess Ellen," for she was his daughter.

I heard nothing else. I am sure I did not clap. My body was falling down a tunnel, down into a bottomless pit, down, down, into a lonely place far far away, far away from Newton School, far away from Ellen and her happiness and Dan and his blond likeableness. My mind, on the other hand, had gotten away and was somewhere else in the room looking back at me. I wanted to get as far away as I could from this horrible election. I was ashamed because I had lost; if nothing else, I wanted to win for my family so that we could be happy, so as not to disappoint, so they would not worry about me. We were not losers; I knew that if I knew anything.

That night, back in the dorm, Becky looked me up and sat with me in one of those veranda-hallways, not a place you would normally sit, and in half light. "I think you may be feeling the way I am," she said. "I think we both were hoping we might be chosen." She had been eligible in the queen category since she was older. I still see her open face, framed by her brown hair, her skin clear now from acne, and her hands in her lap, almost reaching for mine, and her shimmering dress. How I wish we could have gone home together, how I wish we could have gone home to our mother, who might have said to me: *Elaine, you are so much more than a Valentine's princess, you are bigger than that; believe in yourself. Some girls are only princesses but you are a star; you shine without ornament. I believe in you.* That's the sort of thing you want to hear from your mother, absolute, unequivocal support. I think about my son and wonder what sentence he wishes from me.

I continued as usual through the spring, but something was broken that I would never get back, some sureness in my step. Once when I smiled in Oshogbo it had been because I liked myself. Now when I smiled, I was searching other faces to see if they liked me.

Though the Mountains Shake
with the Swelling Thereof

As STUDENTS LEFT the compound in June, the country was splitting open like overripe fruit. Of course, Becky and I didn't go anywhere but across the compound to the boys' dorm where we re-settled in our "own" rooms. Mine was arrayed with pictures of cats and my glass animals.

Throughout the early months of 1966, Ironsi, Nigeria's new leader, had tried to cool the country's competitions by making things more national, less regional. Maybe this way everyone could win, not just the East or the North or the West. Igbos were happy to cooperate; they had sought education and were eager to take up posts all over Nigeria. Yorubas in the West bristled somewhat at the Igbos' ambition but mostly Yorubas can sway this way or that. But Northerners would not be nationals with Igbos; they certainly would not serve *under* them. It began to look to them like the Igbo staged the January coup for this very reason: to take over at every level. Maybe Ironsi, who was Igbo even if he had turned back the Igbo-led coup, was actually part of the plot. Northerners wanted to *discipline those indolent igbos living in the north,* according to one newspaper headline. Even the lack of capitalization was insulting.

It wasn't just religion and history that separated Hausa and Igbo. The Hausa had their power in the way rich people have money; they just do. But the Igbo thought you could earn power through hard work; they would have fit in at Newton School. So when Ironsi announced the Unification Decree on May 24, just a week or so before we finished the year at Newton, he sealed his own fate with Northerners. They could see Igbos moving into their territory like a flood of locusts. And that was when a violent hand swept through the

Northern city of Kano, into the Sabon Garis, the "strangers' quarters" where Easterners lived outside the old wall. And Igbos were killed like chaff before the fire.

It was summer, and for Becky and me that meant our mother would soon set out to prepare our next year's wardrobe. She would make a week-long appointment with the renowned seamstress Mrs. Adebimpe, who would come to visit, and the two of them would set up shop. But many preparations had already been undertaken. Mother purchased fabric from the market stalls for her sewing, but she also depended on cloth she had purchased on furlough. This material was stored in drums along with Butterick or McCall's or Simplicity patterns. Before Mrs. Adebimpe came, Mother would cut out all of the soon-to-be-dresses on the mahogany dining room table, securing the patterns to the folded fabric with straight pins. When Mrs. Adebimpe arrived, the sewing would begin: Mrs. Adebimpe doing the stitching on the machine, Mother following with the finishing work—the hems and buttons. In this manner, the two of them turned out a year's worth of dresses for the three of us. Becky and I would be called in at intervals for the trying on of the garment. These sessions could get tedious, especially when it came to pinning the hem. But the truth is, we loved this yearly ceremonial that began with Mother opening the drums and Becky and me leaning into them, noses first, for a long intake of the smell of America. The fabrics were always colorful and enticing and the time it took for the dresses to be made increased their value for me.

How my mother continued this sewing extravaganza with the world falling down around us I cannot say, but it should give you some idea of her constitution that she did.

One evening as I stood in our apartment living room in the boys' dorm watching the rain pour down, General Ironsi left Lagos, undertaking a tour of the country. He would never return home. Instead, he arrived back in the Western region and Ibadan on the night of the second coup, this one plotted by Northerners.

I did not know at the time of the horror, and now as I read of it I am sur-

prised that the skies were not red with the killing, that the palms did not dry up and fall over even though it was the rainy season, that the ground beneath us did not split. In Ibadan—so close to us—Eastern soldiers were taken to a tailors' shop on the barracks grounds and were locked up in the darkness; thirty-six hand grenades flew through the windows.

In the North, a young Igbo boy is met early by his father at school, where he is lifted onto shoulders and run through the streets, the father's sandals clacking on tarmac. The boy thinks it is a game and laughs.

Ironsi and two others in Ibadan were arrested, stripped, their hands tied behind their backs with wire; then they were flogged with horse whips. When he was forced into a van, Johnny Ironside's spirit left him. After a short ride, the vehicle stopped and all three men were ordered down a footpath into the bush. *Now they are beaten again, their bodies no longer their own. When they come to a stream, they are too weak to cross so they are carried. Finally, they are commanded to run farther down the path and they hear the shots as they are falling.*

I know the landscape along the road outside of Ibadan and I know it was the rainy season. I can see this scene more vividly than I would like: Ironsi's large body, stripped, the broken places on his skin as if he has been painted, his ears still soft and perfect but his eyes swollen shut, his feet surprised by the coolness of the ground, the foliage from the trees swatting against his battling arms, his backward glance at his attackers, his relief when finally they fired.

We must have known in Oshogbo that Ironsi was missing because the Igbos on our compound would have told us; perhaps the *Daily Times* confirmed it.

My response to the second coup was to evangelize; I began to lead my family in evening devotionals.

We are sitting in our living room, Becky and Mother on the couch, my father and I on the mission chairs. Becky is sitting on one leg with the other crossed over it and dangling; she does not believe my parents should be indulging me in this crusade. Becky has always thought I am overindulged. But my parents can hardly refuse. For once I am trying to be less like myself and more like a Christian. I have chosen the scripture though I am not sure what I will say about it. *God is our refuge and strength, a very present help in trouble. Therefore will not we fear, though the earth be removed, and though the mountains be carried into the midst of the sea; Though the waters thereof roar and be troubled, though the mountains shake with the swelling thereof. . . .*

The great summer rains were a godly weeping for all of us. I grieved over the state of every soul I met. I thought if we could witness to more people, we could save the country; this despite the fact that thousands of Christians throughout Nigeria did not appear capable of keeping us from falling into war. And I watched the rain coming down as I stood in that living room feeling helpless because there was so little I could do to save the world.

For three days the country was a horse without a rider. All over Yoruba land, Northerners were in command: in Abeokuta, Ikeja, Ibadan, and the international airport. The coup came late and failed in the East, but it succeeded everywhere else. Eventually Lieutenant-Colonel Gowon, the Northerner who had once aided Ironsi, emerged as Nigeria's new commander. There was one fellow, however, who would give Gowon plenty of palaver and that was Lieutenant-Colonel Chukwuemeka Ojukwu, an Igbo in the East and the governor of the region. No one knew where Ironsi was and Ojukwu thought that other officers superior in rank to Gowon should lead the federation. In Ojukwu's mind, Gowon was chosen only because he was a Northerner.

After the coup, a pogrom burned against Easterners in the North. *A story emerges of a woman arriving back in her village holding only her child's severed head. Her hands will not let it go. She caresses the cheeks and pats down the eyelids. I do not know if the story was a fact or a metaphor or both.*

During that summer as Mrs. Adebimpe and my mother were sewing and I was watching the rain and we were praying in the evenings or listening to Grieg or I was wandering the compound in search of myself, thousands of Easterners were killed.

Ironsi's death would not be announced for six months.

And that was the summer my father was nearly killed again. He was making arrangements for the catering of the yearly Mission Meeting. This meant all sorts of trips to Ibadan, where business proceeded as usual, to order and purchase food. It meant trips to other destinations, in the case at hand, Oyo, where he headed one dull, overcast day not long after the second coup and Ironsi's kidnapping, to buy a large supply of eggs for all the missionary family who were going to show up in a few days in Ogbomosho.

But as he wheels the school van toward the Baptist compound, turning from the left lane across the right lane, for we drive like the British in Nigeria, he is hit by a truck behind him trying to pass in the same lane. For a moment he feels the deep shudder of the hit and sees the windshield break into a field of snow. He realizes he has been hit and thinks to himself, as if the words themselves are written in the air, *I have been hit; I am in an accident; this is how it is.* For one or two seconds, his body lifts into the air and flies, but it feels longer and like a movie. He is actually looking up into the sky but he doesn't know what he is seeing. Finally in a hard landing that seems to take minutes, he is on the ground. Before he opens his eyes he smells the grass. Then he is looking sideways across it, but he does not feel hurt. He thinks he may never move again. It is so quiet on the ground after all that roiling.

My father suffered only aches and pains and a black eye. Still, I was concerned that he kept having these near-death experiences even though he seemed to walk away from them not much damaged. You could never tell when your luck might change.

A Brief Happiness

BACK AT NEWTON, the Igbo and Midwestern men who prepared our meals and worked in the dorms remained even after that
summer of violence. We still thought they were safe as long as they
weren't in the North. They along with my parents would take bread
down to the train stations to meet refugees coming south. And then
just as we were breaking in our new books in September, the Igbos
in the East started feeding the Hausa some of their own medicine. A
Northerner in Igbo land might be "detained" on the road or a young
Northerner who worked for Baptist missionaries in the East and who
had long been befriended by his neighbors might find them ham-
mering on his door at night, demanding his life, which was then taken
from him neatly as a pound note. Gowon tried to calm the conflict,
but he was too late.

In the corner room of the younger girls' wing with Rebecca Russell and Lee Brothers, I was less afraid of the dark. My top bunk rested
next to a window, and I watched the stars at night flickering over the
branches of the mango trees at the edge of the compound. I watched
the stars after reading *Wyatt Earp* in bed before lights-out, and sometimes after—with a flash light. Wyatt Earp was a natural sequel to
Trixie Belden: here were horses and mysteries and sharpshooting, a
dangerous territory delightful to read about because it had for me no
reality. I didn't notice that with adolescence I had had to turn to a
male hero in order to find adventure.

After the Valentine's failure of the year before, I recommitted myself to living for the moment, without regard to reputation or poten-

tial gain. It was the last year of my boarding school life that I allowed myself such luxury.

When I had been at Newton with my parents before, the room I now shared with Lee and Rebecca was not a bedroom at all but a dark, dusty game room, featuring a tired assortment of entertainments like Chinese checkers, Life, and Monopoly. But when Becky, Lee, and I inhabited the room, it was light and airy and full of promise; we were inseparable. Listening to Petula Clark singing "Downtown" and cleaning our room on Saturdays and performing our own plays in the dark after lights-out and reading Westerns one after the other and writing a novella called *The Grasshopper Affair* and learning about sex and whispering over who had *got their period* and lying in the grass in front of the classrooms and sitting together in church on Sundays, we really were sisters growing up.

Lee was a funny girl who cast an austere countenance to the world. Rebecca, whose father worked for USAID, was beautiful, with long, wavy blonde hair and glasses and a face like something out of a baroque painting. I was still tall for my age, with a straight body and a swayback and no makeup. On Saturdays, we wore Keds with white socks and shirts buttoned all the way up. Our underarms were still blank pages. We hated no one yet but cared for few.

One boy chose me that fall, inviting me to every affair. I liked him at first, though perhaps because he was seeking me I was not on fire for him as I had been briefly for Dan. Still, I cooperated in sitting with him at our fall festivities. But then one evening on the way down to the chapel he leaned over and kissed my cheek, and from then on he was toast. I leaked the news to Ellen and a few others that I no longer liked Jon. This was the wrong thing to do because he found out from someone other than me and then hated me, and I gained a slight reputation as a man slayer. This reputation is funny or sad since I had no idea what I was doing and absolutely no sense of how to attract or repel anyone. I never really learned how to tell a boy good-bye, to say "I'm just not ready" and smile sweetly so that I made myself more desirable and also off-limits at one and the same time. I just blinked and bolted. There were no instructions and it seemed to me that the boys had all the opportunities to decide these things and girls had none. Boys could ask girls to go with them and then girls could only say yes or no and it was very risky to say no because you might hurt his feelings and look conceited and then his friends would hate you too. Of course, boys could stop asking you to sit with them or they could break up with you and then everyone felt sorry for the girl, but they didn't hate the boy because, after all, he was a boy and he could like you or not as he wished. It wasn't a crime.

In the mornings, I was awakened daily by the domestic staff coming onto the compound. They must have been talking about the uproar in the country. We had already been through two coups. Many Igbos had fled the North and this exodus meant that the East was filling up with refugees. There were rumors of succession. As usual, the Yoruba were riding the fence (though they didn't care for all those Northern soldiers in their midst). But it looked as though North and East were flexing to a breaking point: the North was ready to chase the Igbo into the sea, and the East, for its part, was ready to drum the Hausa into the ground.

In October, Ojukwu ordered all non-Easterners to leave the Eastern region since he could no longer assure them of their safety.

A gravel road wound around the exterior of that corner room. Before the wake-up bell sounded, around 6:30, just as the sky was turning a soft pink and I could see the shapes of trees and make out the storeroom and tennis court, I would hear the men approaching, talking to one another, their voices mixed with the sound of bicycles on the gravel. I was reassured by their arrival. It was daybreak; the world was still here. With the louvered windows open, I could smell the moist odor of the earth. I did not know that some of those men would not be alive another Christmas. For the moment, our routine remained steady. If we had been closer to town we would have been more aware of the chaos, but out on this high piece of land we were somnolent.

In my world, we had our own politics. The older kids were running for office in the student government. Apparently, those of us below the eighth grade were not sufficiently mature to manage these offices. My sister was running for president. This ambition sort of went hand in hand with her posting of the Declaration of Independence on her bulletin board at home. She was running against two very favorite sons, David DuVall and Kenny Wasson. An odd reality of our boarding school life was trying to figure out your relationship with a boy—in my sister's case—like Kenny Wasson or David DuVall, since their families were so close to ours. Was he a brother, a romantic interest, an intellectual competitor, a political rival? When your family stayed the weekend with his family and you showed up at breakfast with him in your pajamas, what was he then?

Perhaps I realized the awkwardness of my sister's situation, because I became her campaign manager (not that she asked me), coming up with the clever idea of creating a banner that looked like clothes on a clothesline, with each item of clothing spelling one letter: B-E-C-K-Y-F-O-R-P-R-E-S-I-D-E-N-T. This propaganda I strung between two palm trees out in the round field in front of the girls' dorm, positioning it so you had to run into it or duck on your way to and from the chapel. Someone even compared me to Robert Kennedy in his support of his brother John. I assumed this was a compliment. Becky won, though her victory probably cost her being elected Valentine's queen once again, so I'm not sure how happy she was about the outcome.

With my political life on hold, I began a novella with Lee and Rebecca; I still have a copy with Rebecca's illustrations, including maps of the compound. Telling the story of how the three of us rescue the boarding school, it mimicked the subject of new arrivals from the U.S., featuring a boy—Bendailboy West—who shows up midyear, corrupting the school with his unsanitary eating practices. He habitually makes sandwiches of locusts and forces other students to eat his concoctions. This enforced consumption, or learned desire, leads to a plague that infects the entire campus, everyone except for the three of us. We are immune to the illness and come to the rescue when the rest of the school—including all the adults—lie sick and dying. I don't know where the boy's name came from—Bendailboy West—but I am bemused in my adult life to see that we associated masculinity, insatiable consumption, and pollution with the West;

we've even got an allusion to Ben Franklin in there. On our title page we claimed a 1967 copyright by Brorusneman, a combination of bits of each of our last names: "bro" from Lee Brothers, "rus" from Rebecca Russell, "ne" from Elaine Neil. I don't know why we added the "man," though I suppose it was because so many words ended that way; "man" seemed to ratify things. Aunt Marian Leftwich, our house mother, helped with the typing, and we located our fictive publishing house in Ibadan, Nigeria, West Africa. This is our preface:

> One day we were sitting in the swing at the boys' dorm. We wanted a story and came up with this one. We were thinking about the new boy who will be coming to Newton Memorial School next year. This book is mainly fictitious, but we have replaced the names of two Newtonites by the names Sylvia and Cynthia as they do not wish to be known. The setting for this book is at Newton Memorial School. The book is about a very unusual boy who is interested in unusual things.

The boy might have presaged Baden Richards, a "new" MK who was expected to arrive at Newton the next year. If so, this story certainly anticipates the chaos he created in my heart later. But at the time, the story exercised the revenge of the native against the intruder, of the true believer against the imposter, of girls who didn't shave their legs against girls with white fishnet hose, of young girls against careless and flagrantly indifferent boys, of youth against age, of plainness against beauty, of Nigeria against America. We plotted the "newness" of the West as invading Africa and corrupting it. Bendailboy West desired too much and he desired the wrong things. Now I myself have been hungry all my life so perhaps there was some transference in this story. But I also think there is a difference between hungers that grow the more you eat and hungers that grow like curiosity. My American hunger has always had more to do with the first.

In this glorious epic, Lee, Rebecca, and I put ourselves in the place of Nigerians. We were not "new." We belonged here. As natives, we associated ourselves with civility and moderation and imagined the American boy as vulgar and insatiable. We were throwing off learned self-doubt, learned when all those new girls from America kept arriving; they had what the American boy wanted. But we were exposing his wallowing lust. Within the confines of our little book, Bendail-boy West and everyone taken in by him had the illness; by refusing his seductions, we had the cure. At the end, we save the entire compound, adults included, and are well feted indeed.

How brilliant we were, because this tale tells many of the narratives that were flying around us but of which we were supposedly unaware. In the first place, it depicts the ugliness of Western capitalism let loose in West Africa. Remember the oil discovered near Eku and in the East. It was not by chance that a war was breaking out just as the East was finding itself rich in what the West desired. Wrapped beautifully into our story are all the elements of the rising conflict: the ethnic fighting, the self-interest of outside forces, the excesses of power, the greed. How much we knew and how little we knew that we knew it.

For once, if briefly, I was happy at Newton, keeping company with Lee and Rebecca and reading about Wyatt Earp and ignoring brassieres and making up stories to tell the truth.

But then the Igbo men began to disappear. One morning you would get up and go through the cafeteria line and the face that used to greet you and serve your food was no longer there. Mr. Amobi, the Igbo cook who had worked for the Cockrums and whose family I had once known, had left in the night, taking only his wife and children and what he could carry. I remember those sudden absences; the small boys and the Yoruba domestic help now stood in where an Igbo man had been. No one ever heard from most of those men again. When I read about the beginnings of the Nigerian-Biafran conflict now, I think how long it has taken for the sounds of that war to reach my ears, how long my dreaming eyes were shielded on the compound even though I stood out in the sun. I could not see what I could not believe. I could not hear what I could not yet see. Much later, I learned that Mr. Amobi was shot one day in the East when he came out of the bush to go to town to find food and no one I know knows what happened to Nwada, the daughter my age, whose mother fed me gari to eat in my hands.

In January, Gowon met with Ojukwu in Aburi, Ghana, for negotiations because Ojukwu no longer believed he was safe in any part of Nigeria but the East. In fact, the peace summit began on January 4, 1967, my sister's sixteenth birthday. The four of us traveled to Ibadan for the weekend, and while Ojukwu and Gowon met in Ghana, we were having dinner at the new Premiere Hotel up on the hill. Since independence, these Premiere Hotels kept popping up all over the place. They were lovely, huge skyscrapers, full of empty air-conditioned rooms and no smells. Down in the lobby were beautiful little shops for tourists with wildly overpriced silver and gold jewelry and leather handbags and ebony carvings with ivory ornamentation and blouses made of local cloth but pinched at the waist, European-style, none of which we ever bought. These hotels were built to glamorize Nigeria and make the regional Premieres look big, and they were a huge bust. Hardly anyone stayed in them, so they must have been costing the country millions of dollars a year to run. Meanwhile, right down the road there were still no sewers. The dining room was large and full of round tables with white tablecloths and all of the many courses were served on white china. This was the height of luxury in Ibadan. We were there just for dinner.

In Aburi, perhaps Gowon and Ojukwu joked with one another. Perhaps they remembered a time just a few months back when they had been brothers. But as soon as they returned to their regions, they were under pressure to backtrack from what was being called the Aburi Accord. Ojukwu argued that the agreements meant each region could have its own military and keep its own revenue. But Gowon declared that the Aburi agreement restated the authority of the Supreme Military Council on all national matters, in other words, his authority. To clear things up, he published decree 8, which reiterated his command. But Ojukwu just tossed the decree aside like an empty cigarette pack.

So Gowon began a blockade of the East, holding up food. Nigerian Airways flights into the region were suspended.

At Newton I often entertained myself on a swing that hung from a great shady tree. The seat was circular and the rope long. What you would do was hold the rope with the swing dangling below your grip and back up halfway around the tree, then run and jump onto the seat so that the swing curved back in its return around the trunk. Then you would catch the tree with your feet and hold yourself at an angle away from it and begin to work backwards around it, positioning your feet against the trunk, back and back until the rope was wound around as far as you could get it. Then you kicked out from the tree and the rope swung you way out, way way out until your stomach went farther than you did, and then, just then, when your insides were in front of you somewhere out there in the air, the swing began to descend and turn back around the tree in the other direction and then you swung like an arching pendulum back and forth around the great tree in the shade. You just had to watch out as you came back that you kept your face to the tree because otherwise you might slam into it. But if you managed this stunt successfully, without getting thrown against the tree, you did it again and again until you had turned into another person or stopped being a person altogether and become a motion, a wave. It was liberating to be so beside yourself that you forgot who you were and existed only for this motion, to keep it going. This was the opposite of the feeling I had in front of the mirror in Eku, of splitness. This swinging was absolute togetherness. Being the motion was bliss, was heaven.

The swing was a kind of time machine for getting you out of the place where you were and into another place and time. As I reconsider that spring and that story I wrote with Lee and Rebecca, I think the violence got closer to us than anyone knew and thus we tried to deliver ourselves. We were fully exposed and startled to dreaming.

Near the end of the year, Rebecca's father showed up one day, packed her few things, and stowed her away. Perhaps he had to leave the country because of the war. I don't know. We Baptists weren't going anywhere. But I saw Rebecca get into that official-looking van with USAID standing upright across the side and she cruised down the circular drive just like that without leaving a forwarding address or even a fingerprint.

Suddenly, I remember being on the other side of the compound in that open space behind the chapel or between the chapel and the boys' dorm in the hot hot sun. There was only one tree remaining there, way out at the far side away from me, and under that tree a man was chopping a log. I could see his arms lift and hold a moment and then come swinging down, hitting that log. I couldn't hear anything yet, it was so hot and so still and not even the grasshoppers were talking. Then, boom, the sound pounded into my ears. But the man already had the hatchet lifted over his head again and now it was again coming down. When he hit again there was no sound, nothing. Then moments later, as once more he lifted the hatchet, boom, I heard the sound. And that was when I learned about the difference between the speed of light and the speed of sound or the difference between trusting your eyes and trusting your ears. Or perhaps that was when I learned that time is not seamless but incongruous and incommensurate, although I did not at the time fully comprehend just how incongruous.

Fathers

ONE NIGHT AT Newton it began to snow, or it looked like it was snowing. It was evening and the sun was just setting. But in that brief twilight, as we stepped out the front doors of the girls' dorm to head for the classroom building for study hall, little white flakes began to fall from the sky. And then the air was full of them so that you could hardly breathe and you fanned your hands wildly in front of your face. But it wasn't cold and it wasn't even raining. And then we realized that the snow was winged ants, the sort that hatch at certain times of year and emerge out of thousands of unseen nests in the grass to make their brief ascent toward heaven. They looked like snow flying upward. Momentarily forgetful of our books, we ran about like released captives into those startled swirling insects. Many veered indoors, captivated by the light, and fell confusedly onto the tiled floor or landed on the furniture or flew crazily toward the light-bulbs. *Truth and love and mistaken identity* is what I want to write.

Resisting for the moment the lure of any actual boy, I began to focus on GAs, a sororal field of experience for young girls aimed at educating them to Christianity and missions. GA stood for "Girls Aux-iliary," our motto: "Arise, shine, for thy light has come" (Isaiah 60:1). The first time I read that motto it seemed mysterious and powerful, as if some heroic stranger had come to me in the night and opened my window. He came in brilliant light but also with a darkness behind him, so his proposition was risky and absolutely seductive. Our colors were green and white and gold. I suppose we were royal virgins in our salad days, destined to become the brides of Christ. For Southern Baptist outsiders, GAs is an evangelical club for young girls in the church. Here we learned to be missionaries ourselves, becoming educated first in the scripture and in stories of other missionaries, and then learning to emulate them. There were "steps" in GAs that you achieved through spiritual good works. First you were a maiden, then a princess, then a queen, then a queen with a scepter, then queen regent (with a green cape), then queen regent in service by the tenth grade (with a gold tassel and a white Bible).

GAs provided a world of female succession. The meetings we held were a little like something Trixie Belden would dream up, with mottos and club allegiance and programs to arrange and fantastic things to say. And all this glory was divinely sanctioned. Here I could covet greatness openly and not deprive anyone else of it either. There could be lots of princesses and queens. We didn't cancel each other out.

On Wednesday nights the girls split up into two sections. The younger girls went to the chalet, which housed single female missionaries on one-term appointments. They were called journeymen, and I never thought about the misnomer. The older girls went to the Congdons' house where Aunt Esther made delectable oatmeal cookies and yellow cake with chocolate syrup worth paying for. But you didn't have to pay, of course, except with your devotion. For about forty-five minutes, each group of girls held GAs at its respective location and then we had refreshments before going to study hall. This Wednesday night affair was a gracious interlude in a fairly regimented week. Social competitions ceased. There were no boys here, only girls. In this hour, we laid down our weapons and sang:

> We've a story to tell to the nations, that the Lord who reigneth above has sent down his son to save us and show us that God is love and show us that God is love. And the darkness shall lead to morning and the morning to noonday bright. And God's great kingdom shall come on earth, the kingdom of peace and light.

> We sang it as if it were a love song.
> We sang it though there was a war approaching.
> We sang it through the war: *the kingdom of peace and light.*

At the end of our meeting, we closed with a prayer, holding hands as you do in church when you're a girl: you cross your own hands in front of you and then reach out and grasp your neighbors' hands; then when the prayer is over, you twirl under your arms and come out on the other side and let go.

I was dead serious about GAs, not really about missions, per se, or about God really, though maybe about Jesus. What I was really serious about was salvation because it seemed to me I stood in need of it. And I loved the discipline, the accomplishment, the recognition, all of which kept me focused on manageable tasks so that my mind did not wander out above the trees or down the Oshogbo road. I loved "doing things," whether that meant memorizing fifty verses of scripture or writing an essay about my personal relationship with God (a particularly Baptist way of speaking), or creating a notebook on Singapore, or reading a book about the famous missionary Lottie Moon, or coloring a world map to show where all the SBC missionaries were. All these activities made my life appear normal and gave me a history, which is another way of saying they gave me a faith. I liked the assurance that, as I once wrote, "I am God's and God is mine." In GAs you could make claims for yourself that no one could dispute because we were Southern Baptists, and if you felt it and God said it to you, it was true, even if you were a girl. These days, of course, in the Southern Baptist Convention, if you're a girl and hear God calling you to lead, you're hallucinating and stand in need of therapy, or prayer, which is cheaper.

We had authority. In fact, one of our activities as GAs at Newton was to lead the outdoors Nigerian male staff in devotionals on Saturday mornings, and I was always a leader. We younger girls went down to the carpenters' buildings on the lower part of the compound around ten o'clock, passing as we walked the Congdons' beautiful gardens all abloom. A group of four or five men waited to greet us in the shade of large trees, their caps in their hands, their clothes various shades of brown: brown shorts, a brown shirt, a brown cloth in the pocket. Some of the men did not speak English, so one who did would translate for us. We read scripture, of our own choosing, and one of us would speak briefly, explicating the text I suppose, while everyone else sat on the concrete porch of the shed. Then we would pray and maybe sing *Kum-ba-yah*. And then we shook hands, in a kind of friendly solemn way, the men's hands like the roots of plants. And we would part until the next Saturday. The men never failed to show up. Remembering this mission work, I am astounded that we girls were not strictly lectured about the sin of pride before we set forth to save souls, but I am more astounded by the men's sober reception of me. The way they held their bodies suggested a kind of disciplined patience mixed with an accommodating thoughtfulness and perhaps even a little bit of entertained curiosity. I wonder if they thought they would be fired if they didn't show up. Or maybe our arrival just meant they could take a longer than usual break from work. These men were Yoruba. I think they knew what they were doing.

As I write, I wonder how or when I became a person so determined to go ahead when I did not know what I was doing. What compelled me to be a leader in devotionals or to dance in *Swan Lake* when I had never had the first lesson in dance? Even now, I cannot imagine. I desired so much and the channels at Newton were so narrow, like that little blue pool in Ede—meant exclusively for Europeans—where we sometimes went to swim. I took what I could get.

I want to say something about the faces of those men now, as I see them, but how can I say it? I want to say that their faces were open, like a room you could go into. Most faces of the white men I knew, and even boys becoming men, were more like stone walls, like the granite walls of Newton. They came out to meet you and stopped you before you could enter. The bodies of the boys with these faces were like soldiers, legs spread, arms across the chest. When I look at a black-and-white photograph of older MK boys from those years, I am surprised to see how rigidly they stare into the camera. Even my son notices, looking over my shoulder. "What are they mad at?" he asks. Their gazes passed right through you to a space about five feet beyond where you were standing. But the faces of these Yoruba men were milder. Perhaps it was the markings on their faces, lines that looked like wings or leaves etched diagonally across the cheeks. I think the difference was that the Nigerian men's faces registered emo-

tion. Whereas Yoruba culture includes the wearing of masks for religious and cultural ceremonies and festivals, American culture included
no masks save those behind which most American men stood. A few
of the boys around me hadn't yet put on the mask. But they were the
ones who suffered. And my father's face was sometimes open to me.
But sometimes it was also closed, as masked as anyone else's.

When it came time for the GA coronation in the spring, all the
girls dressed in white from head to toe, including barrettes or ribbons, dresses and slips and underwear, socks and shoes, or later, pale
stockings and white pumps. I can still conjure the smooth erotic feeling of stockings under my dress. After everyone was seated in the
chapel and the girls all lined up in the back of the sanctuary according to step, the coronation began.

Each step processed in turn, and when we got to the queen step
and above, someone played "God of Our Fathers," accompanied by
trumpets.

*Today, when I look in a hymnal from my sister's church that I have taken
out on a kind of permanent loan, though I did not ask permission, I see that
the words to the hymn are different. Now the title reads: "God of the Ages,
Whose Almighty Hand." Out loud I say, "no; that's not it." The song is "God
of Our Fathers," in spite of my feminism. What are ages to fathers? No one can
see an age. What does it look like? What is the shape of its hands? What does
it tell you about God to sing "God of the Ages"? I would like to keep the father,
a father without a mask, a father with a face you can walk up to and enter.*

*I have a dream. I am with my mother and sister at Antioch Church in
Ogbomosho. I look out the window and see Dr. Green's first clinic and the two-
storied missionary houses that were part of the original grounds. The church is
full of young Nigerians. And then I see my father, dressed like a Yoruba man
in all of that huge blue and white and cream cloth with a fedora on his head.
He is clapping and singing in Yoruba, looking at me and smiling.*

Wenger

THE MOST FASCINATING person in Oshogbo lived not on our compound but on the shores of the sacred River Oshun, home to the river goddess Oshun, the divinity who showed all the other gods the way down to earth. The woman's name was Susanne Wenger, the second "white-woman-gone-native" I encountered in Nigeria. Her name itself—Wenger—was tantalizing, suggesting she could fly. What was more tantalizing to me was the idea that a white person could *stay* in Nigeria indefinitely, because at this point in my life I could see I was going to have to leave. My sister was bound to take off soon. All MKs in our mission left West Africa at the end of the tenth grade to go to America so we would get the native out of us in time to go to college. But Wenger was staying.

Oshogbo was and is a great arts center. Here one finds the Duro Ladipo Traveling Theatre, the artist Twins Seven Seven, and Nike Davies, maker of batik. Wenger still resides in Oshogbo, at least she did at the last printing of *West Africa: The Rough Guide*. An Austrian-born painter and sculptor, Susanne Wenger came to Nigeria the decade of my birth, the decade before independence. In Oshogbo she devoted herself to Obatala, divinity of creation, that wonderful god riding an elephant whose molding of a few deformed people (when he has had too much palm wine) helps explain an imperfect world. While I was at Newton, Wenger was occupied with local artists, rebuilding shrines and temples in the Sacred Forest of Oshun. Women worshipers in the area even made Wenger a priestess.

Once a year in boarding school, we made a visit to the Oshun. I remember helping Aunt Marian pack lunches of fried chicken and peanut butter sandwiches and bananas in brown paper bags to take on such a trip. The Oshun was approachable only by path through the dense foliage of the forest surrounding it, at least that's the way I remember it, or that's the route we took. The Oshun was not close to our usual haunts in town: the open market or the BP station or either of the cathedral-like Baptist churches.

I have no idea what we were supposed to do on these outings to the Sacred Forest. The trips were not intended to be educational, certainly not religious in nature. I guess these picnics were a diversion. At least we had the decency not to have fun. Because of the steep decline to the river itself, you couldn't run. No one thought to throw a ball or a frisbee. Either one would have been lost in the forest. The one activity that offered itself, and it was sobering rather than entertaining, was to walk across the river on the swinging bridge suspended high above it. I made this vertiginous traversal several times, always enormously frightened.

At the river, we walked in the forest, smelling the odor of crushed undergrowth. You could see the shrines for the goddess: rounded white sculptures close to the ground and rising out of the greenery like a dispersed herd of humped and grazing animals. The temples and Wenger's house, however, were "taller," and here you saw, in painted white concrete, the large circles and flowing lines of modernist art: modern African and European.

On the banks of the river, we were quiet. It was Oshun who talked, rippling in her bed. The brown Oshun was not a river we went into. It was not a swimming river.

I saw Susanne Wenger from afar, imagining her mostly, by seeing her house and her sculptures. She was a woman beyond my ken, a woman outside my line of vision. How could a white woman live in Nigeria like that? What did she do at night with her windows open and the air coming in and the front door open? What language did she speak on her knees in the forest? How did she wear her hair? What did she do with her hands when she was remembering the houses of her girlhood or the teachers she had in grade school or the boys she knew on the street?

I have never known the answers to those questions. And I continue to wonder—but now about myself: What have I been doing with my hands all these years, forgetful of Nigeria? What family have I lost? What history? What spirit?

Since we didn't swim in the Oshun, we drove in the vans over to Ede, about twelve miles from Oshogbo, to swim in that small blue pool—not a very satisfactory body of water; it smelled too much of frogs and paint. This basin was surrounded by a fence. Clearly the pool was intended for the few white folks in the area and not the general population. It was here that I was first told by a sophisticated tenth grader that I had fantastic legs. She told me that they were perfect because they touched at the knee and did not touch again all the way up to my swimming suit and they were long and well proportioned. Unfortunately, this new knowledge did not save me. No one liked me more because of it, and I did not know how to use my legs to advantage. I was entering a stage in which my body was something to be overcome.

✾෴✾

When I left Andy on that Saturday afternoon—Joel staying put because, as he said, *this is my home*—I was only enacting the last in a succession of breakups; I was doing what I know best how to do. Leave. I did not leave my illness; it followed me, a stalker. I did not get my youth back.

While I was gone, my husband purchased flowers on a weekly basis and placed them in the house. I could see them when I came to pick up Joel. I cannot say why he did so unless he was calling me home.

Returning after a bad break is hard but I have finally realized that not doing so is harder.

Andy and Joel do not look at me as though I am ill, and I am grateful because I look to myself as though I am. My flesh grows a catheter while my feet and legs swell beyond recognition. My skin is yellowed as everything is yellowed here in the spring when pollen rains from the pines. My eyes are bloodshot always. To myself, I look like a person I would pity.

One night I awoke with the sense that my bed was on a ship, rolling back and forth with the waves. When I turned over, I lost my balance, though I was lying down. There was an ocean in my ears. The next morning when I sat up in bed I nearly fell over, and when I stood, I did fall. And that is how I lost the hearing in my right ear overnight, just like that, like a light turned out.

I know better than my doctor who tries to diagnose this latest catastrophe. My body is leaving me in parts, winging back to Africa. My ears want to hear their native music. They are not happy with the sounds of American television and American malls and American grocery stores. Give me a Yoruba drum, I beg you.

In Nigeria in 1966, after the rainy season, the West and the North found themselves adjusting to the vacuum left by the flight of the Igbos. Just as our Igbo cooks had evacuated, so many good mechanics had left; public services suffered because so many technicians had gone in the night; intellectuals vacated university posts. The *New York Times* printed a headline about the growing crisis: *A Time-bomb Ticks in Nigeria*. In the East, drums and pans and nails and glass started walking out of the market and into sheds to dedicate themselves to the weaponry of Biafra. In Oshogbo we heard the story of a train coming out of the North bearing an Igbo corpse without a head: what muteness, how great a cry.

One day I left the compound, climbing over the fence behind the athletic field. Before long I found myself on a path. It was hard to see at first because just beyond the fence the woods were thick. Under two trees I saw a woman resting, a load of wood beside her. As I continued I was met by two young men carrying loads on their heads, and they stepped aside into the undergrowth to let me pass. I met a young boy, just younger than I, and I asked him where the creek was. He only pointed back to the way he had come. I kept going and for a long time I saw no one. Then I nearly ran into a very old man with a walking stick, his head facing the ground. He smelled like curry.

This time I stepped aside; he did not even look at me as he passed. His tongue was clicking. I was about to turn back when I saw the ground ahead shift downward and I could see the bright brook and two small logs laid across it. I ran to the brook and then I stopped and only looked. In the water were fish swimming backward.

God with Us

*J*UST AFTER SCHOOL was out that year, my family and I took a trip to visit Aunt Hattie Gardner in Okuta, a town northwest of Oshogbo, right on the border with the country of Benin, then called Dahomey. Aunt Hattie was wiry and small with steel-colored hair braided up around her head. She was a "true missionary" like Aunt Jo Scaggs, one who did not keep up much of an American appearance. Her house in the bush was a tiny one-room trailer hitched up to a one-room concrete structure and no bath. Once at mission meeting, all the other missionaries kept telling her she needed a bathroom. Finally they were going to vote on it. That's when she stood up and declared to the gathering that they could build it as they liked but she "wasn't a gonna use it."

On that visit with Aunt Hattie we drove in her Land Rover to a village where we were witness to the initiation of boys into manhood. The boys already looked like men to me for they were tall and serene; they almost seemed to be on stilts their bodies were so long and skyward. Or perhaps they looked so tall because I was sitting, cross-legged on a mat, part of the audience. Some of the women of the village were dancing all in a wavering line, bending their bodies over as if they were looking for something in the dirt—their hips the largest part of them—while male musicians drummed and drummed and drummed with no apparent end in sight, though the rhythm shifted from fast to slow and back to fast and the dancers followed. It was midday, but fortunately we were seated under some of the compound trees and this shade made it easier for my eyes to look out on the theater in front of me. Palm fronds were waving as smaller children followed the dance in step, imitating the women and looking around at faces with great happiness. With all that moving and drumming and waving the world became fluid. Then suddenly, like a god of wind, two great Masquerades flew from behind a house. I had that sense of needing to swallow over and over again to keep something down. Palm branches and great sticks moved around us without the aid of people, stirring up the smell of roots.

The ceremony was like a dream being overwhelmed by another dream. It was nothing like a church. At last there were just those tall boys in the courtyard, six of them, and all with only a wrap and their chests and backs exposed, reaching up in the sky. And then one by one the boys were beaten until I saw the blood, like a red flame, red like a crayon, running down their backs. Each time the lash went back, I held my breath, and when it came down, I felt that wrenching feeling you have in your gut when you see a violence. I wanted the hitting to stop but I also didn't want it to stop because of the sensation I was having. I felt I might die if the beating stopped, for the beating of drums and boys was the whole meaning of the universe.

There were many boys becoming men and so the initiation was long. There were no shortcuts. It was the most amazing thing, for the boys never wept; in the end they shouted instead and danced in their ceremony of ascension and jumped straight up from the earth as if they had springs on their feet. After the beatings, the women ululated on and on.

This was the sort of thing, I guess, that missionaries were supposed to be saving Nigerians from. But we watched, mute in our sandals. And perhaps, instead, this vision was a kind of preparation for us for what was to come.

Because as it happened, one night while we were in Okuta, there in an empty mission house with the lamps burning, for the electric generator was turned off in the evening, we heard a voice on the radio. It was the deliberate voice of Ojukwu reading the Biafran Declaration of Independence:

> Fellow countrymen and women, you, the people of Eastern Nigeria:
> Conscious of the supreme authority of Almighty God over all
> Mankind; of your duty to yourselves and posterity;

Aware that you can no longer be protected in your lives and in your property by any government based outside Eastern Nigeria;

Believing that you are born free and have certain inalienable rights which can best be preserved by yourselves;

Unwilling to be unfree partners in any association of a political or economic nature;

Rejecting the authority of any person or persons other than the Military Government of Eastern Nigeria to make any imposition of whatever kind or nature upon you;

Determined to dissolve all political and other ties between you and the former Federal Republic of Nigeria;

Prepared to enter into such association, treaty or alliance with any sovereign state within the former Federal Republic of Nigeria and elsewhere on such terms and conditions as best to subserve your common good;

Affirming your trust and confidence in me;

Having mandated me to proclaim on your behalf and in your name, that Eastern Nigeria be a sovereign independent Republic,

NOW THEREFORE I, LIEUTENANT-COLONEL CHUKWUEMEKA ODU-MEGWU OJUKWU, MILITARY GOVERNOR OF EASTERN NIGERIA, BY VIRTUE OF THE AUTHORITY, AND PURSUANT TO THE PRINCIPLES RECITED ABOVE, DO HEREBY SOLEMNLY PROCLAIM THAT THE TERRITORY AND REGION KNOWN AS AND CALLED EASTERN NIGERIA, TOGETHER WITH HER CONTINENTAL SHELF AND TERRITORIAL WATERS SHALL HENCEFORTH BE AN INDEPENDENT SOVEREIGN STATE OF THE NAME AND TITLE OF "THE REPUBLIC OF BIAFRA."

Then in the dark night, in the space beyond the light of the lamps, we could hear the Biafran national anthem, full of pomp and circumstance and sung like a hymn. It had been written by Azikiwe, one of the founding fathers of Nigeria.

I don't know where I was when Kennedy was shot but I know where I was when Ojukwu spoke. I was with my parents and my sister in the dark in a mission house that was designed just like the ones I had lived in in Ogbomosho as a girl. But this one was barren, in the outback of western Nigeria, smelling of lamp oil.

In Igbo land, you might have heard a store owner exclaim: *We done reach independence o. Today now good day for we Biafrans. God with us!*

Bleeding

SOON AFTER WE RETURNED to Oshogbo, my periods began. I awoke one night with a sensation in my abdomen that I had never imagined, a heaviness and a pull, like something being torn. A few days later, playing with friends, I went to the bathroom and found my panties stained red and brown, like the congealing of paints left overnight on a dish. My mother suited me appropriately and I went and sat next to the tennis court that afternoon and watched. I wondered if my father knew. Soon after, I learned to shave my legs, though the first time I undertook this activity, I carved off a long piece of skin from one leg and bled into the tub until the water was pink.

A few weeks later, I drove with my parents to Lagos to put Becky on an airplane for America. She would fly to Atlanta, Georgia, to live for a year with the DuValls, who were on furlough, and attend the local high school. Her primary assignment was to put Africa out of her mind and act like an American.

What our parents did not realize when they put us on those planes, rescuing us for America, was that we were lost already, or at least lost to America. Our souls were already claimed by the prior commitment of our births, our childhoods. How could I forget the silver song of the children under the leaves before I was born, or Ojukwu's voice, or the calabashes in the market, or the smells of the koto, or the long-tailed weaver birds with their boot-shaped nests, or David's tapering fingers, one with the brown freckle, and the driver ants, or women going to market and men on their bicycles when the rain fell like waterfalls, or Abraham with his walking stick? I could never be fully American. Remember, in order to run for president, you have to be born in America. By being sent to boarding school and Americanized, I was made as unfit to be a Nigerian as already I was unfit to be an American. Because as you can see, I was a Nigerian spirit born to an American mother: a crossed star, a mixed message, a long hunger.

Traveling in a school van rather than our Peugeot sedan, we were stopped at roadblocks by young Nigerian soldiers with submachine guns. Our luggage was examined more than once at checkpoints along the way before we were finally told to "pass on." I was not afraid for myself. I was so accustomed to Nigerians being friendly that I could not believe these soldiers would shoot me any more than my father would. Still, everything around me was swelling, or parts of things were swelling. My sister's face was too large and the metal drums on the side of the road were expanding and beginning to fly and the birds in the afternoon sky were big as goats, their droppings large as saucers. The boys with the guns were getting smaller while their guns were getting bigger.

At the mission hostel, the atmosphere was placid as usual. We would all gather in the formal living room before meals. This was a large room with graceful furniture, upholstered but not plush, instead smooth and elegant, and with carefully appointed lamps—a room you might expect the Trapp family to inhabit. When everyone had arrived, we would move to the huge table that could seat twenty people if necessary, always draped in a cloth, always formally set. I never saw the kitchen where our food was prepared, though of course I saw the men serving us. I suppose we were not strong enough to pass the bowls ourselves. One day before Becky left, during the noon meal, we were interrupted by a siren. Rather than getting under the table, we all ran for the windows where we could see military tanks of the Nigerian Army making their way down the street. Like the drums on the side of the road, these tanks were swelling, and for a moment I thought of the huge parade balloons in New York—or maybe I have thought of that association later. You wanted to laugh, as Sam, our cook, had laughed long ago when Nigeria was approaching independence. But instead we sat down like civilized people and finished our meal.

I watched at the old airport in Lagos as Becky walked away from us toward the airplane. In that airport—little more than a bunker with open windows and sand coming in the doors—you could see straight out onto the runway. Becky walked with her escort—one of our "aunts"—out onto the dusty field and then to the concrete runway, the wind whipping her hair and her slender dress. At one point she looked like she was walking on water because of the heat waves rising and then her legs evaporated as if her lower extremities had been blown away. I searched for her among the small blank windows of the Nigerian Airways plane, but could see nothing. She would fly to Accra and then to Paris. Watching her leave was like being in the camera pulling away from the shot. I couldn't tell if Becky was moving or if we were all together moving in that dashing wind and blowing heat. I remember my father looking away as if someone had just cut off his right hand and he didn't know what to do with himself, my mother weeping as if she had lost herself. I looked straight ahead and did not blink in that sand storm.

On the way out of Lagos we were stopped again and often and now the stops were harder to endure because my sister was missing from the backseat.

"You go stop now," the young soldier declared in the perfect logic of Pidgin English, and then he and a few others opened our luggage, looking through it more out of curiosity than anything, almost forgetful of the supposed seriousness of what they were doing. One young man smelling slightly of peppermint even grinned at me before a superior reminded him that he was a soldier, and then a look came over his face as if he had been put in a box.

"You, pass on, pass on," he motioned, done with us now and angry that he had faltered for a moment, had fallen into his humanity.

My mother claims that the first accounts of actual fighting began the day Becky left. That would have been July 6, the day the first Nigerian troops crossed the border from the North into Biafra. We might have done well to have turned around and followed Becky onto the plane. We did not. We headed back up-country.

As we parked the van in Oshogbo, I ran out to the flower bed on the side of the boys' dorm—one my mother had planted—and picked an armful of asters and zinnias so large I could hardly see where I was going as I ran into our apartment. I do not remember what happened next but my mother says I threw the huge bouquet across that mahogany table—that very mahogany table made by those Yoruba craftsmen where Mother and I had written letters to Becky when she was in boarding school, where I had fought with my sister in Ogbomosho when I was three about who had to eat on the plate with the chip, where we had drunk cocoa out of our Micky Mouse cups with the saucers before one got broken, where we had taken our nivaquine and heard our father submit a thousand prayers and my mother had held the world together better than Virginia Woolf's Mrs. Ramsey and where I might as well have been born—and then I wept as if my heart was broken, not for my sister but for myself. Everything had been coming to this. From the beginning everything had been coming to this. From my parents' meeting in Fairfax, South Carolina, and before that, from my great-grandfather's farm, and then after that, the *African Patriot,* and all our houses, and then boarding school, and every lesson in American citizenship, and every Chopin sonata, and every correction of our posture, and every dress that was laid across our breasts, and every courtesy we had ever learned. Everything had come to this parting.

And from the beginning everything had been coming to this. From the first European explorers and even before that from the first wars in that country and after that from the drawing of lines where there should be no lines and from the clash of gods, Allah and Jehovah, and from the importation of weapons and from the interest in oil. *Everything had been coming to this parting.*

And now, as I am throwing those flowers upon that table, the fighting is escalating in Nsukka: The Biafran poet Christopher Okigbo grabs a gun, though he has hardly any training as a soldier, and throws himself into the front of a group of Biafran soldiers. Within hours he is dead. The fighting goes on for a little over a week and the University of Nigeria, opened on the occasion of Nigeria's independence, is destroyed. And when the fighting is over on July 15, you can see a burned-out bus on the side of the road and a public tap with no one waiting, only a white comb stuck in the mud and a blue enamel bowl abandoned by the road, full of wet laundry, and a yellow shirt hanging in a tree, and the letter C drawn on the side of a wall, and on the outskirts of town a burned-out petrol station, even a book, opened on a desk in a house but the house now doorless and a lizard asleep where the door had once been. Only no people, no old men sitting in the shade, no children at the water tap, no middle-aged man on a bicycle, no women with loads on their heads.

Civil War

WE BEGAN TO LEARN who Gowon and Ojukwu were. Everyone and everything from preschoolers to the Nigerian men who worked on the compound to billboards to radio announcers to songs you might hear in the market detailed their lives and exploits.

On the side of Nigeria was General Yakubu Gowon, the thirty-two-year-old son of a Methodist minister and from the minority tribe of the Angas. He had grown up and was educated in mission schools in the Muslim North, joined the army, did his officer training first in Ghana and then at Sandhurst, serving with the Nigerian forces in the Congo, later attending Joint Services Staff College in the United Kingdom and returning to Nigeria to take up a career as an infantry officer. He was young and handsome, smooth-looking. On the side of Biafra stood one General Emeka Ojukwu, a thirty-five-year-old Easterner, born to a millionaire father in the Northern region but an Igbo. Ojukwu entered the Catholic Mission Grammar School and advanced from there to King's College (a private academy); at thirteen, he was enrolled at Epsom College in the hills of Surrey. From there, he moved to Lincoln College, Oxford, where he studied modern history and played rugby. He returned to Lagos, clashing with his father over the family business and opting for civil service. He was sent to the East as an assistant divisional officer, and in two years he joined the army. He attended Eaton Hall for officer training. By 1963 he was a lieutenant-colonel, the first indigenous quartermaster general of the Nigerian Army. He was tenaciously independent, an intelligent man bred for aristocracy. In pictures, he looks moody.

But most of what I know about the war I learned reading books while writing this one. I grieve thirty years later for those who fell but also for myself who did not know my own Nigerian history. Except that I did know it. The earth shudders. Those boys with guns already looked lost. Something changed in the quality of the air. It became heavier and more vacuous all at the same time.

Using an antiquated B-26 and a few Alouette helicopters, the Biafrans struck against Nigeria. A Czech mercenary, "Kamikaze" Braun, piloted the plane, bombing Lagos, Makurdi, Lokoja, Oturkpo, Kaduna, and Kano. Children looking upward might have seen oblong hats descending onto the roofs of houses until they exploded. The stakes of what Gowon had called merely "a police action" against the East were escalating.

In the meantime, the oil war heated up with Ojukwu demanding that Shell/BP make payment to Biafra. But this only led to the Nigerian troops advancing on Bonny Island on the Biafran Coast and the stronger enforcement of Nigeria's blockade against the East.

On August 9, after the Federals took Bonny, after Okigbo had been killed, a Biafran brigade of three thousand men crossed the Onitsha Bridge over the Niger into the Midwest. At Agbor, where David and I had attended that Christmas party years before, the troops fanned out to Sapele and Warri in the south, Auchi in the North, and then to Benin City, the Midwest capital. Perhaps there were children in the road greeting the soldiers, for many Igbos lived on this side of the great stream.

Now the Sapele Kingsway where I had shopped with my father for a birthday present for my mother, where we had picked out a framed picture of lavender flowers in a bowl when I was nine years old, was under Biafran control. The Midwest, including the Eku hospital, was drawn into the war the way dolphins are sometimes caught in tuna nets.

All of Nigeria's oil resources were under rebel hold, though the means of selling and exporting oil were in limbo. With most of the Nigerian infantry still occupied in the North and the East, it looked like the Biafrans could just walk straight to Lagos. So naturally Gowon declared *total war.*

Late that summer, after Becky was gone, I was hoping to get a turntable for my birthday, something to make me more hip at school, though I don't know what records I would have played. I had been saving up Coca-Cola bottle tops that had little pictures of a radio and a turntable and if you got a certain number—maybe ten—you would get this equipment free. I doubt anyone in Nigeria ever got any of it; certainly I did not. But I thought if this plan didn't work, my parents would surely give me a record player for my birthday.

On August 16, my father's birthday, the Biafrans reached the Ofusu River bridge which marks the border with the Western region, our region. On my birthday, August 19, the Biafrans were continuing to advance. All around, the savannahs were quiet; there was a lull in the rains. The air was dry as a stone. Around that beautiful dining room table, I had a birthday party with our little compound clan. I was thirteen and my mother made a white cake with yellow icing and on it she placed a ceramic Siamese cat as a decoration. I wore a dress pink as a carnation. My birthday gift appeared in a small box, a birthstone ring—peridot—in an oval setting, rather plain really, like my face. I didn't like it. I was disappointed. My mother explained that we were in a war and it was not a good time to buy record players when we were so uncertain of our immediate future. She said this to me in our living room after the party and I stared at the philodendron as she spoke, determined not to look at her or signal the least agreement. She could speak if she liked; I would not listen.

The Yoruba had finally got off the fence and appeared to be aligned with the North in its mission to keep Nigeria unified. This was a blow to the Igbos. On the radio you could hear the refrain, *To Keep Nigeria One Is a Task That Must Be Done.*

The next day, August 20, the Biafrans attacked Ore, putting them within 130 miles of Lagos and about 90 miles from Oshogbo where I was unhappily viewing my new ring in its box, for I would not wear it. If they reached either Ibadan or Lagos, the Federation of Nigeria would fall like a bulleted elephant. But just as Gowon was about to flee, the British and Americans intervened. Who knows what happened in Ore. We never knew. But the war turned around. Perhaps today there is an old woman in Ore who was there that day, who saw what happened when the Biafrans stopped and then backtracked. Her eyes may hold the secret.

Running home, the Biafrans picked up refugees with them as they moved eastward. Before long, Eku, which had been in Biafran country for a few weeks, found itself once again in Federal territory. What must it have been like to have armies passing through with the regularity of the sunset? By now in Nigeria, many compounds were more like apartment buildings than family property. Various families might rent from a landlord. So a neighbor who had a grudge could point at you in the presence of a Federal soldier and you knew that your eyes would soon be closed forever. How did anyone secure his soul?

In Oshogbo, my heart was becoming steeled. The gates were locking. But that was inside me. Outside the skies had not changed color. The gloriosa was coming up in the side yard, winding its aerial way straight up out of the ground. There were fresh curtains in the girls' dorm. Our house had not turned around in the dark though there was a new darkness in me. My sister's departure was the ominous sign of a horrible loss that was coming down the path to greet me and not just me but everyone I knew. Everything smelled orange like dampened rust.

As the Biafran soldiers retreated into the East, they crossed the Niger at Asaba and blew up the beautiful new bridge behind them. Little food was getting into the country and the children were dying from kwashiorkor, protein deficiency. Their pictures began to appear on the pages of London newspapers. For them, it was all over that first year of the total war.

When I started my period each month, I would stop by the infirmary—the room that had been my bedroom in the second grade; now it was the girls' infirmary and the house parents had a new apartment. I would open the closet that had been my closet when I was seven, where my Keds had nestled at night next to my Sunday shoes, wait for my eyes to adjust to that darkened space, lean down, reach in, and pull out a box of Kotex sanitary napkins, trying to hold it close to my body, this large awkward box with a picture of a lithe white woman on it with her arms uplifted to the sky. I would try to get to my room, farther down the hall, before anyone saw me. And then fix myself and get back to the dining hall before the last bell rang, smoothing my hair as I walked, and at last finding a place to sit on one of those stiff couches before we prayed, and then after the prayer acting as if nothing had happened.

My roommate now was Jan Barnes, the American girl with long straight brown hair who had arrived so brilliantly in her fishnet hose and who owned every Beatles album to date. I only had the soundtrack to *South Pacific;* this was the sort of album my mother believed in. I should not have tried. I should simply have been myself, but I did not have the nerve to venture something that dangerous. So I tried something even more dangerous, though I did not know it at the time. I tried being someone else. I applied makeup to my freckled face and teased my hair. And I tried to smile without opening my mouth, demurely, so that I looked still asleep or a little drunk. I tried, in short, to be a girl you could like, or rather a girl who looked like someone else, but it didn't work. I became a stranger to myself instead.

I was between continents. Having left the younger girls' hall behind, I had not yet fully achieved whatever it took to be an "older" American girl. Part of the problem was that I was being measured by an outside standard; but I only got lessons in American popular culture once every four years when I went with my family on furlough, so I fell behind. Either I wasn't getting all the messages I needed— about how to grow into a likable girl at an American boarding school in Nigeria, West Africa, in the 1960s while we were in the middle of the Biafran War (I don't think there were any articles on that topic) or I wasn't getting the lessons in order. They came in batches, like letters that had been held up at the post office, so my learning was piecemeal and sporadic. I kept misstepping, being the wrong girl in the wrong place or the right girl in the wrong place or the wrong girl in the right place.

I had been two-faced before, cheating in school, acting happy when I was not, being "nice" to girls I envied. But now I seemed to have only this false exterior, a face untrue to what I had in the past most coveted: my capacity for abandon and daring.

I became insecure about my athletic skills, plummeting from the sport of Eku to the reluctant player at Oshogbo. I learned at Newton to sit out weekend softball games because it was too humiliating to be a girl and to strike out all at once. If you were a boy, you could be decently shamed because you should be able to hit the ball. But if you were a girl you were supposed to strike out or else hit the ball but not too forcefully and then maybe run to first base and actually make it (the crowd was cheering wildly now because you were a *girl* and had run *gracefully* and still made it). You were always acting. The few girls, like Beth, who really could play ball were an odd exception and you weren't envious of them; they were not the ideal. So you couldn't even really be shamed properly. All you could be was a girl.

When I would walk down to the set of rooms reserved for the truly older girls—ninth and tenth graders—I felt as if I were walking onto a movie set. I watched, an onlooker, while Gwen Barnes applied eyeliner or Melba Smith stood in her slip in front of the mirror, her breasts like small European nations. I was amazed and not by grace but by makeup: foundation, blush, eye shadow, all in coveted little boxes that clicked shut. I had not foreseen such a complex future for my countenance when last I was in the U.S. so I had little of this beautiful equipment. In the background on such an afternoon, someone was playing the Beatles' "Nowhere Man." I remember dust motes in the light in the hallway, a feeling of fatalism and sadness—or something heavier than sadness, like the premonition of death, as if we were all waiting for someone who would never show up—and shadows among the hardwood furniture in those dorm rooms. Outside the sun was blazing in an otherwise blank sky and the boys were playing football. But inside, we girls were in our rollers and slips, humming "Nowhere Man" and "Michelle" and "Norwegian Wood" and "Girl" and "I'm Looking Through You." The last song, at least, I understood: *I'm looking through you / where did you go?*

I might have sung that song to David Gaultney, who reappeared just after school had started. One afternoon there stood Aunt Virginia in my mother's kitchen drinking a cup of coffee, looking just as she always had only more robust. But when I saw David, he acted as if we had never met.

Perhaps the boys in my class that year were as stymied by this crossing to maturity as I was. No one in our group dated except for my roommate Jan who dated older boys. She already knew how to kiss. I was made a scapegoat a little and deserved it I am sure for trying to raise votes for myself in a number of venues on various occasions. I was awkward. But JoEllen Norman was the object of the most scorn. JoEllen was the girl I had visited in Joinkrama in the Eastern region who traversed her territory there like a true native daughter and who showed up in Eku briefly. But with the war, she had evacuated Biafra with her mother and two younger brothers and come to Oshogbo. They had left everything behind: their piano and their family portraits and Aunt Lois's cake plate. This was not JoEllen's first year at Newton, only her first year as a refugee. Her father, Uncle Bill, stayed behind at the hospital, tending to war victims. So Aunt Lois was living in the "round house" at Oshogbo. The round house was a kind of architectural marvel, an experiment enacted by the mission architects. It only occurs to me now that perhaps it was an attempt to copy the round structures of many Nigerian mud brick homes. But it didn't work. Though this one was constructed of "superior" materials—granite stone and concrete and Western-style roofing—it leaked in the middle and whereas it should have been light and airy, with windows on all sides, it was cramped and dark, almost like a dungeon, its floors cold and hard and the color of dried blood.

JoEllen sat over on the edge of the eighth-grade class, on the far left in the front row, as close as she could get to her mother down in the round house, for it was on that side of the compound. She was a small girl with curling cropped brown hair, and before the teacher came into the room, the boys would taunt her. Once in an awkward defense, she turned around and called Baden Richards *Raden Bitchards* and then she was taunted for the rest of the day for speaking the word *bitch*. I had to be taken aside at lunch and told what the word meant. The comparison of a female to a dog was so preposterous in my mind I thought I too was being played. In boarding school you need to know things but not show that you know them until a time comes when you can be cool because you know things without showing that you know them. The key is to have enough information to stay calm. JoEllen was naive and let it show. She was also very cute but cuteness did not save her.

I find it curious looking back that this Biafran refugee was the one singled out that year for such treatment. I remember seeing beautiful Aunt Lois and her two blond-haired boys, those brilliant speakers of Pidgin English, walking across the campus, Aunt Lois looking like someone who had been operated on in the night without her knowing and her heart or some other vital organ removed.

On Sunday evenings we attended church services in the new school chapel, constructed of the same granite stone and concrete block, trimmed in the same colors as the dorms and the classroom buildings. It was dusk by the time the service began with all of us gathered in that well-lit place and all around us the quiet compound. What interests me now as I write is not the chapel service or the hymns we sang or the special music or the sometimes moving sermons we heard or the look of those rows of chairs or the memory of how we stood to sing or the feeling of contentment one sometimes had because it was so nice to be dressed up at night or the wet smell of the concrete floor or the awareness I had of being watched. What interests me now is the rest of the compound, silent and open while we were all gathered in the chapel on a Sunday evening.

I think about the air in my bedroom in my parents' apartment in the boys' dorm. I think about the collection of glass animals on the mahogany shelf in that room, those translucent objects in the shapes of a giraffe and a rabbit and an elephant. I think about the pictures of cats—my answer to Becky's politics—cut from magazines, arranged on the bulletin board in that room, in the dark of that room with only the light of the moon. And I think of the moisture in the shower stalls and the gecko lizards hiding there and the cooling breeze down the hall. I think about my cat Molly's feet on that floor. I think about the spaces outside, the paths luminous, the white stones lining the drive, the darkness under palm trees, the steps in front of the girls' dorm where a thousand footsteps hovered. I think of the absence of sound in the dining hall where every mahogany table was surrounded by six chairs, each pushed up in perfect symmetry, and the empty mirror at the end of the hall. I think about the kitchen where no hands moved among the pots, no strong mens' arms ministered above the large table. And the tennis court behind the kitchen. And the field behind the dorm where only insects played at night and a bat flew under an outdoor light and mangos ripened in the dark under the glossy leaves of the trees. I think about the silent desks in the classrooms, sentinels for civilization; the paper, fingered and curled; the books frayed on the edges, heavy and sad. I think about the cocoa pods and the ancient kapok and the benches, cool and serious in their concreteness. I think about the fence around the compound: a thin ribbon, a great wall. I think about the giant philodendron, its climbing roots against the concrete, pulling against that rock, dislodging grains of sand. I think about how in those evenings the compound was already vacant of us, how in that hour nature began to reclaim itself, how our time was up and we were already gone. Only our singing reached a little ways out in the dark. I think about how the earth already knows itself and how the earth in Africa knows itself better than any other. And I think about how the earth knew us better than we knew ourselves, how the earth knew me better than I knew myself.

How the earth knew me.

How I was made from that earth.

How I was loved by that earth.

How I loved that earth.

Now, so much that happened didn't happen; so much that was spoken was not spoken; so much that was meant was not expressed. There was a war going on and we never spoke of it. We listened to the Beatles instead. I never told my parents that I wished a boy would like me. I never told them that instead he laughed at me. I never told them that the face of a Yoruba man who has lost a child was not bearable to me because he let you see his pain. I never told them that I did not know how to go back to fixing my hair in any decent way. Everything was said with a look, a glance. And even what was said meant something else. A boy's taunt meant that he was standing on a thin ledge and feared looking down. A girl's silence meant she hated him. A house parent's thin "goodnight" meant "God help me." A teacher's rebuke meant "I have no words to tell you how helpless I am."

Here we were curling our hair. Here we were with white legs in short skirts. Here we were listening to a scratched LP: *Yesterday all my troubles seemed so far away, now it looks as though they're here to stay.* And there were guns in the distance. Sleeping at night in the heat with only the hint of a breeze and the sheet more than I could bear so that it was pushed aside and wound around my feet, I began to dream of the Ethiope. I began to visualize that green water as I lay down to sleep. I stopped saying my prayers and composed myself in the river instead. I stood on the shore and drank in its beauty, its swift current, its surface brilliant as an eye, the green vegetation tilted inward as if bowing. I swam across. I pulled myself upstream. I gave myself to the river as to a lover. I dove. I surfaced. I was alone. I was not alone. I should never have let that river out of my sight, the place where my body between my legs shivered in ecstasy, the place where David laughed with me, the place where eternity began.

Those days, when I went to the Oshogbo market with my peers from school, I was still called *oyinbo* by the Yoruba children, person without skin. When I was young, I had pronounced freckles and so I could imagine the story behind *oyinbo*. It was as if African skin had evaporated, leaving behind only these drops. Young children still came up to me and ran their hands gently up and down my arms. Their faces were still as open as hibiscus at noonday. Older boys were less friendly but no less aggressive. In their trays they carried dozens of watches on an array of bands, carefully arranged. On each arm they displayed eight to ten samples. They wanted me to buy one for the boyfriend I did not have. The market women spoke to one another, noticing me only if I asked a question or picked up an item or acted as if I would buy. I was likely to buy but not much. I did not need any dishes, any soap, any cloth. If anything, I might buy a scarf, perhaps a small piece of ornamental china; in fact, I remember buying a small white china dish with a lid and on the lid was painted the scene of an eighteenth-century English gentleman and a young woman walking in a garden. As I walked I was cautious about the ditch between the road and the market stall and its stench of rubbish and decomposition in the sun. But the woman I traded with wore beautiful cloth, her headdress green with gold trim and so large it might serve as an umbrella. There were so many angles in the preparation of her cloth, she could have been an inspiration for Picasso. She kept her money tied in the tip end of her wrap, near her heart. Yet somehow she seemed hungry and surprised by it, like she hadn't been hungry before. She was angry with her son and kept slapping him on the head.

On a day like that in Oshogbo, we might leave the market for the shops. For every twenty Yoruba shops, you would find one owned by a man from Syria or Lebanon. Now that the war had begun, Mr. Manu's store was closed. He was Igbo and his establishment had been burned out. Downtown we used to stop at Mr. Manu's, piling out of the warm bus one after the other. He kept a fine establishment about the size of a small American grocery. Everything was in it: Rowntree's Smarties, Trebor mints, Pepsodent toothpaste, Lux soap, Ovaltine, Hero jams, Odorono deodorant, Lyle's Golden Syrup, toilet water and powders and lotions, household cleaners and laundry detergent, canned foods including hams and tuna fish, cold Cokes and Sprites and Fantas, fresh fruits near the checkout, cigarettes, women's lace underwear, brooms and mops, clear plastic shoes with buckles, a small selection of apparently gold jewelry, chewing gum, and finally, blow-up toys called Hug-a-Bears, I think, in loud colors like lime green and pink. But Mr. Manu was gone. Approaching that section of the street and looking at the vacancy was like looking at the face of a person who has had a horrible accident so that his cheek is blown out but still his eyes and his mouth are there and everything else intact but that cheek.

When I got back to the Newton compound, my feet were sandy and brown inside my shoes.

The war was now so old we could hardly remember it. England remembered, though it wanted to appear neutral or at least not actively committed. It was in a tight spot because Nigeria made it clear it would turn to the Soviets for arms if the British held out. Indeed, Nigeria found itself in possession of two Czech Delphin L-29 jet fighters and twenty MiG-15 fighter-trainers and two hundred Soviet technicians as well. Oddly enough, the jets were piloted by Egyptians who turned out not to be such expert gunners or else weren't that interested in getting killed since they generally missed their targets and rushed back to the landing base. The British supplied arms but never men. China registered on the side of Biafra, not because Biafra was pro-Communist—after all, it was being led by a millionaire—but because the Russians were on the other side. France also championed Biafra, along with Israel, Rhodesia, and South Africa. It was quite an odd assortment. There were already 1.5 million refugees in the East at the beginning of the war and almost no food coming in. More people died of starvation than fighting, thousands a day. (Later, historians would debate whether Gowon caused these deaths through pushing or Ojukwu through holding on.) The one zone that kept guns and food arriving was the Uli "airport," really just a long strip of highway covered by palm fronds in the day and "opened" at night, lit for about thirty seconds at a time, so that friendly planes could see the strip and land. We actually had a missionary stationed at Uli although he was supposed to be unloading only food.

The Biafrans fought back with land mines, *ogbunigwe,* or "destroyers of all," milkchurns filled with scrap metal and petrol.

Every once in a while Gowon would announce that Nigeria was on the cusp of victory, but he was wrong. The war was just coming to a boil.

Driving into an Igbo town, you might spot the End of Nigeria Garage or the Hail Biafra Bar. Biafra started turning out its own gin and brandy as well as some very beautiful postage stamps. But many minority tribes and many ordinary people had little ambition for the war. They only lost and lost.

As I write this book, finally, I see pictures of the war: a tall young man, probably my age at the time, with huge unbooted feet and a cap on his head, in a pullover sweater turned up to his elbows and dark pants, assisting an older but much shorter man with a blanket over his shoulder and army fatigues and a belt of bullets around his waist and also something that looks like a Western-style jacket, like he might wear in London on an afternoon having coffee, except that the jacket is torn and they are leaving the battlefield; the shorter man has a questioning across his brows that I think must never have left him, and he looks to me as familiar as that photograph of Ishola. And another picture of wounded soldiers sitting on a stoop outside a hospital, two missing legs and each holding a single crutch, another man with white patches taped over both eyes, his hand held by one of the amputees next to him who looks into the camera as if he is watching the calamity that brought him to this place.

That year I was a queen at the GA coronation. After we marched in and arrived on the podium, each girl had a turn telling about something she had done to earn her step. I almost always quoted scripture. It seemed to me you could not improve on this language. What could I say that would top Isaiah or Psalms? For once, I knew my limits. I was actually humble before my God. My favorite scripture that year was Psalm 91, which I learned and recited. I was heady with it:

> He that dwelleth in the secret place of the most High shall abide under the shadow of the Almighty.
>
> I will say of the Lord, He is my refuge and my fortress: my God; in him will I trust.
>
> Surely he shall deliver thee from the snare of the fowler, and from the noisome pestilence.
>
> He shall cover thee with his feathers, and under his wings shalt thou trust: his truth shall be thy shield and buckler.
>
> Thou shalt not be afraid for the terror by night; nor for the arrow that flieth by day;
>
> Nor for the pestilence that walketh in darkness; nor for the destruction that wasteth at noonday.

I stood and spoke these words and believed them. One had to believe.

Pestilence, terror, destruction.

Perhaps it is not as absurd as it seems that mission children were becoming missionaries. If no one else needed saving, we needed saving: from drowning in too shallow a pool, from being "protected" from the things we should not have been protected from and thus being exposed to our own callousness and pettiness. Incongruence had followed us all of our lives; we were well while others suffered. We rode in cars through poor villages and enjoyed the scenery. But we were damaged by this enclosure and its power. And we were damaged in our own lives. Yet we had no words for the damage. Children never do.

On a monthly visit to the dialysis clinic, one of the nephrologists decides to unburden himself. I guess because I am a white woman and better educated than most, he believes I will be sympathetic. He thinks I will see myself on his side, so he begins by telling me he has to discipline his patients at work just as he disciplines his children at home. His voice rises as he enumerates the hardships visited on him by clients who eat salt and guzzle liquids. He brings to mind a Belgian colonial in Africa complaining about the ungratefulness and laziness of the natives, of whom I am now one. He is almost testifying, so taken up is he by his narrative: "One woman came into hemo one day twenty pounds heavier than she was two days before. She must have sat around those two days trying to drown herself!" he proclaims. Then he tells me about a woman who eventually "killed herself by sipping salt ice twenty-four hours a day. She drank herself right into a heart attack!"

I am sufficiently horrified, but not by the stories of the patients. Instead by the doctor. He has no knowledge of the disease he treats, no knowledge *in his own body* of why death can be preferable to life like this. Most of his patients are not on the transplant list; they will never get "better."

I speak with one of the technicians. I tell him how it seems to me that dialysis patients are treated like second-class citizens. We are not wealthy. Most are black and not well educated by society's standards and not very bold in their demands. I ask him how people who are not aggressive or articulate enough to demand better treatment survive this ordeal. He answers without expression, as if I have only observed the obvious: "They don't," he says. "They die."

Uncle Connell

OUR PARENTS AND house parents did not know that the war was pulsing through the air and into the ground like nuclear radiation. Some of us were growing horns.

One day I went to practice the piano as I always did, but I noticed that Molly was more skittish than usual. When I bent to pick her up, I saw that her whiskers were gone; they had been cut off, close to her face. As it turned out, some of the older boys, displeased with my parents or with themselves, had pulled this prank. Looking back, I think those boys were infected; their eyes were beginning to bleed.

One day we awoke to find ourselves visited by Federal forces circling the perimeter of the compound and every building. They were there to search the premises, which they did, entering each dorm, each apartment for house parents, each classroom, each private dwelling, looking into closets and drawers. They were on the hunt for shortwave radios, believing we were somehow in communication with the enemy. Nothing in the way of radios was discovered. What I think was discovered instead was our whole way of life. I doubt the soldiers' barracks were nearly as nice as our dorm rooms and I wonder if the military takeover of the compound that occurred two years later was connected with this search.

The truth is that after all these years, I hardly remember that early morning investigation. My father told me about it recently. What I remember from the late spring of 1968 instead is Uncle Connell.

Uncle Connell and Aunt Eunice Smith lived in Ogbomosho in the house Gary Lynn Williams had lived in when I was young, the house next to ours. Uncle Connell was a surgeon and Aunt Eunice worked with the local Women's Missionary Union. Uncle Connell was a compact man, shorter than my father, with cropped hair. He wasn't really stern but he was certainly no-nonsense, and not one to make small talk. Aunt Eunice was elegant and tall, with smooth, almost translucent, skin and eyes like gemstones they were so soft and luminous. She was the sort of woman who seemed to wear hose in Africa in the afternoon. Whether she did or not, I don't know, but she *seemed* to. The Smiths had two children at Newton, Melba and Loy. Melba was one year my senior. Loy was one year behind me. He didn't like me, or perhaps he thought I didn't like him, because one night before study hall, he launched a huge toad across the classroom in my direction. I diverted the poor animal with my open palm as it came flying through the air, and so it hit the wall instead.

It was seldom the case that missionaries took trips to the U.S. between furloughs, but Aunt Eunice had because her sister was ill, so Uncle Connell made the trip to Lagos to fetch her at the airport. On their way out of Lagos that morning, they stopped to visit briefly with the Dahunsis, who were leaders in the Nigerian Baptist Church; he was the pastor of First Baptist Church, Lagos, the church that had been brought over piece by piece in boats from Savannah, Georgia, after the American Civil War. After tea the Smiths got back in their car to drive up-country to Ogbomosho.

That very same day I was on a field trip to Ogbomosho, my original home. (How blazing is that notion: a field trip home.) The eighth-grade health class, led by my mother, our teacher, was there to visit the hospital. The big event of the morning had been a viewing of the operating room and an explanation of sterile procedure. The surgical ward was Uncle Connell's arena, of course, since he was a surgeon. I suspect he was more at home and more relaxed in an operating room than on the tennis court or even at his own dining room table. Perhaps that morning as we toured, someone mentioned that Uncle Connell was away for the day but that the next morning he was scheduled for such and such a surgery. Perhaps he had two or three surgical procedures lined up for the next day.

Our tour of the hospital was over, and we had all gone over to the Edwardses' house for lunch. At this point in time, the Edwards family was living in the house that my family had made camp in that summer between Oshogbo and Eku when I was seven going on eight, and my mother was sick, and Becky was out gallivanting around, and I was making those huge chocolate milk drinks, and Susie got lost. We were having lunch in that house. The meal was special because adult missionaries were serving us and treating us well. Most of all, we were away from the older ninth and tenth graders. But then someone wrenched open the front door and flew into the room. As if choreographed, aunts and uncles and my mother huddled together, their voices dangling with sharp words softly spoken, like knives under a napkin. Anyone could tell something was wrong. I remember going out to the front porch and seeing Nigerians streaming past, because there was a little path that cut through by the house connecting the compound road with the hospital. Men were walking their bicycles, not riding them, because they were too distraught to ride. They had heard the news before we had. The meal was over then, though not because we were through eating. We were told that Uncle Connell had been killed in a car accident on the road from Lagos. Our field trip was over.

As was almost always the case, we did not get the full story. We were always being "shielded" from the latest trauma. But in reality, this form of caretaking had the opposite effect because in our not knowing the whole story, Uncle Connell's death became huge, the way the shadow of a lamp becomes huge against a wall. You really should not try to raise children in the midst of a war and pretend it isn't there. How can it not breed all sorts of evil? You become callous because you are going about your daily life as if nothing is the matter, as if your little world is all that matters; you hide your own small concerns because everyone is so busy being nonchalant.

Uncle Connell's death was the truth our parents could not deny, and still they did not give us all the facts right away. And even when, finally, I learned what had happened, it was told to me in whispers as though somehow maybe we could keep it small, not let it overwhelm us. I remember no one in that company of white people in the Edwardses' living room letting out a groan or weeping outright or calling out to God or demanding an answer for this senseless death. I am sure we MKs would have been better off in the company of the

Nigerian staff at the hospital who would have been weeping appropriately and loudly: a medical doctor in Nigeria, and especially a surgeon, red or yellow, black or white, is a beloved person.

Instead, we climbed into the van for the return trip to Oshogbo. But on the way we crossed paths with another vehicle which was carrying Loy and Melba to Ogbomosho, where they would be reunited with their younger brother, Brian, and wait for their mother and the body of their father. We stopped, and I saw my own mother leave the van and go embrace Loy and Melba as they got out of the car. It was an ordinary stretch of road with grass growing tall on the shoulders, everything green except for this thin strip of blacktop. I have never seen any lonelier people than Melba and Loy getting out of that car and standing there. They might as well have been waiting for a firing squad. Watching them knowing their father had died, I knew there were things I would never be ready for. But I have to confess that I envied them my mother. Other people always seemed to need her more than I did, and usually I had to agree that their case was worse than mine. This would certainly be so a few years later when I wanted my parents to come to the U.S. with me but they were scheduled to do refugee relief work in the former Biafra. Whatever else is true about my mother, she has the look of someone who will not be moved, who could stare down death and then finish her lunch. Maybe she learned this composure in New Orleans in nursing school.

And this is what happened to Uncle Connell and Aunt Eunice. Returning from Lagos in their new French Citroën and not far from the city's outskirts, they were hit by an oncoming Federal truck driven by army recruits. *You can hear the skidding tires, the crash of metal, the burst of glass and then the sound of that glass, like hail, hitting the tarmac; you can see the trees nearby unmoved by the tumult, their limbs stationary in the noon white heat, and hear the voices of the men in the truck cascading through the air. You can see the truck careening down the highway, because it does not stop though the car is destroyed and the Smiths are left for dead in that open stretch of road, for there was not even a bend or a hill. Uncle Connell is dead in the middle of the road but Aunt Eunice is still alive in the ditch looking at her husband and unable to get to him.*

That road from Lagos to Ibadan, at least in those days, began in swamplands and the forest was low and flat there. Often off to the side of the road you would see water covered with green algae and water plants and sometimes lilies and then slowly the swamp would turn to dry land. I imagine this is how the land looked where Uncle Connell died, low and green and sweltering, the road dipping occasionally to a bridge, not a haunting road but an indifferent one, a land between sea and forest, a land not as yet committed to any one thing. Writing that sentence, I think, *Nigeria is a country not as yet committed to any one thing.*

All of us from Newton went to the funeral, along with hundreds, perhaps thousands, of Yorubas. How small and lost and white Melba and Loy and Brian looked sitting at the front of Oke 'lerin (Mountain of Elephants) Baptist Church where the service was held, the sound of the great organ escaping those open windows. I remember watching the waves of people leaving that church, waves of yellow and orange and blue fabric. I remember it from a bird's-eye view because I was flying away over Ogbomosho, away over the market stalls—I saw only their brown rusted roofs—away over the patch of earth where Thomas Bowen had built his first compound, away over the hospital. *Uncle Connell was buried on a slight hill just thirty feet or so from our first home.*

Back in Oshogbo at boarding school, it was no longer possible for me to speak an honest sentence. It was as if words would only go forward and you could not back them up or make them go sideways. They were like the words of the war; they kept advancing and there was no retreat. And because they would only go forward, you could not say what you really meant. You would start and then realize that you needed to detour, that what you really meant was way off over here to the left. One Saturday, through the windows of my room, David Fuglie called me "a goody two-shoes," and I didn't even know what he meant. But I replied with bravado: "Same to you." Immediately, I realized that I should simply have cried. Such a guileless response would have thrown him off his game. Instead I tried to meet his charge and of course my response led only to his pitying laughter. And how could he have thought I was even *trying* to be good?

When I walked, I kept running into walls. When I wrote my name, it looked back at me in judgment. I was a hollow girl, not a good one.

Though it seemed there might be some hope that Wednesday at recess when David Gaultney asked me to go with him to the movies Friday night. I was standing on the open porchway outside the classroom and no one else was there but David. He was leaning against one of those stone columns that held up the roof, his hands behind his back, wearing brown shorts and a white shirt and worn tennis shoes. His skin was still olive brown, his hair still with a wave in the front, and he was older but still the quiet boy from Eku. I stood facing him, my back to the classroom, feeling tall and unsure of my arms and hands. He asked me simply if I would go with him on Friday night to whatever event was in store. I suppose I simply said "yes," though I was surprised and did not know what this invitation meant. Was it a joke? The sun was shining out on the grass while we stood there in the shade for a moment before parting, like two leaves on a branch before they are torn from it and scattered in the wind.

Preparing for our "date," I looked at myself in the mirror and saw a too-tall girl whose teased hair made her even taller and whose straightened bangs elongated her already long face; a too-tall girl with makeup that gave her an overcast look, a heavy shadow on her pale skin; a girl whose smile had become practiced and hard like the flowers in those plastic arrangements that had to be dusted. I thought— like I did about words—that I could only go forward with this facade. I could not go back to myself, or back to my mother's marigolds in a vase on the mahogany table or back to the river at Abraka. I had to go ahead in this terrible masquerade because all the words went forward. So I had to tease my hair even though it was not my style and I had to tape my bangs even though doing so made my face look lifeless and old and I had to apply this makeup that turned my skin to dust. I had to because there was no other language. There was nothing to do but try to be pretty and if one was not pretty, why then one had at least to fail in the attempt.

When I met David in the breezeway at the end of our hall, I felt I dwarfed him with my height and that he was already regretting his invitation. He never asked me to sit with him again and I never knew why he cast this life preserver in my direction that one time. The longer I was at Newton, the more doubtful I became of myself, and the further I was from the girl in Eku or the further she was from me. I was not a girl you could like. I no longer even liked myself. I had come to believe that there was no power aside from that which was assigned to me by the admiration of outsiders. Nigeria was falling apart, but we were indifferent because we were leaving.

And now as I write, I think: what if outsiders had entered Africa with a true interest *in* Africa instead of *out of* Africa? Ah, what a difference it would have made. We should have needed at least five hundred years just to soak up the news that would have greeted us there.

And now as I write, I think: in Oshogbo in those days, I was not only losing myself, I was losing my country. In the afternoon, lizards and small birds rushed in four directions and then came back and crossed each other and ran, mindlessly, in another direction. At night the birds died and we swept them up off the porches in the morning. But sometimes the feathers were caught in my mouth. And all day long I could not cough them up.

The year ended, and before long I was with my parents on a two-week European tour, headed for the U.S. In Switzerland, we saw thousands of posters about the plight of children in Biafra. And then we were back in America, or rather, we were in Atlanta, Georgia, a city I had never seen in my life.

In my home in Raleigh, North Carolina, I practice the piano. I play Chopin's "Valse brillante" opus 34, number 1, one of my recital pieces at Newton. Halfway through, I remember something about the air in the afternoon in Yoruba land. You can see it like a thin veil. Perhaps it is the humidity, perhaps it is the desire of the people, perhaps it is the skirt of the goddess Oshun, perhaps it is the sun's rays, perhaps it is the children who have not yet been born, perhaps it is the gleaming of Ife's crown, perhaps it is young soldiers going to their graves.

The Spirit of Malice

NOTHING WAS REAL. *Everything now was just film. That's how I felt in America. It makes sense to live among people you hardly know, to go to school in a place you have never been, with teenagers who find a reason for living in American popular culture. I just had to learn to dress for the part and I expect I might have lived happily ever after—but I was a failure at the part. I was not pretty or coy. I was not entertained by the ideas of my new acquaintances. Trying to be an American teen in Nigeria where failure was almost guaranteed was one thing. In America, trying to be an American teen was like being lost at the fair with lots of money so you kept spending but really there was nothing you wanted to buy. I nearly died of boredom. Not that I knew it at the time. At the time I simply thought I was a failure.*

I began high school in Decatur, Georgia. This is where I had traveled since beginning kindergarten: Ogbomosho, Eku, Winston-Salem, Oshogbo, Eku, Easley, Oshogbo. Now it was 1967 and I was in Atlanta, the "new" South. Unfortunately, there was no *Rough Guide* to help me on this journey.

We were living in a "missionary house" sponsored by First Baptist Church, Decatur. The DuValls had lived in the house the year before and Becky had lived with them. Now David DuVall was living with us because he was "too old" to return to Newton. He was sixteen.

I got braces that year. My father would drive me to the orthodontist all the way down in Columbus. Maybe he was giving my family a special rate; I don't know why we went so far. But getting braces was horrible. I swear they hammered those things on. And then I had to wear rubber bands on my front teeth so that when I opened my

mouth to speak, it looked like a little cage with bars. This is how I
went forth to conquer the world in Decatur, Georgia: in homemade
cotton dresses, with braces and rubber bands on my teeth, and Nigeria still in the bend of my knees. You'd be surprised how well I did.
I actually made some friends and wasn't a total outcast, although one
very svelte girl who overheard me one day say something about coming from West Africa lifted her nose and looked sideways and said,
Queer.

I became short-tempered with my mother. She was working hard
for us, packing lunches every night, fixing breakfast at the crack of
dawn, coming up with a wholesome dinner every evening. This was
before you ate out half the time. We ate in all the time. She was also
trying to clothe Becky and me on a small allowance, and it is hard to
build a winter wardrobe for a whole family in one or two fall months.
You know that whatever you buy you will wear only a short time
because then you'll go back to Africa and before you get back to this
climate everything will be out-of-date and outgrown. But if you're
the child, that doesn't matter; you *need* to be wearing what everyone
else covets.

I bought the Beatles' *White Album,* but mostly I listened to "Hey
Jude" until my mother said she was going to scream. She did not
approve of rock and roll. We didn't have a decent stereo, just a little
box of a turntable, and it was in the dining room. The house we were
borrowing was passable but nothing special. It was small, with what
I called "false flowers" in the vase on the mantle and gas logs in the
fireplace and a plastic green tablecloth on the dining room table and
little heaters in the wall. It was not a house that many of the well-to-
do members of First Baptist Church, Decatur, would live in but it was
good enough for missionaries. Things were always turned around
when we came to the U.S. Rather than being the wealthy members
of the community who could afford to give bread to the less fortunate, we were the ones living on the edge of poverty, receiving wel-
fare from the white folks.

Becky and I would take the bus and go downtown on Saturday
and shop at Rich's. Shopping didn't mean purchasing big items like
dresses or shoes though I remember looking longingly at a pair of

brown patent leather shoes one day and a matching purse. What our shopping meant was buying hair products or some new eye shadow, small things you could afford on five dollars a week. We would eat at the downtown Woolworths where I ordered club sandwiches without fail and a fountain Coke. Together my sister and I went to the Fox Theater to see *Gone with the Wind* which I didn't realize was about my own life.

I watched the popular girls with a hunger I hadn't felt since the last time I was in America. Their faces were pink and smooth, their hair all went in the same direction, their hands were petite, and they wore little wool skirts and white cotton shirts and these very itchy but necessary button-up sweaters and kneesocks and saddle oxfords, which was okay for them because their feet were small, but on me they looked like boats.

I overheard my sister talk with our mother about visiting the grave of Martin Luther King Jr., and somehow it became clear to me that during our last tour in Nigeria, he had been killed. My young life was full of experiences like this. I would catch some movement out of the corner of my eye, or some bit of news would get lodged in my ears like the buzz of a fly—like that time I overheard my mother talking to Aunt Mary Evelyn about the Beatles—and then years later I would hear the fuller story and put it all together. My whole life has been a jigsaw puzzle and I'm still missing some of the pieces.

In Decatur I became aware of racial tension in our high school, something I had never encountered before. In fact, it was in Decatur that I first saw "black" people. The neighborhood was still a wealthy white enclave, but there was a sizable black minority, enough for my white peers to feel threatened. In PE, the white girls clustered together to dress and the black girls did the same. One African American girl was clearly the best athlete in our class. Though she was short, she outran everyone, especially on the basketball court. But instead of her achievement making her confident and easy, it seemed to make her defensive and brittle. I did not understand the hostility that emanated from her tightly turned pigtails. I had never seen a Nigerian girl bristle like that. For my part, I felt threatened primarily by the rich white kids who were privy to a script I didn't understand

and who were happy to flaunt your difference and then ignore you. If I had gone to sit with them at lunch, they would have fainted from shock.

At church, Becky and David and I were members of the Youth Group, which, now that I think of it, has the sound of some Nazi organization for teens. Most of these youngsters were very suave. They did not spend any time with me. At weekend get-togethers, I would wander endlessly *between* groups so that it wouldn't show that I wasn't *in* any. On Sunday nights, I found myself rehearsing a contemporary musical, a very odd invention intended to keep teenagers interested in church. The name of it was *Good News*. I would have found it good news if the rapture had come and I had been lifted out of that chiseled band of white Americans. Not that anyone said anything unkind. The messages were in the manners, the way three girls would close in together like a flower taking in its petals, and you were the one dropped off.

I complained when my parents decided we would go to Fairfax for Christmas and spend it with my mother's mother. I wanted to stay home, whatever that meant. But I lost that argument. We went to Fairfax. For Christmas, I received a blue formal gown I had picked out with my mother that I would take back to Nigeria to wear to the Thanksgiving Banquet at Newton.

Back in Decatur on a winter day after Christmas, I was sitting in my English class when a secretary came down the hall to our classroom and motioned to the football coach who was supposed to be our teacher. He went to the door and then called me to the front and told me to go to the office. I was terrified. I thought my parents were dead. And then when I got to the office, I saw my father, and I thought my mother was dead. My stomach was full of bats. My father approached me as if in slow motion, half smiling, his head turned a little, his hands out reaching for mine, and then he said softly as if we were in church, "Grandmother Thomas died this morning." I was so relieved I could have kissed him. We went to the funeral and I saw my mother cry. My Uncle Robert with the bad eye wept inconsolably. He sat out on the enclosed porch on a single bed, crying with the grief of Job. And I saw my cousin Franklin, who had been more or less raised by my grandmother, nearly lean over and fall down into the grave with her. He looked like a refugee.

Once again, I overdosed on television. I was particularly enamored with a drama series depicting a northwestern logging town run by men. They had imported a coterie of women as prospective brides. I thought the plot was very sexy and did not at all see the horror of it. My mother tried to get me to do more homework and watch less TV, but that was a losing battle. And while I watched, I ate. I gained about twelve pounds and then I went on a diet. All the girls were on diets. That was about the time I bought a pink two-piece bathing suit and started lying out in the sun. This was not an activity I had ever indulged in in the tropics, but it was a serious pastime for white girls in Georgia. *The Age of Aquarius* was a hit and I would listen to it on the radio in the back yard sweating in that two-piece suit. In the privacy of that same back yard, I tried to practice being a cheerleader, but it was too late. I could not get myself to do a cartwheel for fear of breaking my neck. Paisley was in. *Laugh-In* was a big draw on television and I watched it because David liked it, but I didn't quite get the humor.

One evening, as we were gathered for dinner, eating in that darkish dining room at the table with the green plastic tablecloth, my mother told me she had some bad news. My cat Molly, whom we had left in the care of another missionary family in Oshogbo, had disappeared. Molly was a totem for me. She was beautiful and independent and demanding and mysterious, as most cats are. I had loved cats all my life with a kind of fierceness usually reserved for religious objects. And now, like my beloved Susie, Molly had disappeared or was probably dead. There was obviously nothing to be done; we were on the wrong continent to undertake any kind of reconnaissance effort. I couldn't even mark her passing in any kind of symbolic way.

I must have thought about David Gaultney on and off while in Decatur. There are some people who have once been so close to us that we must think about them. They are in our heads like a dear piece of furniture or a book we read and reread until we can anticipate whole passages. David was like that for me. Though we had only been intimate friends those two years in Eku, the conversation had been so intense and daily, had gone so deep and been so exclusive, that we were, in my mind, bound like twins. In our isolation and hunger for adventure, we had developed our own special language that we spoke to no one else except maybe Bruce and Stevie. In any case, when I thought of David it was to imagine a return to utopia. I would dream of meeting him on the compound road in Eku: he would smile at me, and without speaking we would begin walking in the same direction. It was a dream of friendship and belonging, a very old dream that I had need of that year in Atlanta.

Once that year in my home economics class a makeup consultant visited and I got a facial makeover. I think I was chosen as the girl in the class who needed the most making over. But it didn't matter. The year was ending, my sister graduated from high school, and we were out of Georgia like breakaway thieves.

While I was in Atlanta, the Biafrans were carrying on like the good businessmen they were. Lawyers still wore white wigs in their courtrooms. At Uli airport, you still went through a careful customs inspection: *Please, have you got anything to declare?* From the bush, Radio Enugu continued to broadcast, while in Nigeria, GOWON was the password: *Go On With One Nigeria!* There was no question in the East about winning even though the Federals were squeezing tighter and tighter. Shell was supplying fuel to both sides. I suppose the Nigerian leadership, and the British, were afraid that if Biafra were successful, the rest of the country would splinter like those mud houses David and I blew up in Eku, scattering into a thousand fragments. Hank Wharton, a German American airline operator, was running his three ancient Super-Constellations under the name of Biafran Airways. Biafran boys were marching to the front line singing, with five rounds of ammunition apiece. Nigerian soldiers were often fighting on a diet of Star beer and marijuana. Sometimes to make it sound as if they had machine guns, the Biafrans would run a stick up and down a piece of corrugated iron.

In Eku, after the Federals swept through, several of their officers made periodic visits to the hospital; one of these, a Tiv from the

North, kindly informed the missionaries one day that he was listening in on their radio communications every night. Thereafter, the missionaries tried to communicate by secret code. Another officer, Colonel Benjamin Adekunle, nicknamed "the Black Scorpion," had already made a reputation for himself in the war as one of Nigeria's most successful and controversial field commanders. Now he was lodged near Eku and was much less friendly toward the missionaries. One day he rather stiffly announced to one of my uncles that he, the Black Scorpion, should have blown up the hospital when he had had the chance; he hated missionaries. Who knows, maybe he had been keeping his armory in Eku.

This is what I really think happened to Molly. I think some of the MK boys in the dorm might have done her in. Several of them had chosen her as an object of their fury the year before; they were still at Newton but now my family was out of the way. Molly was a scapegoat. This possibility has an ugliness to it that is beyond my capacity to narrate. And yet I believe it; I can see it.

Sometime that year while I was in Decatur, learning to wear a girdle and hose and blue eye shadow and alternately eating and dieting, I think the Spirit of Malice took up residence on the Newton compound. It had been there before but for the most part only visited, leaving footprints around the perimeter fence. It seemed to appear in those moments of sudden violence when someone was hurling an insult like a cleaver through the air or twisting an arm or torturing a lizard or walking into a younger boy's room and closing the door. This creature's prints were like a large bird's, like those you sometimes see on a beach but bigger, and the indention was especially pronounced in the toes as if he bent forward as he walked. Perhaps it was a manifestation of Eshu just fed up with our white ignorance. Perhaps it was our own image stalking us.

Whoever this spirit was, it had never lingered before because before it had been overcome by some wise and powerful adults who would not put up with its shenanigans and who, when they saw it hanging from a corner of the living room ceiling or creeping down the hallway, would give it the boot. Perhaps it had grown cannier through the years or perhaps no one was awake enough to spot those yellow eyes gleaming in the dark. But by the time I was back in Nigeria and the new school year had begun, the spirit had made itself so at home and so secure that we would have needed dynamite to separate it from the outer walls of the dormitories. It sat on its haunches on the roof during the day, reveling in our discontent and misery. But the sun was so bright that we never lifted our eyes high enough to see it there. It grew lean and hungry, waiting for us to weaken, and when we did weaken, it picked us off like young sheep. If we had been traditional Yorubas and aware of the necessity of placating the divinities of evil as well as the divinities of good, we might have tamed it or kept it busy eating up the offerings we left. But we were not Yoruba so we were not sufficiently respectful of the demon on our backs.

Last Chance

WHEN I FINISHED MY dialysis this morning, I saw that the drain bag had a small hole in it because it was leaking all over the living room rug, staining a good half of it. I can't imagine that the rug can be saved. Still I tried, first putting down old towels and sopping up as much as I could and then taking them upstairs to the bath and squeezing the towels out and rinsing them—then sitting some minutes out of exhaustion and nausea—and then going back down for more of the same. The solution has a smell, not really like urine, but a kind of spoiled sweet smell.

Sometimes Joel's friends come into the room while I am hooked to the bags—I refuse to isolate myself four times a day. Though this is what the dialysis manual tells me to do: go into a room and close it, close all windows and vents, mask yourself and anyone else in the room, and so on. But I refuse. So his friends see me with a tube mysteriously extending out from under my clothes and this yellowish liquid filling up the bag on the floor and they do not know what to think. I am sure they are disgusted. I do not try to explain. It is too hard. And then, too, it is disgusting.

We left Atlanta. I got back to Nigeria and found myself sinking fast.

One afternoon I was swimming in Ibadan in the prodigious new pool at the Ambassador Hotel. For a price, you could order a salad or a hamburger from the café. Once my mother ordered one of those salads expecting a tossed salad but she got only lettuce. When she complained, she was notified forcefully: *Please, Ma, eh-tis a* green *salad.* The changing rooms were nice and didn't smell rank with old standing water.

I was wearing that two-piece pink suit from Georgia, feeling very inadequate even though I was just back from America. It doesn't matter who else was there. Baden Richards was. Over the loudspeaker we could hear the Rolling Stones singing "Honkey-tonk Woman," and he was singing along. It was like that time I saw the Barnes girls step out of the car at Newton. I was in over my head, already falling in love with this fifteen-year-old, but he was singing along with the Stones and the song was hard and menacing and everything smelled of chlorine, a fitting prelude to my last year at Newton. I knew this was the last year: the last year I could hope to date the boy I wanted; the last year I might be Valentine's royalty; the last year I would perform in the piano recital; the last year things might go well. But already they were not. What I should have been thinking was: *this is my last year to live in West Africa,* but I was not thinking that. The shape of American desires had for a long time been robbing me of Nigeria.

My family was actually stationed in Ogbomosho that year—well, my family without Becky, whom we had once again left in the U.S., and without me, once the school year began. We were living in a new house, not the one we had occupied before. And everything had changed. The Williamses weren't in their house; not even the Smiths were there. Instead the Doshers had taken up their residence. Rose Cottage was gone, demolished. I guess it was considered old and no longer useful. It went the way of the monitor lizard though we had killed the monitor in the yard of Rose Cottage, presumably to safeguard it. Only the circular drive that wound up to the lost front steps was left, so now there was just a blankness where the house had been. The Edwardses were in the U.S. and the Richardsons were in their house and the Wassons were going on furlough and the Tolars were moving into what long ago had been our house, the first one I remember, where I heard "Joy to the World" outside the windows on that Christmas morning. Everything had shifted.

Still, I liked the new house. It was back behind our old one on a new road, at the apex of the hill that the compound occupied. Across from it was a huge semicleared area that ran up to the fence. From there you could see an unpaved road and on it, every day, men would be directing cattle to southern markets; they came by this road to bypass Ogbomosho proper. A few dwellings were growing up on that side of the compound. I remember a two-storied house in particular that was clearly visible on the other side. It had one of those upstairs porches Nigerians are so fond of with a concrete latticework wall to keep you from falling off. And there was a guava tree in our back yard which I visited for fruit but never climbed. I decorated my own room, choosing pink and orange and going for psychedelic. When you came down the hall, a glow emanated from the doorway. I liked the effect and even painted a little bookcase that Becky and I had had since we were girls, which had a scalloped border, to match the room. I would give a thousand dollars for that bookcase now, ten thousand if I had it. My parents planted zinnias in the bed in the back yard and they grew like giraffes with long necks. Dad developed a large aquarium that he placed on the half-wall separating the dining room from the entry hall. At meals we were entertained by the slow melodic movement of fish. In the living room were the mission chairs and the wood-inlaid table and the long table made of Sapele wood with the cushions for sitting and the couch we had had *titi laelae,* forever and ever, though it had been re-covered more than once, and a tim-tim or two and the coffee table Dad had commissioned for Mother when we lived in Eku and Mother's collection of green and blue glass. This house was more windows than walls, so you could sit and look out at the world; it felt once again like that screened porch where just the three of us ate in the evenings in Eku.

For my fifteenth birthday, my parents gave me a record player; I had waited for two years. It was plastic, a kind of caramel color. It did not have the look of a record player you would purchase in Atlanta. I kept it in my room on my little mahogany desk, unless I packed it up to take outside or to someone's house for the afternoon.

One night that summer, my father called me to come outside. When I did, he was looking up at the sky with his glasses on and his head tilted back and he informed me that the first men had landed on the moon and we should look at it and so we did. Of course, it looked no different for having been recently colonized. I could not see the American flag. But the next day many Nigerians from the hospital and from town came by to salute us on our moon landing; they came as they often did, not riding their bikes but walking beside them. There was also the man in Biafra, however, who asked an American why it was that his country could put a man on the moon but could not get food to hungry people in the East. "Why is that?" he wanted to know.

I remember walking home in the evenings to that house. I remember the curve in the road just behind the Williams/Smith/Dosher house because there was bamboo there and it inserted itself into the road just at that turn. The sky was bending down by this time, pulling in the fluffy corners of the sky, and everything around was quiet. I remember being conscious of myself, as I have been on and off in my life since that time in Eku when I passed through the mirror. I remember a sense of expectancy.

And did I not have the sense to know, nine months later, all that I was leaving when I packed up so blithely with a one-way ticket to America?

There was much still to come before that.

At Newton, I was guardedly optimistic. I was now a truly "older" girl; no one could look down on me, or so I thought. I had a room in the very last wing of the girls' dorm, the wing where all those glamorous older girls of former years had resided. Surely some of their style was left behind on the walls and I would pick it up through osmosis. I was a little concerned because the numbers at Newton were down and we were hardly a school that could afford any attrition. In fact most of the "older" girls had a room to themselves, whereas in earlier years we had always had a roommate. Now I think how lonely that made all of us, stretched out so thin on those hallways. We needed everybody we could get in order to have enough people to seem like a quorum. What was happening to Newton, though I did not recognize it at the time, was that more parents were sending their children to the North to Hillcrest, the international school. I always viewed this move as the choice of traitors. Newton was *our* school, I thought. And besides, I never put much stock in the North, that faraway and inconsequential region. Little did I know.

It didn't take long for me to fall hopelessly in love with Baden. As far as I could see, there was nowhere else to place my affection. David Gaultney was just a few steps away, but he was too much like a lost brother, and besides I didn't want to risk being rejected by him.

Falling in love with Baden was like being possessed. In the presence of his perfectly ironed green short-sleeved plaid shirt and his poised pitcher's arms and the square planes of his face and neck and the swath of brown hair falling across his forehead, I no longer owned myself. Instead, I was taken over by a force greater than a river, a force like a riptide.

I don't recall what happened first. It seems to me we observed Sadie Hawkins Day early in the year, that one day that a girl could ask a boy for a date. I asked Baden. And miraculously, on that night, he kissed me.

We were sitting down on the concrete bench out in front of our classroom building; it was placed in a grove of palm trees that almost smelled of fermentation in their thick branched growth. Some distance behind us was a single compound light, so we were in shadows. We had been sitting there for about fifteen minutes, talking about nothing in particular. He had one arm perched around my shoulders, so we were very close and could hear each other breathing. And then, abruptly, he leaned slightly forward and toward me and he began kissing me. There was no building up to this intimacy except for that one arm stationed over my shoulders. I remember how oddly cold were his teeth and how determined his mouth was on mine like the pressure of the Georgia dentist putting on my braces. His tongue seemed occupied with searching out every corner of my mouth, while my shoulder blades were pressed against the back of that concrete bench. Baden would stop momentarily and then another kiss would begin where the last one left off, all of them relentless. No tender touching of lips, just a timed thrusting. This was the first kiss, really, of my life, since you couldn't count that time Jon Mosley kissed me on the cheek. I remember thinking about the kissing as it was occurring: "Well, this isn't what I thought a kiss was— I thought it would be sweeter—but what do you know! This is what a kiss is like." I kept thinking that: "This is what a kiss is like. I am now being kissed. I am being kissed by a desirable boy. This is the thing that should be happening to me and it is."

Later in my room, I began to turn the evening and the kiss into a romantic fantasy. It had been lovely with the soft glow of light around us and this must just be how boys are: hard and fierce and demanding. I rescripted the evening with Baden so that it began to look like *The Magnificent Obsession*. I must have liked what had happened, I reasoned, because this is romance. And it's a very beguiling romance because this sort of thing must have happened to the incomparable Susan Levrets who dated Baden last year but is now at Hillcrest. Replacing Susan in Baden's eyes was like stepping into the leading lady's shoes. But this interpretation was a struggle, and at another level, I wasn't sure I really liked Baden. Still when he asked me for a date the following weekend, I of course said yes. All I was thinking about was that this is how things should happen. A certain sort of boy should like you and he should take charge and ask you for a date and you should then get to spend all sorts of time preparing and thinking about it and sort of brushing off the younger girls' questions because you knew things and they didn't. Baden and I had a second date, this time at the swimming pool in Ede. After the swim that night, the older group were actually allowed to walk part of the way back to the compound on the Oshogbo-Ogbomosho road in the moonlight. We talked and walked with our arms around each other although this was a difficult dance as I was taller than Baden and so I hardly had room to maneuver.

On our third date, we sat on a different bench, a more private one, in a beautiful cluster of trees. I was very happy to have found myself so liked by a boy I had always thought of as aloof and superior. Again, Baden's arm was around my shoulder, but he wasn't kissing me. And then he began slowly, in the way someone speaks when the news isn't good: "Elaine . . . you know . . . I like you. But, well, last year I went with Susan, and . . . I still . . . like her. So . . . I don't want to date just one girl." I might as well have been hit by a lorry. I was desperate somehow to turn things around before the evening was over, somehow to convince him that he was mistaken. How could I hold his attention, amend his words so that I had some hope as I went into the dorm, so that my heart did not stop as if I had been bitten by the gaboon viper? But alas, I had already lost his attention or I never really had it. And so it was that at the beginning of the year, I lost my heart like a green pearl-drop necklace I wore in Eku that just disappeared one day. The initial shock was bad enough but to have to continue living after this sting was torture. The farther Baden moved from me, the more desperate I became to revive our romance, and the more desperate I was to revive our romance, the more distant he grew, until finally he became downright mean and made fun of me for my attentions. At night in study hall, he would turn around in his seat and look at me and mimic my look at him, lonesome and sad and hopeful all at once I should imagine, and then his face would crinkle and he would laugh, almost whinnying, as he might at an animal behind bars in a zoo.

One night I decided to sneak out and go over to the boys' dorm as a way of impressing Baden with my daring. I didn't think this adventure up on my own; some of the boys had already made such a visitation to our hall, showing up outside our windows and waking us and then talking to us through the screens. I was always misinterpreting such events. What I should have understood was that boys want to have experiences that girls don't have. Instead, I imagined Baden would be impressed if I snuck over to his dorm one night. I made my plans, talking several other older girls into going with me. Ellen was planning to accompany us but then at the last minute remembered herself and changed her mind.

We slipped out the kitchen back door and were on the lookout for the night watchman, but becoming frightened, we ran straight out in the open across the campus to the boys' dorm—our white legs could have been spotted a mile off in the moonlight. If the night watchman saw us, I'm sure he thought we were spirits. I talked to Baden outside his window that night. He was not too unfriendly, but by the next morning, in the daylight, he remembered that what I had done detracted from his male privilege; I only suffered further humiliation for my trouble.

I was slow to learn the lesson of female passivity. In fact, I simply could not conjure enough passivity and self-restraint to convince a boy that my primary desire was to shape myself to his. I realize now I would have been much more attractive to my male peers had I simply accepted my fate calmly. I would have seemed serene and a little mysterious if I had kept quiet and to myself, waiting, waiting, never talking back but still smiling, as though I had a secret.

But always I wanted to know what to do. What could I do? And the anguish of that last year at Newton was that I didn't know what to do after being jilted by Baden. I still had a whole year of school to get through. If years are like songs, this one had a scratch so large across it you didn't hear the music at all, only the scratch. But, of course, I did not act in the least hurt and did not for a moment lose my public composure. So when another boy asked me out, I went, although I had little admiration for him. And when he asked me to go steady, I said yes, like someone in a dream taking directions to hell.

So little was left. We didn't witness to the carpenters on Saturday mornings. I was much too old to skip rope or throw frisbee or even swim properly. When we went to the pool, the older girls just lounged around in the water. We no longer enjoyed those "club" nights we used to have one evening of the week in which we signed up to learn cooking or nursing or some other fine art. In some uncanny way, the faculty and staff at Newton were acting as if we had seceded and our poverty was to be expected.

We students, however, were required to participate in the most stringent PE classes. Jon Lowe, a former MK, was at Newton as a journeyman and he thought we should all be athletes. Our usually desultory exercise classes were turned into high-powered drills. The older boys actually had PE during rest time at two o'clock, the hottest time of the day. You could see them out on the field, their eyes squinting, the sun's rays glancing off their bodies like bullets. Then around three, after the bell rang, the girls would take the field. We now had uniforms to help us take our physical training more seriously. We ran timed laps and worked at our soccer game as though we were going for Olympic trials, or better yet, as though we were training for the army. I played right forward and paid for it with bruised shins to match my bleeding heart.

But all the spirit had gone out of everything. God had left. There were no butterflies around those big flowered bushes in front of the girls' dorm. Like hyenas we began turning in circles and eating ourselves. Another girl would walk up and in the light of day report some viciousness that was circulating about you. Or a younger boy, seeming bold in his starting maleness, would glance at you and toss his head. You yourself would pray for another's downfall and feel your heart restrict.

The war stagnated. No one was giving an inch, least of all Ojukwu. Still, soldiers from one side would ask about their "brothers" or *omoni* on the other. I have read somewhere that sometimes the front lines were ignored by both sides as they engaged each other in a soccer match or as they set up market—beer was a favorite item of trade— and that at noonday everyone stopped for a rest. Count von Rosen, a Swedish flying ace, managed to help the Biafrans import a number of small aircraft called Minicons. They flew low—just over the tree-tops so they weren't detectable by radar and couldn't easily be hit by antiaircraft. He flew numerous missions over Nigeria, causing palaver among the Federals and for a while lifting the spirits of the Biafrans. Several Nigerian aircraft were destroyed, but enough survived to continue nightly bombing attacks on Biafra. In the end, Rosen's heroics did not change the outcome of the war; they merely prolonged it.

Until finally, in December, the Nigerian Army managed to cut what was left of Biafra in two, capturing the last rebel-held town of Owerri. And in January, just like that, the war ended like the setting sun; Biafra had been called "Land of the Rising Sun."

Already Uncle Bill Norman, JoEllen's father, had left the little Joinkrama hospital; he wasn't in Biafra proper anyway, but in the rivers area. Perhaps as he left he locked his house up, but I guess it didn't matter. I suppose what they lost in Joinkrama was more than the children's portraits and their piano and Aunt Lois's cake plate. Ojukwu left the country of Biafra at 2 A.M. on Sunday, January 11, 1970. He departed from Uli airport, the last holdout, which fell on

Monday. On the front of the *Daily Times* a photo appeared showing the first group of jubilant Nigerian soldiers running with arms up across the tarmac. That same day, at 4:30 in the afternoon, Radio Biafra, which had been playing Beethoven's Seventh Symphony, announced that the new leader, Major-General Philip Effiong, would make a statement. Declaring the end of the war, he prayed: "May God help us all in this hour of our need."

And so the Biafran War is my Vietnam, the war that shaped my youth, the war I saw in sudden absences and read of in the headlines, the war I witnessed in burned-out vehicles by the road, the war that made JoEllen a refugee and gave me names I will carry forever: Gowon and Ojukwu, Ore and Uli. But the sound of the war for me was not Beethoven's Seventh Symphony. It was Grieg's Piano Concerto in A minor, opus 16.

At night in the soft light of the living room lamps that December—when I was home for the holidays—we listened to Grieg. The kitchen was quiet, the smells of dinner having exited by the back door, and the mahogany table was long and dark. The sound of the music was the very essence of longing, as my youth was slipping away like badly spent money. Nothing would be left. To the aching beauty of Grieg, I read books and otherwise held my mind blank to be filled by the voluminous rhythm of a sound that perfectly suited my mood. Or was my mood created by the music? In the East hungry and battered people lay in shelters, their faces motionless, while our living room was the perfect emblem of civilization. But we were incapable of doing anything but listening to Grieg.

On Wednesday, January 14, exactly four years after the first coup, Ojukwu's spokesman surrendered in Lagos.

Sometime after Christmas and after the war, I developed my second case of filariasis, that noxious disease I suffered when I was first in Eku. My legs swelled up like the long tail of the boa constrictor, but I was left more or less on my own in my room to sweat it out.

In my present life, I have a dream. I am floating in an African river with my mother and my son, Joel. It is the river I swam in as a girl but the clear, shearingly cold, pale green water has turned dark and murky, like water that has stood too long in a small-mouthed vase of dying flowers. We are floating downstream, holding each other up, when I see the serpent arise from the water behind us. His head is yellow and large as the headlight of a car. Suddenly, the water beneath us churns, the currents warm around our legs. I feel the slick horror of the snake and know I have been bitten, though I hold my child up out of the water and manage to pull us three to shore and safety. Then I see my legs: green from venom. Swollen and deformed. I cannot say if I lived.

After the war was over, Ellen was crowned again at the Valentine's Banquet. This time she was the queen. If ever I smiled that year, it was in agony.

As I write this book, it occurs to me that Ellen might really have been my friend. She wanted to be. But I was too envious of her beauty and her older brother and her ability to cry. And besides, like all the girls at Newton School, we had been thrown into competition from the moment we arrived: competition for a boy's attention and the other few prizes available to us, most of which required an active passivity, a state of being I have not yet achieved, not even with kidney failure.

I do have memories of selfhood that last year, but only when I was alone, and even these are bittersweet. I see myself glissading down the front veranda of the girls' dorm. It is a school-day afternoon; the sun is setting, creating a diagonal lacework of shadows on the wide floor, a dream web. Dust motes dance downward in the air as if the shadow were a fountain. But in reality it is the dry season. Only the croton and giant philodendron still prosper. I'm walking down the hall alone, on my way to practice the piano. I hear someone's clumsy playing of Brahms, the clicking sound of dying insects, a clang of pots from the men in the kitchen preparing our dinner. A boisterous scream from underclassmen down the younger girls' hall reminds me of my age. At the end of the veranda is a full-length mirror. I see myself approaching: a tall girl with lackluster hair and a fading smile. While I am critical of my appearance, I am proud of my piano acumen. My recital piece this year is "Premiere Ballad" from Chopin's opus number 23. No one's suitcase is packed for evacuation, but on that afternoon I am aware that I walk on shifting sands. This despite the fact that I confess Jesus as the rock of my salvation. Martin Luther King Jr. and Robert Kennedy are dead as are Tafawa Balewa and Aguiyi-Ironsi.

I pause before the mirror; frown. At the piano, I practice vigorously for thirty minutes before showering for dinner.

Whatever anger there was smoldering among the students flamed out at the end. Alas, the Spirit of Malice reigned, with its red head and chameleon shorts and smoking cigar. It seemed to me that Baden was fanning the inferno, though perhaps my perspective is shaped by the fact that he still held my beating heart in the palm of his hand and he appeared very careless about it. He was indignant. Perhaps he had been happy playing baseball on some red Georgia field when his parents announced one day that they were going to Africa to be missionaries and he was to go with them. I guess he was another sort of displaced person. So he exercised with the force and witness of a fallen angel. As I remember it, he wouldn't have anything to do with RAs, or Royal Ambassadors, which was the boys' equivalent of GAs, and during recognition ceremonies he sat in his chair with his arms folded across his chest like a suspect refusing to be questioned. He seldom smiled but dressed impeccably, and that last year he assumed a vengeful leadership among the older boys. He was ringleader in their "secret" club; it had the code name STAG, not a code hugely difficult to decipher. The primary mission of this group seemed to be to intimidate and humiliate everyone below them, a grouping that included the older girls. During study hall we were pelted mercilessly with spit wads. Or a STAG member put Kotex in your desk and then had a big laugh, reenacting the facial expressions of the poor girl who found it. At such moments, I would look at Baden and observe his crisp collar and his clean white hands and the shaft of brown hair that fell over his forehead. Here was a code I could not read. I might as well have been tied up and left standing in that circular field in front of the girls' dorm; that's how humiliated I felt. *Even now I dream of awakening in the middle of the night to Baden crouching in the corner of my room, he knowing his intention and I not.*

Perhaps the terror I felt had a history, starting in the reverbera-

tions of an earlier cry still shuddering in the grass. Because much later
I learned that beginning the year before, the older boys' tactics were
much worse than I had suspected. I hear phrases like *sexual hazing* and
ritualized beatings, acts that shatter the heart if not the bone. We were
scrapping bone that last year. I remember the look of less powerful
boys coming to school in the morning, this one with his shirt tail out
and a brush of dirt across his back and here another with sweat across
his forehead like writing. Apparently, these marked ones were receiving worse than I, and I was actually lucky to be a girl and merely
taunted. Those young boys who appeared to me already to be flexing their muscles were really twitching from some event of the night,
their bodies reacting late after a damage so complete there would
never anywhere be recompense. One wonders who had beaten the
older boys.

Everything smelled like pressed clothes and trampled grass.

In my present life and after these reports, I dream of being chased
across a field and it is Baden running for me but the dream is not a
romance. I am running for my life.

When the rules of decent behavior began to fray at Newton, the
whole fabric started to unravel. And none of the adults on campus
was really in control. Perhaps in their stern effort to ignore the Nigerian Civil War, they also ignored our local embattlement.

That spring, the older kids went on our senior trip. The year
before, this group had gone to Eku, which seemed a fine destination
to me; but this year we were awarded only a short trip to Ibadan. I'm
not sure what we had done to deserve such a delimited destination;
it would have been better if the adults had confronted us, saying
something like, *You all have behaved rather badly, and as a result your trip
is curtailed.* Actually, they should simply have left the boys and taken
us girls; I think we might have enjoyed ourselves. Instead, nothing
was said and we were left guessing about our crimes and who had
recorded them, though I did wonder if someone out of malice had
reported that one night's crusade I had led to the boys' dorm. Mostly,
I had the feeling all the adults were just worn out. So we slouched
over to Ibadan. We might as well have stayed home. By that point in

the year we were hardly talking to each other. The boys would whisper to one another and laugh and you knew you were the butt of the joke. No one liked anyone. Ellen's boyfriend had broken up with her, a rare occurrence. In Ibadan we watched a British film that was all about spies and women in short skirts, the sort of film that had nothing to do with any human being I had ever met. On Saturday, we girls were privileged to watch the boys play football on a borrowed field. The whole event was a letdown from start to finish. It was a relief to get back to Oshogbo and be able to go to your own room and shut the door and weep into your hands before dinner.

The war killed two million civilians and one hundred thousand soldiers and thousands died after the war was over; many more were wounded.

The End of This World

FINALLY, THE CALL comes: 3 P.M., November 11, 2000, a beautiful Sunday afternoon; it's seventy-five degrees outside. I'm at the flea market in Raleigh when my beeper goes off. I ask a man who sells outdoor furniture if I may borrow his phone, and I call home. Andy answers: "Duke called. They want you to come as soon as possible." To the man I do not know, I announce triumphantly: "I'm going to Duke to have two transplants!" He looks at me as if I'm a peacock.

Outside I hear my university band playing because there's a football game that afternoon and the flea market is close to the stadium. We're the Wolfpack and I hear a howl and realize our team has just scored. The sunlight is slanting the way it does here in late fall, making everything light and dark at the same time. Inhaling the grandeur of hot dogs and popcorn, I feel an escalating joy and nearly start to run, and then I begin to weep.

In the car, driving home to pick up Andy and my suitcase, I listen to the end of the game. We win in the last thirty-eight seconds. And then I notice everyone passing me on the beltway because I am driving slowly, perhaps stalling before surgery, or trying not to kill myself just before I am saved. I hear the ringing in my deaf ear.

At home I cry again, standing at the top of the stairs, calling down to Andy, who comes and holds me against him.

The nurse at Duke has trouble with the IV and tries three times before she finally gets it right. I sign a consent form that says, of course, that it's not the hospital's fault if they kill me. For some reason, I begin to see Nigeria: the apartment at the boys' dorm in Oshogbo, the laundry building in the back, the marigolds my mother planted, the Peugeot and Molly the cat lounging on the boot, the palm trees, the way the land crested down from our apartment front door and the gloriosa that glided into the air, the big front window with mother's glass, the lavender couch without arms and the black telephone in the hall, our great sign of progress.

I drink something called Golytly and then I sit on the toilet over and over, every few minutes, feeling as though I am being turned inside out. The fixtures in the lavatory are cold and I shiver all over while groaning at the contractions in my belly. These are loud groans. I do not hide.

I meet a resident from Germany: Marcel Geyer. He says I am an excellent candidate for the transplants and holds my hands and rubs them because I am still shaking. The nurse leans into the room and announces that I will go to surgery at 11 P.M. Then she pulls my hair up in the back and twists it a little, stuffing it into a blue net. Only Andy goes with me down to surgery and he is there when Dr. Collins arrives at 1:20 A.M. and tells me we cannot go ahead. "The pancreas has some polyps on it." So around 2:30 I am ferried back to the elevator and then to my room. I will go back to Raleigh and wait again. I am not surprised. But the next day, at home, I cannot plow through the depression. I turn over to sleep.

Somewhere in my last Nigerian year, a morning of brief rains that raised the odor of the earth, we were called down to the chapel. Maybe it was a Saturday. Uncle Wallace, who had been the school principal pretty much since its beginning and who had always walked with as much purpose and grace as my father, got up, looking older than himself, walked up to the podium, and announced to us that Newton School would close after this year. We were defunct. I suppose there were warning signs for this ending that came as suddenly as the war's, but I didn't see them at the time, only in hindsight. For example, there was the defection to Hillcrest. Apparently the mission saw the writing on the wall. Everyone was going to the North, so why keep this Southern school open? It was too expensive. We walked out of the chapel like people without a country—or at least I did. It was all over, but it wasn't quite over. We still had to finish the year. We still had to go to PE in the afternoon, and fix our hair for dinner, and go to devotionals at night, and endure study hall with those boys who had gone mad with their unchecked power, who could say anything to you and walk away smiling.

I never thought about it at the time, but Newton was a casualty of the war. It makes such elegant sense. The North had won. The North had always been winning. Hillcrest, in the North, flourished; we, in the South, were shut down like a bad movie.

Once in those last days, one late afternoon, I traveled with "Uncle" Jon Lowe, for he was now an adult, and Daniel Hill and Aunt Marian Philips over to Ede to sing at a banquet for Nigerian students. This is either funny or sad because I can't imagine we were much good. I have never been able to sing, although I tried, as I tried with everything. On the way back from the performance, we stopped the VW van at a bridge in a valley over a small river. We got out and walked onto the bridge and watched the water and the moonlight on it and listened. Such a detour was beyond the boundaries of the normal for us. How odd and beautiful and even daring that brief stop seemed to me. What I think now is that it reflected the needs of the adults around us. If we MKs could not get "out," neither could they—and I don't mean out of the country or out of the war but out of ourselves and our painful betrayals of one another. There were no pure hearts among us. So for a moment that night—in the quiet breeze and the huge air undisturbed by any artificial light—we escaped briefly.

One evening late in the year I found myself sitting with David Gaultney out on one of those concrete park benches after dark. I don't know why we were together or what we were doing. We weren't on a date. But I remember how I longed to tell him about my heartbreak, about how much I missed Eku and all that I had lost since we were together as children. We had been one together, in a marriage before laws, in a country before the Niger Bridge was blown up, in a time when monkeys still drank at the Ethiope. I wanted to pour out my tribulations to him. But I did not. I didn't have the language for it. So we hardly talked; we just sat there, facing the girls' dorm, on that very same bench where Baden Richards had told me so many months ago that he liked me but not that much. We watched people coming and going out of the girls' dorm. I felt time running out, but I could think of nothing to say.

At the end of the school year, we had our recital. For once, I was brilliant. Even David said so; he said so softly afterward out in front of the chapel, with his head down and cast to one side. He said, *you really knocked that out.* I knew it was a compliment. Of course, my parents had come from Ogbomosho. Each year some senior won the citizenship award, and I did not win. My father was disappointed. I remember getting into the backseat of the Peugeot with them in the front, closing the door, and driving away from Newton as if I had never been there, as if I had never walked barefoot down those roads or flown on that rope swing beside the dorm or played in that sandpile with Vicky and Nwada, who was probably dead now from the war. As if I had never closed my eyes and prayed to God for the boy I loved, as if I had never fixed my hair or tucked in my shirt or gotten Kotex out of that closet or dreamed about being the Valentine princess or wound my cat around my neck or waited for my mother to tell me good night or drunk from the cold water fountain in the dining room or looked at Tommy Wasson across the table or worked geometry problems in the afternoon after lunch or read a novel after dark with a flashlight. I left like the foreigner I was. I left the way I always left: without a tear.

Breaking the Calabash

I DON'T REMEMBER TOO much about those last weeks in Ogbomosho after leaving Newton School. I was back at the beginning, the place where I was born. The war was over, and everything except the tops of trees had gone gray. My relations with the other MKs on the compound, including Jud Dosher, with whom I had not been entirely true that year, and his younger sister Delene, who had disliked me for it, had grown staler than British biscuits in the rainy season. We were a sorry lot together with Steve Hart and Cathy Miller, who lived with her family over on the seminary compound. We had all been at Newton the year before, but now in the presence of our parents we were a little more civil. I remember sitting with Cathy once on the top-floor porch of her house—for it was one of the original Victorian houses on that compound—looking out toward the seminary. The sky was so big from there, you could actually forget your troubles, and that was saying a lot in those days. From there you had the sky and beneath it the bougainvillea that grew up around that house and on one side the thick branches of mango trees and on the other side the tall fanlike fronds of a clump of banana trees. There were so few places in Nigeria that I viewed from the second floor. Most all of the houses were one story. So I remember that afternoon sitting there with Cathy, momentarily escaping our peers.

Cathy used to try to have parties at her house in the evening and Delene would do the same at hers. I at least knew better than to attempt this at home. We tried to dance like Americans, looking at each other or upward a little in order to avoid the face right in front of you. We did not know how to dance like Nigerian women, bent over and looking at the ground to watch our feet. It occurs to me now that it is very important to look at the ground you are dancing

on, to know it, in order to know yourself. But we were always dancing looking up and were thus disoriented and unsure of where we
stood.

We had these parties without adults, and all the teenagers and
would-be teenagers on the compound came. If we had been orphans,
and I guess we were in a way, no one would have adopted us. I would
try to dance with some of the boys though I was generally three inches
taller than any of them. The summer before, Walter Richardson had
been in Ogbomosho visiting his parents. He was a college student
then, so much older than we and more worldly. I danced with him
one night on the tennis court. He told me just to follow and let him
lead. I did and it was wonderful how he could make us move like the
tall grass. He was handsome and had blond hair and a grown man's
body and he knew what he was doing. I didn't bother to fall in love;
he was clearly beyond my reach.

That last summer there were many of these parties that we should
not have tried to have. They were like Fourth of July parties without
the fireworks or birthday parties without the cake. They were as flat
as those tennis courts. Still, I could see the desire in Delene's eyes;
like me, she wanted so much. But try as you might, you cannot turn
a Baptist mission compound in southwestern Nigeria into a social
hot spot. It could not be done. We might have gotten some lessons
in highlife in town, but we weren't allowed.

One day Delene and Jud got the idea of painting a huge peace
sign on the floor of their garage. Of course, like all garages on our
compounds, this one was not used for cars. I don't know when that
garage had seen its last car—not for years and years.

So Jud and Delene were going to transform their garage into a
dance hall and the way you would know this was by the huge peace
sign they painted on the floor. This effort was perfectly in keeping
with our hope always to stay abreast of whatever was hip in the U.S.,
and the peace movement was big at the time. It was 1970, the year of
Kent State. For once, we were on track with our American peers, not
two to five years behind. At the time I did not even consider the
relevance of this huge symbol. What did we know about campus
demonstrations and napalm? But now I wonder if the sign was as

clear as those green branches Nigerian boys carried after each coup. Perhaps at last we were conscious of the Biafran War just ended.

I remember well the night of the first dance. The record player was going on and on in that paint-scented room with something like *In-A-Gadda-Da-Vida,* which, I have recently learned was first written, "In the Garden of Eden." In the mythological garden we certainly were not; the evening air had sat down on its haunches at the garage doorway and we were sweltering inside: Jud and Delene, and Cathy and Steve, and his younger brother, and me, and there must have been a few others. I don't remember dancing though someone must have because by the time Mission Meeting arrived and we reconvened in that garage with a larger group of MKs, the peace sign was already badly chipped.

I suppose I was lucky to have had such an unsatisfactory last year in Nigeria. It made it easier for me to imagine how enticing it would be to leave everything I knew and once more head for America, the land of the better haircut and the home of the interstate. Soon, I would transfer to Richmond, Virginia, where my sister was in college, and I would live with friends of my parents and finish high school.

But Becky was taking a break from the University of Richmond, where she had been a less than happy freshman, and had flown out to Arkadelphia, Arkansas, where she was living for three months with the Wassons, our family friends from Ogbomosho who had resigned from the field just the summer before. She made arrangements to take French lessons from a friend of theirs, Pat Chambliss, who taught at Ouachita Baptist University, which was in the same town, and I suppose Becky made herself useful at the Wasson household. Aunt Lil and Uncle Mel still had young children in the house and Becky found herself liking the environment. Why shouldn't she? Being with the Wassons was almost like being at home—for Becky especially, since she had always dreamed of babies overflowing the crib. As far as I was concerned she could have her dream. Being "gifted," I wanted more than babies.

In the end, my sister decided not to return to Richmond but to stay in Arkansas and transfer to Ouachita. Thus it happened one day that a letter arrived, and when I came in that afternoon, Mother approached me in her usual way, serious and methodical. We went to my psychedelic room down the hall and she laid out the new plan. Instead of going to Richmond to live with a family I hardly knew, how would I like to go to Arkadelphia and live with the Wassons while I finished high school? Or better yet, there was a young couple there, the Chamblisses; they had a beautiful brand-new house and would love for me to come stay with them in a private apartment upstairs.

I had not exactly been enthusiastic about the Richmond plan. So I jumped like a fish to the bait when Arkansas and the Wassons were held out to me. At least I would know someone. And Becky would be there.

This is how the mornings were that last summer in Nigeria. You would wake up and maybe the first thing you would see would be that clear pinkish nail polish you had applied the night before. When you got up and went to the window, the African morning was there bold as ever. A Nigerian morning, by the way, is like a book fully open on its spine, whereas an American morning is like a book two-thirds open, if that much. You could see the low trees at the compound's edge. If you went outside and, say, took a walk along one of those local paths that skirted the compound, you might come onto a slow rise and see how serious and quiet the fog is resting on the branches of the trees and hovering down over the footpath. The path is itself damp and brown with the fog just rising, and here and there are some trees and maybe one larger tree; then after a while, you could see the hill rising, and when you climbed it you could look down in places and see the valley dipping below, and all around the dense quiet of the morning until you saw a man coming along the path wearing a blue knee-length overshirt with tan shorts. He hails you and in that moment the sun pierces the calm and day begins.

Except that I did not go out for a morning walk. It was not part of my life now to wander and explore.

Instead of exercising, I stayed in bed late and read *Reader's Digest* novels, looked over and over at the *Seventeen* magazines I had brought from the U.S. the year before, listened to Simon and Garfunkel and the Beatles and—I blush to say it—Tom Jones. Once I did get up, I tried to sunbathe in that relentless heat, if ever the sun would show through the clouds, my towel poised upon a thousand mud stools in the front yard (little dirt castles made by insects in the night), and I wearing that pink two-piece bathing suit. What a stranger I must have been to any Nigerian who could see me.

Before leaving for the U.S., I decided to go on a diet. The rumor on the MK circuit—which, by the way, was amazingly swift, if not accurate—was that the girls at Hillcrest had gone on a diet the year before. And the lead dieter was the beautiful Susan Levrets, who was eating something like three green beans a day. She was reportedly as skinny as Twiggy. Some of these girls would be coming to Mission Meeting, so it was imperative for me to shed some weight. Delene and I closed ranks around this goal. At the time I weighed 140 pounds; in other words, a normal weight for a girl who stood five feet, eight and a half inches tall. In fact, I needed to lose weight about as badly as I needed to learn to be polite at the dinner table. But of course such determinations at such an age have nothing to do with reality and common sense.

So the second diet of my life began. This summer I intended to get way past normal to subnormal. I wanted to look downright skinny.

It was hard work. For one thing, I was no longer that active physically. There was no swimming, no running. Though for a while Delene and I took turns exercising in each others' houses in the evenings, doing all the moves we had learned at boarding school and others we had learned from our girl friends (I use that term guard-edly; boarding school is a wonderful place to learn to be suspicious of your friends forever). Sometimes Delene and I would put on music and try to run in place in the living room for thirty minutes. But these exercise gigs were on and off, not regular.

For another thing, meals were a chief entertainment of mission life, and every lunch and dinner of my life we had had dessert. Dessert was something you *had,* like iced tea. But I was determined not to have it anymore. Instead I learned to bake all kinds of rich desserts for other people to eat. Perhaps I thought that if those around me gained weight, I would look as though I had lost even more. As others gobbled down the four-layer chocolate cakes I had made, I secretly practiced tightening my abdominal muscles. And when I was standing in my room alone, I would try to determine whether my pelvic bones were poking out any farther. I scrutinized the sides of my knees when I sat down to see if they curved inward. What you wanted was a kind of hollowed-out look. Of course, I see now how scandalous this was. There were children in Biafra still starving in the cold aftermath of the war and I was trying to achieve a genteel level of starvation, a kind of romantic Western thinness, the sort that applies only to women. The look I had in mind was planned for, brisk as new money, every hair in place and your fingernails groomed and your eyes kind of vacant-looking. Hungry children's eyes are not vacant. They are full to the brim.

I have always been hungry, but that summer I denied myself food for the greater satisfaction of becoming enviable, either that or I was crying to my mother, and anyone else who might hear, to save me, to alter my destiny, to make it possible for me *not* to have to choose between my mother country, Nigeria, and the country that apparently claimed me, the United States of America.

If you've ever been on a diet, you know that all you think about is food. It consumes you since you're no longer consuming it. Your whole life becomes a dream of food: what you might eat, what you manage not to eat, what you did eat. Your mental landscape is reduced to meals and the time between them. You go to bed early to be away from the obsession and because when you do get up you can have half a grapefruit and a boiled egg and a piece of dry toast. How you eat becomes ritualized: how you put the egg on the toast, how you cut it, how many pieces you make, how long it takes. You take more interest in other people's food than they do. Denying yourself becomes the route to self-congratulation; you pity those who eat well. The extra pounds come off slowly like a bad reputation. But eventually you really do start to look different and you smell just a little like powder instead of sweat and this is what you meant.

I have never known a Nigerian to diet for reduction, only the other way, to diet for gain. Obviously, I had completely forgotten anything I had ever learned about being Yoruba. Obviously I obsessed about weight loss as a way of avoiding the true losses I was facing. Obviously what I was really doing was getting ready for the hunger of America.

When Susan Levrets showed up at Mission Meeting, she certainly looked different; she looked like an older sister of herself, only smaller somehow. Her blue eyes shone out of her face as though she had a fever. I guess she would have been the perfect fulfillment of the Victorian ideal with her wrists not much bigger than a finger. I saw I had a long way to go to get down to her size. She never made things easy for the rest of us.

One Mission Meeting night, the older MKs convened at Jud and Delene's dance hall. We were always on the lookout for a romantic interest, and in the first few days of the annual get-together I had become vaguely aware of Robert Parham, a boy whom I had known only by reputation in the past. Robert was an MK living outside the law. I had a secret admiration for such boys. If I had known them in the U.S. they would have been smoking cigarettes in the parking lot and skipping class. Since Mission Meeting had begun, I had been watching Robert Parham in his aloofness and indifference, hanging out at the edge of the MK social set like a lone cowboy. When he showed up that night at the Doshers', I was briefly hopeful. But then in the time it might have taken me to blink, his eyes lighted on Ellen DuVall sitting there in her impenetrable calm and he went to her. I gave up without a struggle, without even a momentary surge of jealousy, this outcome so frequent a story that I no longer had the energy to try to alter it. I simply turned my head. I might even have smiled, because after a while a regular disappointment becomes a kind of ally. You can count on it.

My mother objected to my dieting, of course—at least she did after I lost the first ten pounds or so. She didn't understand that dieting is not undertaken by girls in order to reach an ideal weight. It's a competition like drag racing. The point is to see how far you can go, to reach the limit, and then to exceed it. I guess the ultimate victory would be to kill yourself.

I have often wondered if that summer was the beginning of the end of my health. In the U.S. at age twenty-five, I was diagnosed with diabetes. There is no evidence, of course, that dieting leads to diabetes. But what dieting in the extreme certainly does lead to is imbalance, which is a feature of diabetes: blood sugars racing up and down like fingers on piano scales. The next summer when I returned with Becky for a visit with our parents, I took my dieting to extremes, going from about 155 pounds to 105. I hadn't weighed so little since the fifth grade. Now I think that those summers were my only way of speaking, of saying that I am losing something I desperately need. *Help me, I beg you, to hold onto it.* Less fortunate Nigerians were always saying, *I beg you.* And now I was saying it. But no one heard me.

I didn't even hear myself, because I have no memory of consciously wishing to alter my plans. I don't remember ever thinking: "I can't do this. I can't leave my parents and my country and travel to a place I have never been to go to school with people I have never met." I would not have spoken this sentence because my country and my tribe had already been lost to me. And besides, I had never been asked to do anything I had not been able to do, although the last year at Newton had badly eroded my confidence. So I proceeded like the Scotsman Mungo Park exploring the Niger, determined against the odds because I didn't even perceive the odds. I was caught in the rapids and going down fast and I didn't have a clue. I accepted a one-way ticket to America; I walked into the fire; I drank the poison; I welcomed the sword; I lay down my life for my country. As Mark Twain might say, it was a bad trade. As Ken Saro-Wiwa's character says in *Sozaboy,* his novel about the Biafran conflict: *"The world don spoil."*

In my present life, I read about possible spiritual causes for the onset of diabetes: *Longing for what might have been. Deep sorrow. No sweetness left.* I catch my breath.

Two years, seven months, and four days ago, I experienced kidney failure, a long-term fallout from diabetes, no, a long-term fallout from my loss of Africa: *my flesh and my heart faileth.* Perhaps kidney failure signifies my body's refusal to give up anything more because now even my poisons are locked inside me. I was so strong as a girl: quick, passionate, hot, and sturdy as those bungalow houses we lived in. Always I lean toward Nigeria like a plant toward a window, but I'm leaning so far I topple.

My home was Africa.

And one needs a country as one needs a lover as one needs a child as one needs milk as one needs a mother as one needs a father as one needs a god.

Sometime, perhaps even that summer, after we closed out that last year at Newton, the Nigerian Army moved in on the Newton School compound. The land had always been on loan, of course, and the mission wasn't going to be using the buildings anyway. I never went back to see the place after that. But I have wondered if all the furniture was left, or was it sold, or was it stolen: the bunk beds and desks in the bedrooms and the long couches in the living rooms and the solemn tables in the dining room and the pianos in the chapel and the desks in the classrooms, still lined up in rows for our evening study hall? And what about our playground equipment and the pots and pans and dishes in the kitchen? What about the bookshelves and coffee tables and the thousand minor items like the medicines in the infirmary and the scales? And what about all of those carefully tended outdoor gardens? Did the Nigerian military refresh those with water? Did they avoid parking on the grass? Did the Spirit of Malice still dwell there in the space behind the chapel and crouch under the leaves of the tomato bush in the afternoon, eating the fallen fruit? How did Uncle Wallace bear it the last time he locked the doors and drove away down that drive with his family, with Ellen and Aunt Pearl and Ricky and Kathy and Becky?

I can see the army trucks and lorries lumbering onto that compound. And I can see the screens coming off the windows and cooking fires built outside the kitchen in the courtyard where Ellen and Vicky and I staged weddings. I can see women coming onto the compound with their children to set up shop just inside the gates, lining up their goods on patches of cloth laid on the ground. I can see their children hugging their legs as their mothers bargain with the soldiers, and perhaps the braver young ones step out from behind the maternal skirts to survey the grounds. One of them hears our lost voices and talks back, throwing stones. I can see the paint slackening on the walls of the dorms and broken chairs collecting in the corners of the chapel and scores of young men bearing arms and practicing their drills in the soccer field and the legend of the Nigerian flag flying above it all.

I wonder if any of the men who worked for us on that compound stayed behind to labor for the army. What met their eyes as they reviewed the transformation? Did an old gardener stay on? Was he saddened to see the decay and fall of the flower beds or was he relieved to be through with that business, to have no more responsibility for watering, weeding, and planting? Was he glad to have no more to do than keep the grass down, which wouldn't have been difficult with all those marching feet and hungry goats that would have been part of the landscape?

Were the tennis courts ever used and was the grapefruit harvested off of the trees and did anyone ever wander to the front fence to find the pitanga cherry trees that Ellen and I would sometimes visit to eat that bitter fruit? Was the fence torn down or did it remain?

Did any of the rooms of those buildings become rooms of detention and was anyone tortured there or forced to confess to alleged crimes?

I never thought about these things at the time. I was through with Newton.

Late that summer, some of the adults on the Ogbomosho compound staged a little going-away party for me. It was held at Caladium Cottage, the single missionary women's villa that was built when Rose Cottage was torn down and which sat next to its ruins on the compound road. The party wasn't a large affair; not everyone was invited. But someone gave me a silver pin of Africa. I did not cherish it at the time. As with many such gifts, I undervalued it in my youth. It was African, after all. The workmanship appeared a little rough in my eyes. I was on my way to becoming, once again, an American teen. What would I want with a little silver pin in the shape of Africa?

In my garden in Raleigh, everything grows huge like the Baptist church. But my own body is crumbling.

Before I left Nigeria, my mother prepared me to leave. Well, she did not so much prepare me to leave as she prepared a wardrobe for me with which I could leave. I have come to think that my mother never learned in her family how to express her feelings. Perhaps she feels too deeply and cannot bear it, and in my youth perhaps she held in her tears until nighttime when she could show them to my father like hibiscus leaves she collected in the daytime. The tears spill over in me. I am the reservoir she saved up all those years. So she sewed my dresses and never said to me: "My blood is spilling out on this cloth like the thread." Or, "My heart is split within me like the country." Or, "You are my starlit night, my best wish, my roundest wisdom." Or, "Your leaving is the end of all sweetness." If she had said any of those things, she would have fallen down and wept and she would not have been able to prepare me for America.

I remember the yellow dress she made me. I think now it was a poem for the daughter with the blonde hair and the determination of waterfalls. I wore it the afternoon we departed from Lagos. We were at the hostel as usual and Mother was going with me, taking me to Arkansas where she would deposit me with my sister and the Chamblisses. She and I were standing under the canopy of trees that shaded the drive, waiting for my father. And then we drove, as we had rehearsed with my sister, to the old airport, the one I had always known. It smelled like oil and sand. I remember nothing until we were on that plane and I was in the window seat. As the airplane turned for departure, I could see my father standing outside the terminal, sort of leaning against it, the wind whipping up his slight hair, his frame long and thin and his arm raised to shield his eyes and everything bleached by the light and the sand. Finally his hand lifted in a kind of half wave, half salute, and I thought, "There is my father." And for the very first time I realized that I was leaving Africa and all of my life since then I have seen my father holding up the terminal, or was he collapsing against it, and that bright light and that wind and that small window I was looking through and palm trees in the distance. And that is Nigeria to me. As I told you in the beginning, for all I loved there, it was not mine to hold.

Wandering through Lifelong Years

WHEN JOEL WAS LITTLE, around two or three, he would sometimes stay with friends or with my parents for a weekend and he would be perfect while Andy and I were gone. We might even see him as we returned, before he saw us, and he would be happily occupied with some object—turning the pages of a book or manipulating knobs on a toy. But then he would see us and his little arms would go up as if in prayer or lamentation and before he could cry, he would run to us, arms outstretched, leaning forward in a way that his feet could not keep up with him. He would fall before us, weeping, because only then did he really understand that we had been gone and he was indignant and his heart was broken for the loss that could never be recovered. We had left him. And that was what I felt so much of my life but could not say. My whole family had lost too much time that we should have had and I could never get it back. But I did not even know at the time that that was what I was feeling. I could not have told you. I could not have said what I had lost in losing the compounds and moving to America where people live in suburbs and the nuclear family rules. I could not have said, *I have lost my family, all the faces—white and black and brown and gray—that I have known all of these years, even the faces of my enemies, and the spaces between our houses, the afternoon tennis, the marketplace, the monitor lizard, the petty envies, the singing of hymns in lamplit places with the windows open, the old grudges, the lingering hopes.* Not until writing this book could I say, *all the relations of my early life were ripped from me like hair by the roots. Losing the whole cradle of your childhood, wandering through lifelong years having lost all those relations and influences and contexts and loves and even hates is like losing a mother. You seek her for the rest of your life. You ache for her.*

Such a separation creates a sharp division in your soul. When other people talk at the dinner table you gaze into a place beyond the room; you cast yourself back to a time when you had a mother and you were whole. When someone speaks to you about some issue of the day, you stammer and call yourself back over highways and rivers and paths but your return is listless and insincere. You never turn to the present entirely. Doing so would be a betrayal.

Restoring the Calabash

I DREAMED THAT I WAS on the road to Abraka—to the river. I was with my family in a car. But then we had to park the car and we were led by a local man through several houses, of several stories, going up and down stairs and through hallways that were decorated with colored chalk drawings. We finally came out of the last house—Becky, Mother, my father, and I—and we were in a small town. A dark gray cloud was approaching and I could tell it was going to rain. Suddenly Andy appeared, smiling, and he took my hand and we started on foot to the Ethiope, walking down the side of the busy road. The rain was pelting us by now but there was no thunder or lightning. "I never thought I would see the river again," I mused, "but now I will." And we kept walking through the rain.

Now I think that one of the reasons I forgot Nigeria for so long is the trouble all of us were in when I left. Even on that return visit, I did not really see that I was home because I had left home so completely after I left Newton. But a girl cannot just walk away from her past or even her trouble. Or she can, but she will pay. She will be lost. Her feet will not know their country and her eyes will dim waiting for a true sunrise. Because her country, like her body, is her treasure: memory and bones, kidneys and blood, vision and the heart.

I am back at Duke Hospital. The transplant nurse phoned last night around ten o'clock, Thanksgiving evening. I am familiar with the presurgery routine: an X ray, another EKG, Golytly, agony of the toilet, two physical exams, a visit from the social worker to go over my insurance, a visit from the anesthesiologist. I am perfectly calm and at ease.

When I wake from surgery, all I know is that I am alive and safe. I can smell the antiseptic aftermath of surgery. My family is with me; the operation has been a success. While my husband and my son and my sister succumbed to sleep, my parents stayed up all night, vigilant. Dr. Collins approaches them in the waiting room. I can see them standing to greet him.

Later I see my abdomen, bruised in lavenders and blues, almost like flowers abloom. My new organs hum finely like worker bees. I have visions of donors in my room. They do not frighten but they are serious as men at war.

Perhaps each of us is paid for by someone else. We all spin in space on one side or the other of this evolving life. None of us is merely ourselves. When I went into surgery, after looking into Joel's face, I said yes to life and yes to death. This was the crossroads if ever I knew it. I could have gone either way. But Dr. Collins brought me back into this world, though it took him eight hours of careful stitching. He makes me think of my grandmother. She could sew that long.

At home, I dream of seedlings everywhere, sprouts in early dawn, small patches of young growers, green and green under the waking sky. I receive notes and cards from mission aunts and uncles who have remembered me in the soft round of supplication.

Now when I get up at six o'clock—for I no longer face that agony of the morning, that dull terror of dialysis—I sit at my living room window drinking tea and the sky is ribbons of pink and blue. I feel well and whole and balanced for the first time in twenty years: *like sitting in the guava tree with no fear of falling, like running down Eku compound roads, like holding my hand out the window of the Chevrolet station wagon to catch the rain.* Dr. Collins says I may travel back to West Africa in a year. Friends tell me Nigeria is too dangerous; I tell them the U.S. is too dangerous for me.

I want to go and see a hibiscus bush large enough to pass for a tree and a market stall where a young man sells books, for Nigerians still covet books even if Americans do not, and a village where an old gentleman sits on a stoop in front of his house playing checkers with his neighbor. I want to see those cattle with horns broad as a car. I want to see a green-and-yellow taxi on the road.

I suppose I will see much trouble too when I return.

When Andy and I visited in 1980, we rendezvoused with my parents in Lagos, for they were serving a four-year tour in Ghana where my mother worked with students at the University of Kumasi and my father was the mission treasurer and liaison with the Ghanaian government. Coming into the new Lagos airport, we were met by armed guards. The end of the war in Nigeria wasn't exactly the end. The country remained under military rule. While we were in West Africa that summer, a headline in the local paper read, "No Coup Today." That was the summer Joel was conceived.

Often in my illness, I thought, "Why should I be spared any more than any other Nigerian?" I know that many many Nigerians who were born with me on August 19, 1954, are already dead. I, on the other hand, survived childbirth and hepatitis and death by lorry and the Biafran War and a finger pointed in my direction and loss of home through fire and a knock on the door at night and the tsetse fly and drowning in my own fluids and an abundance of sweetness that means *no sweetness left*.

At the end of the twentieth century, military rule was finally suspended and democratic elections took place in Nigeria. I dare to hope. Still Muslims and Christians are fighting, Northerners and Southerners. There is great conflict over shari'a law. Someone is flogged. Someone is stoned. It will take some time, if we are lucky, for generations to grow up not in war but out of it.

One of the nontruths that middle-class Americans learn is that everything can be fixed without waiting. But sometimes it takes decades just to begin to fix a thing. Dreams can be sold, but they can't be bought.

Shopping in a local mall after the transplants, after my energy has returned, sitting eating a muffin and drinking pungent coffee with milk, for now I am free to eat what I desire, I see across the way a

Latino man cleaning tables, working, I suppose, for minimum wage, and I wonder: could he receive a transplant if he needed one? Who would pay?

Christmas approaches; I consider the family of my donor.

Sometimes in my wellness, or only in my wellness, I begin to understand the cost of illness. Sometimes when I stand and walk, I have sparks in my eyes and a white sheen overtakes the world and I feel I will faint and must sit in honor of the fractures my body still remembers.

Sometimes in my wellness, I begin to understand the great circle of return. Soon after my return to work in the English department, I learned that an Igbo professor of religion was visiting our campus to lecture for a year on traditional African religions. I gave him a call; he seemed quite surprised to hear from a white American woman just a few offices down who could talk about Ogbomosho and Onitsha and Port Harcourt and Biafra. We made a date to meet.

On that day, I saw him walking down the hall. I knew it was Obed Anizoba just by seeing him, the way his legs moved without hurry, the pattern in his sweater, the squareness of it on his upper torso, the density of his color, the familiarity of his bone structure, the straight-lined indentation across his chin, the planes of his cheeks, the compactness of his entire body.

I introduce myself; we shake hands, and then we sit in his office. He tells me how he came to be here. Briefly, I rehearse my history. I tell him about my book. He understands exactly when I narrate my growing up in Nigeria and then losing the whole country and being sent to America. He agrees that something is missing in American churches; he cannot name it.

When I begin to gather things to leave, he clasps my right hand with both of his and raises it to his chin and presses it there. I ask him what this gesture means and he says, "I take you into my heart, into myself"—he says this rolling his hands in front of his chest as if folding dough—"without reservation." He might as well have been Jesus.

In my department I am dangerous with energy, like a young male waking into adolescence. I swerve around corners, walking into people. But the next day, I am tired. I overdid it.

I have never been safer than when I was surrounded by danger, the snakes in Eku, my pregnancy with Joel, my near death from kidney failure. In my present life, I must work to stay close enough to death. Close enough to remember.

I have found the truth about my life but it is not some fabulous revelation or some pure shining thing. Instead it is the mundane truth of a crazy mix of faith and accident, hope and boredom, love and privilege. I was an ordinary girl in extraordinary circumstances. Every girl is.

In a dream, I am in the U.S. in a car with Andy, and we stop at a kind of fair or community get-together. People are displaying valuable antiques. After looking about, I decide to display my own object even though it is plain and seems unremarkable. It is that very box I buried in the earlier dream, out under the guava tree in Ogbomosho: a small dingy white box with drawers and pulls. I set the box down and look at it on the table and I think: "Okay, there it is." And I know now that the box is my calabash, my story, my body, from Nigeria, and it is my essential self, my inner head, however flawed and wounded, however dislocated and forgotten. I have no choice but to claim it.

Something inside of me is waiting to be born. It is my own ivory coast. It is the promise of my salvation.

The sky has cleared. I am running now, barefoot. I lost the knapsack a while back. The path is sandy, so sandy that in places I can hardly get a foothold. I have torn off my jacket. I duck to avoid fronds and branches. My bare arms are scratched. One leg is cramping but I keep loping forward and now I can't even feel my legs. I am coming to a curve and the path opens to the breadth of a single-lane road. The sand is blond here and hot. I run faster. I am almost there. And finally I see what I have been running to. I have vaulted clean through. I am here. Here. I am here. Whole as the monitor lizard before it was shot.

When I dive into the river, the water does not even break.

IN MEMORIAM, Lloyd Houston Neil
AUGUST 16, 1917–NOVEMBER 8, 2001

Coda

IN THE SPRING OF 2001, after my successful transplants, my father's walking began to deteriorate, he who had always walked so bravely, so certainly. I remember his telling me one day out in that deep front yard in Eku that he would never die, he would just fly away one day with the wind. He said this coaxingly and with a smile because he was so thin in those tropic hours. On November 6, 2001, he experienced a massive brain hemorrhage. He died two days later. My grand father. Surely a noble man.

How grateful am I for his love, for my mother's love, always imperfect, always dear.

And in the very end of this all, in the very end of this writing, David Gaultney returned, writing to me one day as if we had only parted yesterday. And, of course, it was yesterday. Time is only the river of memory.

Works Consulted: A Quixotic Bibliography

Achebe, Chinua. *Beware Soul Brother: Poems.* Oxford: Heinemann, 1972.

————. *Home and Exile.* Oxford: Oxford University Press, 2000.

————. *No Longer at Ease.* 1960. Reprint, New York: Anchor Books, 1994.

————. *Things Fall Apart.* 1958. Reprint, London: Heinemann, 1979.

Ademoyega, 'Wale. *The Federation of Nigeria: From Earliest Times to Independence.* London: George G. Harrap & Co., 1962.

Adetoro, J. E. *A Primary History for Nigeria.* Book 3. 1965. Reprint, Lagos: Macmillan, 1976.

Africa Special Report. Washington, D.C.: Bulletin of the Institute for African American Relations. 1955–1959.

Alden, Peter C., et al. *National Audubon Society Field Guide to African Wildlife.* New York: Alfred A. Knopf, 1995.

Annual Report 1994. Ibadan: International Institute of Tropical Agriculture, 1994.

Appiah-Kubi, Kofi, and Sergio Torres, eds. *African Theology en Route.* Maryknoll, N.Y.: Orbis Books, 1983.

Ayandele, E. A. *Nigerian Historical Studies.* London: Frank Cass, 1979.

Bedford, Semi. *Yoruba Girl Dancing.* New York: Penguin, 1991.

Beier, Ulli. *The Hunter Thinks the Monkey Is Not Wise . . .* Ed. Wole Ogundele. Bayreuth, Germany: Eckhard Breitinger, 2001.

————, ed. *A Dreaming Life: An Autobiography of Twins Seven-Seven.* Bayreuth, Germany: Eckhard Breitinger, 1999.

————, ed. *Yoruba Poetry: An Anthology of Traditional Poems.* Illus. Susanne Wenger. Cambridge: Cambridge University Press, 1970.

Bowen, Laurenna. Unpublished diary. (Copy in author's collection.)

Bowen, T. J. *Adventures and Missionary Labours in Several Countries in the Interior of Africa from 1849 to 1856.* 2d ed. Intro. E. A. Ayandele. London: Frank Cass & Co., 1968.

Boyd, William. *A Good Man in Africa.* 1981. Reprint, New York: Avon, 1994.

Bradbury, R. E. *Benin Studies.* London: Oxford University Press, 1973.

Buchanan, K. M., and J. C. Pugh. *Land and People in Nigeria*. London: University of London Press, 1955.

Cloudsley-Thompson, J. L. *The Zoology of Tropical Africa*. London: Weidenfeld and Nicolson, 1969.

Courtright, Gordon. *Tropicals*. Portland, Ore.: Timber Press, 1988.

Crowder, Michael. *The Story of Nigeria*. London: Faber & Faber, 1962.

Davidson, Basil. *The African Awakening*. New York: MacMillan, 1955.

————. *The Black Man's Burden: Africa and the Curse of the Nation-State*. New York: Times Books, 1992.

De Gramont, Sanche. *The Strong Brown God*. Boston: Houghton Mifflin, 1976.

De St. Jorre, John. *The Brothers' War: Biafra and Nigeria*. Boston: Houghton Mifflin Company, 1972.

Drewal, Margaret Thompson. *Yoruba Ritual: Performers, Play, Agency*. Bloomington: Indiana University Press, 1992.

Ekwensi, Cyprian. *Jagua Nana*. 1961. Reprint, Oxford: Heinemann, 1987.

Euba, Femi. *Archetypes, Imprecators, and Victims of Fate: Origins and Developments of Satire in Black Drama*. New York: Greenwood Press, 1989.

Fadipe, N. A. *The Sociology of the Yoruba*. Ibadan: Ibadan University Press, 1970.

Flint, John E. *Nigeria and Ghana*. Englewood Cliffs, N.J.: Prentice-Hall, 1966.

Free, Lloyd A. *The Attitudes, Hopes, and Fears of Nigerians*. Princeton: Institute for International Social Research, 1964.

Fuller, Aletha B. *More than a Memory*. San Angelo, Tex.: Anchor Publishing Co., 1986.

Graf, William D. *The Nigerian State: Political Economy, State Class, and Political System in the Post-Colonial Era*. London: James Currey, 1988.

Green, M. M. *Ibo Village Affairs*. 1947. Reprint, New York: Frederick A. Praeger, 1964.

Hallen, Barry. *The Good, the Bad, and the Beautiful: Discourse about Values in Yoruba Culture*. Bloomington: Indiana University Press, 2000.

Hemingway, Ernest. *Green Hills of Africa*. 1935. Reprint, New York: Touchstone, 1996.

Hudgens, Jim, and Richard Trillo. *West Africa: The Rough Guide*. London: Rough Guides, 1995.

Hull, Richard W. *Modern Africa: Change and Continuity*. Englewood Cliffs, N.J.: Prentice-Hall, 1980.

Huxley, Elspeth. *The Flame Trees of Thika: Memories of an African Childhood*. 1959. Reprint, New York: Pyramid Books, 1966.

Hymns, Psalms, and Spiritual Songs. Louisville: Westminster/John Knox Press, 1990.

Idowu, E. Bolaji. *Olodumare: God in Yoruba Belief*. London: Longmans, 1962.

Ike, Chukwuemeka. *Toads for Supper*. Glasgow: Fontana/Collins, 1977.

Jacobs, Dan. *The Brutality of Nations*. New York: Alfred A. Knopf, 1987.

Kingsley, Mary. *Travels in West Africa*. 1897. Reprint, abr. and intro. by Elspeth Huxley, London: J. M. Dent & Sons, 1976.

Kwamena-Poh, M., et al. *African History in Maps*. Essex, England: Longman, 1982.

LeClezio, J. M. G. *Onitsha*. Trans. Alison Anderson. Lincoln: University of Nebraska Press, 1997.

Lessing, Doris. *Martha Quest*. 1952. Reprint, New York: Plume, 1970.

Leuzinger, Elsy. *Africa: The Art of the Negro Peoples*. Trans. Ann E. Keep. London: Methuen, 1962.

Lucas, J. Olumide. *The Religion of the Yorubas*. Lagos: C.M.S. Bookshop, 1948.

Lyons, Robert, photographer. *Another Africa*. Essay and poems by Chinua Achebe. New York: Anchor Books, 1998.

Maddry, Charles E. *Day Dawn in Yoruba Land*. Nashville: Broadman Press, 1939.

Maraire, J. Nozipo. *Zenzele: A Letter for My Daughter*. New York: Crown, 1996.

Markham, Beryl. *West with the Night*. 1942. Reprint, New York: North Point Press, 1983.

McCullin, Don. *Sleeping with Ghosts: A Life's Work in Photography*. New York: Aperture, 1996.

Morton, J. K. *West African Lilies and Orchids*. London: Longmans, 1961.

Ndibe, Okey. *Arrows of Rain*. New York: Delta, 1996.

Nwampa, Flora. *Efuru*. 1966. Reprint, London: Heinemann, 1976.

Ojaide, Tanure. *Great Boys: An African Childhood*. Trenton, N.J.: Africa World Press, 1998.

Ojo, G. J. Afolabi. *Yoruba Culture: A Geographical Analysis*. Ife: University of Ife and University of London Press, 1966.

Okri, Ben. *Stars of the New Curfew*. New York: Viking, 1988.

Olusanyan, G. O., ed. *Studies in Yoruba History and Culture: Essays in Honor of Professor S. O. Biobaku*. Ibadan: University Press Limited, 1983.

Osaghae, Eghosa E. *Crippled Giant: Nigeria since Independence*. Bloomington: Indiana University Press. 1998.

Owen, D. F. *Animal Ecology in Tropical Africa*. Edinburgh: Oliver & Boyd, 1966.

Paton, Alan. *Cry, the Beloved Country*. 1942. Reprint, New York: Charles Scribner's Sons, 1948.

Perham, Margery, and J. Simmons. *African Discovery: An Anthology of Exploration*. London: Faber & Faber, 1957.

Perkins, W. A., and Jasper H. Stembridge. *Nigeria: A Descriptive Geography*. 2d ed. London: Oxford University Press, 1963.

Reed, John, and Clive Wake. *A Book of African Verse.* 1964. Reprint, London: Heinemann, 1976.

Richards, P. W. *The Tropical Rain Forest: An Ecological Study.* Cambridge: Cambridge University Press, 1952.

Roedelberger, Franz A., and Vera I. Groschoff. *African Wildlife.* English version by Nieter O'Leary and Pamela Paulet. New York: Viking Press, 1965.

Saro-Wiwa, Ken. *A Month and a Day: A Detention Diary.* Intro. William Boyd. New York: Penguin, 1995.

————. *Sozaboy: A Novel in Rotten English.* Intro. William Boyd. New York: Longman, 1996.

Smith, Robert. *Kingdoms of the Yoruba.* 1969. Reprint 3d ed., Madison: University of Wisconsin Press, 1988.

Soyinka, Wole. *The Lion and the Jewel.* 1962. Reprint, Oxford: Oxford University Press, 1996.

————. *Myth, Literature, and the African World.* 1976. Reprint, Cambridge: Cambridge University Press, 1995.

Thompson, Joseph E. *American Policy and African Famine: The Nigeria-Biafra War, 1966–1970.* New York: Greenwood Press, 1990.

Thoreau, Henry David. *Walden.* 1854. Reprint, Philadelphia: Running Press, 1987.

Udo, Reuben K. *Geographical Regions of Nigeria.* Berkeley: University of California Press, 1970.

UPA [Urhobo Progressive Association] Fifteenth Year Anniversary Banquet (program). N.p.: Double A Printing, 1977.

Van der Post, Laurens. *The Dark Eye in Africa.* New York: William Morrow & Co., 1955.

Visona, Monica Blackmun, et al. *A History of Art in Africa.* New York: Harry N. Abrams, 2000.

Willett, Frank. *African Art.* New York: Praeger, 1971.

Williams, Harry. *Nigeria Free.* London: Robert Hale Limited, 1962.

Wiwa, Ken. *In the Shadow of a Saint: A Son's Journey to Understand His Father's Legacy.* South Royalton, Vt.: Steerforth Press, 2001.

Youdeowei, Anthony, Fred O. C. Ezedinma, and Ochapa C. Onazi. *Introduction to Tropical Agriculture.* Essex, England: Longman, 1986.